The nature of adolescence

Adolescence and Society

Series editor: John C. Coleman
The Trust for the Study of Adolescence

The general aim of the series is to make accessible to a wide readership the growing evidence relating to adolescent development. Much of this material is published in relatively inaccessible professional journals, and the goal of the books in this series will be to summarise, review, and place in context current work in the field so as to interest and engage both an undergraduate and professional audience.

The intention of the authors is to raise the profile of adolescent studies among professionals and in institutes of higher education. By publishing relatively short, readable books on interesting topics to do with youth and society, the series will make people more aware of the relevance of the subject of adolescence to a wide range of social concerns.

The books will not put forward any one theoretical viewpoint. The authors will outline the most prominent theories in the field, and will include a balanced and critical assessment of each of these. Whilst some of the books may have a clinical or applied slant, the majority will concentrate on normal development.

The readership will rest primarily in two major areas: the undergraduate market, particularly in the fields of psychology, sociology, and education; and the professional training market, with particular emphasis on social work, clinical and educational psychology, counselling, youth work, nursing, and teacher training.

Also available in this series

Identity in Adolescence
Jane Kroger

Titles in preparation

Young People's Understanding of Society
Adrian Furnham and Barry Stacey

Adolescents and the Family
Pat Noller and Victor Callan

The nature of adolescence
Second edition

John C. Coleman
and
Leo Hendry

Routledge
London and New York

First edition published 1980
by Methuen & Co Ltd

Second edition published 1990
by Routledge
11 New Fetter Lane, London EC4P 4EE

Simultaneously published in the USA and Canada
by Routledge
a division of Routledge, Chapman and Hall, Inc.
29 West 35th Street, New York, NY 10001

© 1990 John Coleman and Leo Hendry

Typeset by J&L Composition Ltd, Filey, North Yorkshire
Printed in Great Britain by
Richard Clay Ltd, Bungay, Suffolk

British Library Cataloguing in Publication Data

Coleman, John C. (John Christopher,) *1940–*
   The nature of adolescence. — (Adolescence and
   society)
   1. Adolescence
   I. Title   II. Hendry, L. B. (Leo Brough) *1935–*   .III.
   Series
   305.2′ 35

Library of Congress Cataloging in Publication Data

Coleman, John C., Ph. D.
   The nature of adolescence / John Coleman and Leo Hendry. — 2nd
   ed.
   p.   cm. — (Adolescence and society)
   Bibliography: p.
   Includes index.
   1. Adolescence.   I. Hendry, Leo B.   II. Title.   III. Series.
   HQ796.C642   1989
   305.2′35 — dc19   89–3594
                                                                              CIP

ISBN 0–415–01484–0
ISBN 0–415–01485–9 (pbk)

Contents

Chapter one

Introduction

The way in which we understand adolescence has been changing slowly but perceptibly over the last few years. To some extent this is as a result of the major social changes which have occurred in western countries, many of which have had a direct effect on young people, and thereby focused attention on this particular group within society. Equally important, however, is the fact that new and valuable research is being carried out, much of it linked to and inspired by major advances in theories of human development. These advances have led to a more realistic, as well as a more sophisticated, view of the teenage years, and brought the study of adolescence to a more central place within developmental psychology.

As far as social changes are concerned, the most striking is undoubtedly the marked increase in youth unemployment. This has had a number of consequences, for apart from forcing governments to take more responsibility for the older adolescent, and placing post-16 training squarely on the political agenda, it has also made us very much more aware of disadvantage and deprivation among young people. Other social changes which may be mentioned include the growing importance of 'equal opportunities' policies, and the impact these have had on education and careers; the changing nature and composition of the family, with higher divorce rates and greater numbers of single and step parents; and an increased awareness of and anxiety about the sexual abuse of young people. All these issues have served to move the adolescent years closer to the centre of the stage. Their impact, however, has been heightened by the theoretical advances mentioned above. The growing strength of lifespan developmental psychology, as well as the widening impact of the work being carried out in the field of social cognition, have undoubtedly had a profound effect on studies of adolescence. These new trends have added substantially to the more traditional approaches to adolescence, contributing a new and important perspective on growth and change from puberty onwards.

Closely associated with these developments is a growing acceptance that events in the first five years of life are not the only events which have fundamental implications for later development. For many years it has been widely believed that what happens in infancy represents the foundation stone for later personality development, and that many of the effects of the experiences of these early years are irreversible. However, it is increasingly recognised that experiences during other critical phases of development, especially during adolescence, have an equally important bearing on what happens later in life. This realisation, that adjustment in adolescence has critical implications for adult development, as well as for the health of society in general, has led to a new surge of interest in the adolescent years.

Another change which has occurred in the last few years concerns a shift of emphasis in the way adolescence is portrayed. Today writers are far less likely to describe this period in static terms as a single stage, or even a series of sub-stages, in the life cycle. Empirical evidence has clearly shown that too much individual variation exists for young people of the same chronological age to be classified together, and there is now a preference for viewing adolescence as a transitional process rather than as a stage or number of stages. To conceptualise the period in this way implies that adolescence needs to be understood as a time during which the individual passes from one state – childhood – to another – maturity – and that the issues and problems faced by individuals during this period are predominantly the result of the transitional process.

This transition, it is believed, results from the operation of a number of pressures. Some of these, in particular the physiological and emotional pressures, are internal, while other pressures which originate from peers, parents, teachers, and society at large, are external to the young person. Sometimes these external pressures hurry the individual towards maturity at a faster rate than he or she would prefer, while on other occasions they act as a brake, holding the adolescent back from the freedom and independence which he or she believes to be a legitimate right. It is the interplay of these forces which, in the final analysis, contributes more than anything to the success or failure of the transition from childhood to maturity.

So far two classical types of explanation concerning the transitional process have been advanced. The psychoanalytic approach concentrates on the psycho-sexual development of the individual, and looks particularly at the psychological factors which underlie the young person's movement away from childhood behaviour and emotional involvement. The second type of explanation, the sociological or social–psychological, represents a very different perspective. While it has never been as coherently expressed as the psychoanalytic view, it is none the less of equal importance. In brief, this explanation sees the causes of adolescent transition as lying primarily in the social setting of the individual and concentrates on the nature of roles and role conflict, the pressures of social expectations, and on the relative influence of different agents of socialisation. Unlike these two approaches, lifespan developmental psychology takes an interactive stance, arguing that all factors need to be taken into account, and that, furthermore, the individual and the environment are likely to have a reciprocal influence upon each other. Both the traditional approaches, together with that of lifespan developmental psychology, will be described in some detail here, for they form an essential background to the main body of the book, one of the aims of which is to look at the strengths as well as the deficiencies of theory as an aid to understanding adolescence.

Psychoanalytic theory

The psychoanalytic view of adolescence takes as its starting point the upsurge of instincts which is said to occur as a result of puberty. This increase in instinctual life, it is suggested, upsets the psychic balance which has been achieved by the end of childhood, causing internal emotional upheaval and leading to a greatly increased vulnerability of the personality (Freud 1937). This state of affairs is associated with two further factors. In the first place, the individual's awakening sexuality leads him or her to look outside the family setting for appropriate 'love objects', thus severing the emotional ties with the parents which have existed since infancy. Second, the vulnerability of the personality results in the employment of psychological defences to cope with the instincts and anxiety which are, to a greater or lesser extent, maladaptive. An excellent review of recent psychoanalytic thinking as it applies to adolescence may be found in Lerner (1987).

Peter Blos may be taken as one of the leading writers in this field. His views are well summarised by Muuss (1980, 1988). Blos has described adolescence as a 'second individuation process', the first having been completed towards the end of the third year of life. In his view (Blos 1962) both periods have certain things in common: there is an urgent need for psychological changes which

3

help the individual adapt to maturation; there is an increased vulnerability of personality; and finally, both periods are followed by specific psychopathology should the individual run into difficulties. Furthermore, an analogy can be drawn between the transformation in early childhood from a dependent infant to a self-reliant toddler, and the adolescent transition to adult independence. In the latter the process of disengagement, that is, the finding of a love object outside the family, involved the renunciation of dependency and the loosening of early childhood ties which have, until puberty, been the major source of emotional nurturance. In some senses just the reverse has happened in early childhood. The child, in an attempt to become separate from the loved one, namely the mother, internalises her. This allows him to become independent while retaining inside himself a representation of the figure he needs. In adolescence, however, the individual has to give up the internalised figure in order to disengage himself and make possible the search for new love objects in the outside world.

If, for the psychoanalysts, disengagement is one key to the adolescent process, another is the significance of regression, which usually means a manifestation of behaviour more appropriate to earlier stages of development. It has been shown how the process of individuation is dependent upon the severance of childhood emotional attachments; however, these attachments can only be surrendered, so it is believed, by a re-animation of infantile involvements and patterns of behaviour. As Blos (1967) explains: 'The adolescent has to come into emotional contact with the passions of his infancy and early childhood in order for them to surrender their original cathexes; only then can the past fade into conscious and unconscious memories ...' (p. 178). The French have a phrase: 'reculer pour mieux sauter', which roughly means: to retreat first in order to leap further, which seems to describe succintly the psychoanalysts' view of the importance of regression.

Blos provides a number of examples of regressive behaviour. One such example is the adolescent's idolisation of famous people, especially pop stars and celebrated sporting personalities. In this phenomenon, he argues, we are reminded of the idealised parent of the younger child. Another example of behaviour in which can be recognised reflections of earlier states is the emotional condition similar to 'merger' – the sensation on the part of the individual of becoming totally submerged by or 'at one with' another. In this condition the adolescent might become almost completely absorbed in abstract ideas such as Nature or Beauty or with political, religious, or philosophical ideals.

Ambivalence is another example of behaviour which reflects earlier stages of childhood. According to the psychoanalytic view, ambivalence accounts for many of the phenomena often considered incomprehensible in adolescent behaviour. For example, the emotional instability of relationships, the contradictions in thought and feeling, and the apparently illogical shifts from one reaction to another reflect the fluctuations between loving and hating, acceptance and rejection, involvement and non-involvement which underlie relationships in the early years, and which are reactivated once more in adolescence. Such fluctuations in mood and behaviour are indicative also of the young person's attitudes to growing up. Thus while freedom may at times appear the most exciting of goals, there are also moments when, in the harsh light of reality, independence and the necessity to fight one's own battles becomes a daunting prospect. At these times childlike dependence exercises a powerful attraction, manifested in periods of uncertainty and self-doubt, and in behaviour which is more likely to bring to mind a wilful child than a young adult.

A consideration of ambivalence leads us on to the more general theme of nonconformity and rebellion, believed by psychoanalysts to be an almost universal feature of adolescence. Behaviour of this sort has many causes. Some of it is a direct result of ambivalent modes of relating, the overt reflection of the conflict between loving and hating. In other circumstances, however, it may be interpreted as an aid to the disengagement process. In this context if the parents can be construed as old-fashioned and irrelevant then the task of breaking the emotional ties becomes easier. If everything that originates from home can safely be rejected then there is nothing to be lost by giving it all up.

Nonconformity thus facilitates the process of disengagement, although as many writers point out, there are a number of intermediate stages along the way. Baittle and Offer (1971) illustrate particularly well the importance of nonconformity and its close links with ambivalence:

When the adolescent rebels, he often expresses his intentions in a manner resembling negation. He defines what he does in terms of what his parents do not want him to do. If his parents want him to turn off the radio and study this is the precise time he keeps the radio on and claims he cannot study. If they want him to buy new clothes, the old ones are good enough. In periods like this it becomes obvious that the adolescent's decisions are in reality based on the negative of the parents' wishes, rather than on their own positive desires. What they do and the judgements they make are in fact dependent on the parents' opinions and suggestions but in a negative way. This may be termed a stage of 'negative dependence'. Thus while the oppositional behaviour and protest against the parents are indeed a manifestation of rebellion and in the service of emancipation from the parents, at the same time they reveal that the passive dependent longings are still in force. The adolescent is in conflict over desires to emancipate, and the rebellious behaviour is a compromise formation which supports his efforts to give up the parental object and, at the same time, gratifies his dependent longings on them.

(Baittle and Offer 1971: 35)

One final matter associated with disengagement needs to be mentioned as an integral feature of the psychoanalytic view of adolescence. This is the emphasis placed on the experience of separation and loss which occurs as a result of the severance of the emotional ties. For some writers (for example, Root 1957) this experience is close to the adult phenomenon of mourning and grief which follows the death of a loved one; for others it is sufficient to stress the inner emptiness with which the adolescent must deal until mature emotional relationships are formed outside the home. To describe this state Blos has coined the term 'object and affect hunger'. He believes that the adolescent need for intense emotional states, including delinquent activities, drug and mystical experiences, and short-lived but intense relationships, may be seen as a means of coping with the inner emptiness. Blos includes here the need to do things 'just for kicks', which he argues simply represents a way of combatting the emotional flatness, depression, and loneliness which are part of the separation experience. He also indicates his belief that both 'object' and 'affect' hunger find some relief in the adolescent gang or peer group. This social group is often, quite literally, the substitute for the adolescent's family, and within it he may experience all the feelings so essential for individual growth such as stimulation, empathy, belongingness, the opportunity for role–playing, identification, and the sharing of guilt and anxiety.

To summarise, three particular ideas characterise the psychoanalytic position. In the first place adolescence is seen as being a period during which there is a marked vulnerability of personality, resulting primarily from the upsurge of instincts at puberty. Second, emphasis is laid on the likelihood of maladaptive behaviour, stemming from the inadequacy of the psychological defences to cope with inner conflicts and tensions. Examples of such behaviour include extreme fluctuations of mood, inconsistency in relationships, depression, and nonconformity. Third, the process of disengagement is given special prominence, for this is perceived as a necessity if mature emotional and sexual relationships are to be established outside the home. In addition, there is one further aspect of psychoanalytic theory, the stress placed on identity formation and the possibility of identity crisis, which has not yet been mentioned. This feature of the theory is most closely associated with the name Erik Erikson, whose views will be described in detail in Chapter four. His theoretical approach, however, fits closely with that of Anna Freud and Peter Blos, and all three represent a view of adolescence which might be expected to result from experience in a clinic or hospital setting. Central to this view are concepts of difficulty and disturbance, and closely allied to it is the theme of adolescent turmoil. The validity of such notions will be considered once the empirical evidence has been reviewed.

Sociological theory

As has been indicated, the sociological view of adolescence encompasses a very different perspective from that of psychoanalytic theory. While there is no disagreement between the two approaches concerning the importance of the transitional process, it is on the subject of the causes of this process that the two viewpoints diverge. Thus while the one concentrates on internal factors, the other looks to society and to events outside the individual for a satisfactory explanation. For the sociologist and the social psychologist 'socialisation' and 'role' are two key concepts. By socialisation is meant the process whereby individuals in a society absorb the values, standards, and beliefs current in that society. Some of these standards and values will refer to positions, or roles, in society, so that, for example, there will be expectations and prescriptions of behaviour appropriate to roles such as son, daughter, citizen, teenager, parent, and so on. Everyone in a society learns through the agents of socialisation, such as school, home, the mass media, etc., the expectations associated with the various roles, although, as we shall see, these expectations may not necessarily be clear-cut. Furthermore, socialisation may be more or less effective, depending on the nature of the agents to which the individual is exposed, the amount of conflict between the different agents, and so on. During childhood the individual, by and large, has his or her roles ascribed by others, but as he or she matures through adolescence greater opportunities are available, not only for a choice of roles, but also for a choice of how those roles should be interpreted. As will become apparent, it is implicit in the social–psychological viewpoint that both socialisation and role assumption are more problematic during adolescence than at any other time.

Why should this be so? In attempting to answer this question we may first of all consider roles and role assumption. It is the belief of most sociologists that a large proportion of an individual's life is characterised by engagement in a series of roles – the sum total of which is known as the role repertoire. The years between childhood and adulthood, as a period of emerging identity, are seen as particularly relevant to the construction of this role repertoire, for the following reasons. First, features of adolescence such as growing independence from authority figures, involvement with peer groups, and an unusual sensitivity to the evaluations of others, all provoke role transitions and discontinuity, of varying intensities, as functions of both social and cultural context. Second, any inner change or uncertainty has the effect of increasing the individual's dependence on others, and this applies particularly to the need for reassurance and support for one's view of oneself. Third, the effects of major environmental changes are also relevant in this context. Different schools, the move from school to university or college, leaving home, taking a job, all demand involvement in a new set of relationships, which in turn lead to different and often greater expectations, a substantial reassessment of the self, and an acceleration of the process of socialisation. Role change, it will be apparent, is thus seen as an integral feature of adolescent development.

Elder (1968) advances this argument by distinguishing two types of role change. On the one hand the young person experiences 'intra-role change'. In this the individual is exposed to new role demands, since as he or she gets older expectations gradually increase. The role remains the same, but within that role different things are expected – the teacher may expect better performance, the parents more independence, and so on. On the other hand, the individual also acquires entirely new roles. Evidently this discontinuity is more abrupt, and is often more difficult to cope with. The change, for example, from school to full-time work usually requires very considerable adaptation, and remnants of the dependent student role are often seen in the young worker. The acquisition of new roles is usually coupled with gradual changes of an intra-role nature, and the two facilitate or hinder each other depending on factors such as the part played by the parents or other significant figures, the relevance of past learning skills to new role demands, the range of the adolescent's role repertoire, and so on. In general it is argued that adolescents experience more or less discontinuity, and that as the degree of role change increases successful adaptation to the new set of role demands becomes more problematic.

While role change may be one source of difficulty for the adolescent, it is certainly not the only one. Inherent in role behaviour generally are a number of potential stresses, some of which have been elaborated by Thomas (1968), and which would appear to be particularly relevant to young people. In the first place Thomas describes role conflict. Here the individual occupies two roles, let us say son and boyfriend, which have expectations associated with them which are incompatible. The individual is thus caught in the middle between two people or sets of people, who expect different forms of behaviour. Thus in the case of son and boyfriend, the teenage boy's mother might put pressure on him to behave like a dutiful child, while his girlfriend will expect him to be independent of his parents and to care for her rather than for anyone else. Such a situation is one which few young people can avoid at some time or another. Next, Thomas mentions role discontinuity, a phenomenon to which we have already referred. Here there is a lack of order in the transition from one role to another. Many years ago, Ruth Benedict (1938) drew attention to the fact that primitive cultures provided more continuity in training for responsibilities, sexual maturity, and so on than western societies, and the situation has hardly improved today. Role discontinuity is said to occur when there is no bridge or ordered sequence from one stage to the next, or when behaviour in the second stage necessitates the unlearning of some or all of that which was learned earlier. One only has to think of the problem of transition for the young unemployed (e.g. Willis 1977), or the grossly inadequate preparation for parenthood in our society to appreciate the point. Third, Thomas draws attention to role incongruence. Here the individual is placed in a position for which he or she is unfitted; in other words the role ascribed by others is not the one that the individual would have chosen. Good illustrations from adolescent experience would be parents who hold unrealistically high expectations of their teenage children, or who, alternatively, fight to maintain their adolescent sons and daughters in childlike roles.

Implicit in these theoretical notions is the view that the individual's movement through adolescence will be very much affected by the consistent or inconsistent, adaptive or maladaptive expectations held by significant people in his or her immediate environment.

Two other writers may also be mentioned as having contributed to this point of view: Brim (1965) and Baumrind (1975). Brim was particularly interested in the adolescent's views of the prescriptions or expectations that adults hold concerning the behaviour of young people. He argued that the more we know of these perceptions, the more likely we are to understand the roles that adolescents adopt:

> We should attempt to describe personality by reference to the individual's perceptions of himself and his behaviour, and of the social organisation in which he lives. We should be interested in the kinds of people he says are of the greatest significance to him, and interested in what he thinks others expect him to do, and in what they think about his performance. We should also know whether or not he accepts what others prescribe for him as right and legitimate, or whether he thinks their expectations are unfair . . . .

> (Brim 1965: 156)

In Brim's view, then, the development of role behaviour will be determined to a large extent by an interaction between the individual's relationships with significant others and his or her perceptions of the expectations of those significant figures. Such an argument accords closely with that of Baumrind. In her discussion of adolescent socialisation she introduces the concept of 'reciprocal role assumption', that is, the effects which prior role assumptions by other family members have on the role the individual may assume. An example which she gives is a situation in which both parents are exceptionally competent managers, thus preventing the young person from developing managerial skills since, while readily available for modelling, such skills are not needed within the family setting. Another example might be a mother who assumes a childlike dependent role, thus forcing her daughter into a maternal role because of the void which she, the mother, creates.

Up to this point our discussion has concentrated on the features of role behaviour which lead sociologists and social psychologists to view adolescence not only as a transitional period, but as one which contains many potentially stressful characteristics. However, the process of socialisation is also seen by many as being problematic at this stage. In the first place the adolescent is exposed to a wide variety of competing socialisation agencies, including the family, the school, the peer group, adult-directed youth organisations, the mass media, political organisations, and so on, and is thus presented with a wide range of potential conflicts in values and ideals. Furthermore it is commonly assumed by sociologists today (e.g. Covington 1982; Marsland 1987) that the socialisation of young people is more dependent upon the generation than upon the family or other social institutions. Marsland goes so far as to call it 'auto-socialisation' in his description of the process:

> The crucial social meaning of youth is withdrawal from adult control and influence compared with childhood. Peer groups are the milieu into which young people withdraw. In at least most societies, this withdrawal to the peer group is, within limits, legitimated by the adult world. Time and space is handed over to young people to work out for themselves in auto-socialisation the developmental problems of self and identity which cannot be handled by the simple direct socialisation appropriate to childhood. There is a moratorium on compliance and commitment and leeway allowed for a relatively unguided journey with peers towards autonomy and maturity.
>
> (Marsland 1987: 12)

Both the conflict between socialisation agencies and the freedom from clearly defined guidelines are seen as making socialisation more uncertain, and causing major difficulties for the young person in establishing a bridge towards the assumption of adult roles. Brake (1985), in his discussion of youth sub-cultures, makes similar points, and it is a common assumption among those writing from the sociological point of view that the social changes of the last twenty years or so have created ever increasing stresses for young people. In particular it should be noted that most writers see little of value in what they believe to be the decline of adult involvement and the increasing importance of the peer group. Among such writers the adolescent peer group is frequently described as being more likely to encourage antisocial behaviour than to act as a civilising agent, and though it is accepted that the effects of peer involvement depend on the standards and activities of the peer group, there is undoubtedly a general feeling that when young people spend a considerable amount of time with individuals of their own age more harm than good is likely to come of it. While, on the one hand, there is clearly some logic in the view that the adolescent who is deprived of adult company is at a disadvantage in the transition towards maturity, on the other hand research does not bear out the myth of the all powerful peer group (see Chapters five and six), and it is still very much an open question as to what effect increasing age segregation has on the socialisation process.

To summarise, the sociological or social–psychological approach to adolescence is marked by a concern with roles and role change, and with the processes of socialisation. There can be little doubt that adolescence, from this point of view, is seen as being dominated by stresses and tensions, not so much because of inner emotional instability, but as a result of conflicting pressures from outside. Thus, by considering both this and the psychoanalytic approach, two mutually complementary but essentially different views of the adolescent transitional process have been reviewed. In spite of their differences, however, the two approaches share one common belief, and that is in the concept of adolescent 'storm and stress'. Both these traditional theories view the teenage years as a 'problem stage' in human development, and in contrast therefore it is important now to review briefly a quite different approach.

Lifespan developmental psychology

Lifespan developmental psychology has emerged as a powerful theoretical position over the last ten years. Its basic tenets have been stated in a variety of books and articles, and useful sources are Belsky *et al.* (1984) and Sugarman (1986). At its simplest level this approach to human development carries with it a number of fundamental assumptions. These may be summarised as follows.

There is a human ecology or context of human development

The intention here is to underline the importance of the environment in its widest sense, and to point out that, for children, the context of development is not just the family, but the geographical, historical, social, and political setting in which that family is living.

Individuals and their families reciprocally influence each other

This principle underlies the fact that neither a child nor a family is a static entity. Each grows, develops, and changes and, most important, each influences the other at all times. The young person's maturation produces changes in the family, but at the same time alterations in family functioning and structure have effects upon the young person's development.

Individuals are producers of their own development

Attention is being drawn here to the part that all individuals, of whatever age, play in shaping their own development. This is probably the most innovative of the four principles, having very wide implications for social science research. While it may be generally accepted that child and adolescent development results from an interplay of a variety of causes the idea that the individual young person might be an 'active agent' in shaping or determining his or her own development has not generally been part of the thinking of researchers in this field. Once pointed out, however, the idea is obvious and, as we shall see, the principle is already influencing the design of studies of adolescence.

A multi-disciplinary approach must be taken to studying human development

This may seem like a statement of the obvious, but the fact that lifespan developmental psychologists have laid particular stress on this principle has had surprising results, and has brought together biologists, paediatricians, sociologists, ecologists, and so on in co-operative projects on human development which are undoubtedly paying substantial dividends.

While the principles of lifespan developmental psychology have had a widespread impact in a variety of areas, we are obviously here concerned with the effects of these concepts in the field of adolescence. As one illustration of this we may take the work of Brooks-Gunn and Petersen (1983), and Brooks-Gunn *et al.* (1985), work we shall be referring to in greater detail in subsequent chapters. These publications, the first an edited book, and the second two special issues of the *Journal of Youth and Adolescence*, document what has been called a 'new wave of socio-pubertal studies'. This research investigates the biological and psycho-social development of girls in early adolescence, attempting to disentangle the multiplicity of variables which affect the timing of puberty, and to look at the way in which rates of maturation in turn relate to other aspects of adjustment.

These studies have been conceived within the lifespan developmental framework, and reflect all the principles mentioned above. The research is multi-disciplinary, deliberately avoiding single-discipline models of change. The research takes account of the ecology of human development, by considering the effects of family, career choice, and even the school upon the timing of puberty. The research considers the question of reciprocal influence, in that note is taken not only of the variables which may be seen to contribute to the onset of puberty, but also of those factors which appear in their turn to be effected by pubertal timing. Lastly, the research acknowledges that adolescents themselves can be 'active agents', and may have the power to hasten or slow down the pace of their own development. By studying a group of young dancers for example, Brooks-Gunn and Warren (1985) were able to suggest the strong possibility that the social context and the individual's desire to be in step with demands of that context could lead to a delay in the onset of puberty.

There is no doubt that this is imaginative and highly significant research. It is important in its own right, but it is important also as a reflection of the potential influence of the principles of lifespan developmental psychology. The quality that distinguishes this theoretical model from other approaches is its interactive stance. It stresses reciprocal influences, it brings together different professional disciplines, it underlines the interaction between individual and family, and between family and the outside world. Lifespan developmental psychology is not specifically concerned with adolescence, yet it is critical to the studies of adolescence because it provides an all-important perspective. A striking example of this may be found in Lerner's (1985) paper entitled 'Adolescent maturational changes and psychosocial development – a dynamic interactional perspective'. Here the author considers three ways in which the adolescent interacts with the environment and thereby affects his or her own development. Lerner draws attention to the adolescent as *stimulus*, eliciting different reactions from the environment; as *processor* making sense of the behaviour of others; and as *agent, shaper, and selector* doing things, making choices, and influencing events.

Lerner's viewpoint cannot help but alter radically the way in which adolescence is conceptualised. Here is a three-dimensional view of the developmental process, and by comparison other models appear somewhat limited. Whether the lifespan developmental model can be translated into an adequate research design is a question we will be considering in the course of this book. For the moment, however, we need only note the potential impact and importance that this approach is likely to have in contributing to a better understanding of adolescence.

Thus we have seen how the two traditional theories, with their emphasis on stress, conflict, and difficulty, lead to a view of adolescence as a problem period. By contrast, lifespan developmental psychology avoids this judgement, setting out basic principles which, it is believed, should inform all studies of human

14

development. As we have seen, this approach has already generated valuable research, and will no doubt continue to do so. In the rest of this book we will be considering empirical evidence as it relates to various aspects of adolescent development. We will also be considering Erik Erikson's approach to identity development in Chapter three, and theories of social cognition in Chapter four. This will make it possible, in the final chapter, to evaluate the three theories outlined here, to match theory and evidence, and to consider to what extent new theoretical approaches are necessary.

Chapter two

Physical development

Puberty and the growth spurt

Having considered three theoretical approaches in the previous chapter we may now turn our attention to the different aspects of growth and change which together make up the adolescent experience. The first of these is physical development. In considering the picture as a whole there seems little doubt that some of the most important events to which young people have to adjust are the multitude of physiological and morphological changes which occur during early adolescence, and which are associated with what is generally known as puberty. The word derives from the Latin 'pubertas', meaning age of manhood, and is usually considered to date from the onset of menstruation in girls, and the emergence of pubic hair in boys. However, as we shall see, these two easily observable changes are each only a small part of a complex process involving many bodily functions. Puberty is accompanied by changes not only in the reproductive system and in the secondary sexual characteristics of the individual, but in the functioning of the heart and thus of the cardio-vascular system, in the lungs which in turn affect the respiratory system, in the size and the strength of many of the muscles of the body, and so on. Puberty, therefore, must be seen as an event in the physical life of the body with wide-ranging implications, the most important of which will be considered in this chapter.

One of the many physical changes associated with puberty is the 'growth spurt'. This term is usually taken to refer to the accelerated rate of increase in height and weight that occurs during early adolescence. Typical curves for individual rates of growth are illustrated in Figure 2.1. It is essential to bear in mind, however, that there are very considerable individual differences in the age of onset and duration of the growth spurt, even among perfectly normal children, as illustrated in Figures 2.2 and 2.3. This is a fact which parents and adolescents themselves frequently fail to appreciate, thus causing a great deal of unnecessary anxiety. In boys the growth spurt may begin as early as 10 years of age, or as late as 16, while in girls the same process can begin at 7 or 8, or not until 12, 13, or even 14. For the average boy, though, rapid growth begins at about 13, and reaches a peak somewhere during the fourteenth year. Comparable ages for girls are 11 for the onset of the growth spurt, and 12 for the peak age of increase in height and weight. As we have noted, other phenomena associated with the growth spurt are a rapid increase in the size and weight of the heart (the weight of the heart nearly doubles at puberty), an accelerated growth of the lungs, and a decline in basal metabolism. Noticeable to children themselves, especially to boys, is a marked increase in physical strength and endurance. Sexual differentiation is also reflected in less obvious internal changes, as Katchadourian (1977) points out.

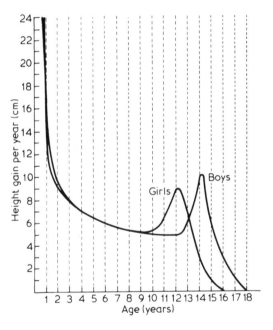

Source: J. M. Tanner, R. H. Whitehouse, and M. Takaishi (1966) *Archives of Disease in Childhood* 41.

Figure 2.1 Typical velocity curves for supine length or height in boys or girls. These curves represent the velocity of the typical boy or girl at any given moment.

Physical development

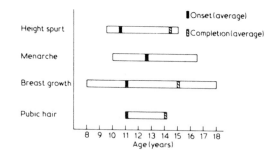

Source: J. M. Tanner (1973) *Scientific American* 229.

Figure 2.2 Normal range and average age of development of sexual characteristics in females.

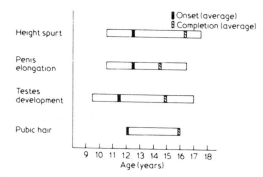

Source: J. M. Tanner (1973) *Scientific American* 229.

Figure 2.3 Normal range and average age of development of sexual characteristics in males.

For example, changes such as the increase in the number of red blood cells, and the increase in systolic blood pressure are far greater in boys than in girls. The extent of such differences, which seem likely to be evolutionary and to be associated with the male's greater ability to undertake physical exertion, are illustrated in Figure 2.4.

It may be noted that it is the action of the pituitary gland which is of the greatest significance for the regulation of the physiological changes which occur during early adolescence. This gland, located immediately below the brain, releases activating hormones. These in turn have a stimulating effect on most of the other endocrine glands, which then release their own growth-related hormones.

18

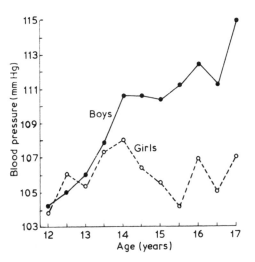

Source: W. Montagna and W. A. Sadler (eds) (1974) *Reproductive Behavior*, Plenum.

Figure 2.4 Differences in systolic blood pressure between boys and girls at puberty.

Among the most important of these are the sex hormones, including testosterone in males and oestrogen in females, which stimulate the growth of mature sperm and ova. However, these hormones also combine with others such as thyroxine from the thyroid gland, and cortisol from the adrenal gland, to activate the growth of bone and muscle which leads to the growth spurt.

Sexual maturation is closely linked with the physical changes described above. Again, the sequence of events is approximately eighteen to twenty-four months later for boys than it is for girls. For boys the first sign of the approach of puberty is most commonly an increase in the rate of growth of the testes and scrotum, followed by the growth of pubic hair. Acceleration of growth of the penis and the appearance of facial hair frequently accompany the beginning of the growth spurt in height and weight, and it is usually somewhat later than this that the voice breaks, and the first seminal discharge occurs. In girls, enlargement of the breasts and the growth of pubic hair are early signs of puberty, and are followed by the growth of the uterus and the vagina. The menarche itself occurs relatively late in the developmental sequence, and almost always after the peak velocity of the growth spurt. The

19

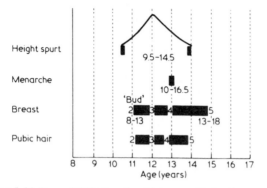

Source: J. M. Tanner (1962) *Growth at Adolescence*, Blackwell.

Figure 2.5 Diagram of sequence of events at adolescence in girls. An average girl is represented; the range of ages within which some of the events may occur (and stages in their development) is given by the figures directly below them.

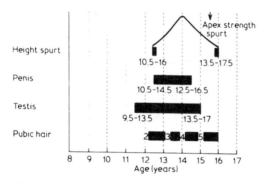

Source: W. A. Marshall and J. M. Tanner (1970) *Archives of Disease in Childhood* 45.

Figure 2.6 Diagram of sequence of events at adolescence in boys. An average boy is represented; the range of ages within which each event charted may begin and end (and stages in their development) is given directly below its start and finish.

sequence of events in boys and girls is illustrated in Figures 2.5 and 2.6.

Tanner (1978) has drawn attention to an important difference between boys and girls in the relative positions of the height spurt in the whole sequence of events at puberty. It was only realised, as a result of detailed longitudinal studies (Eveleth and Tanner

1977), that girls experience their height spurts considerably earlier than boys. The differences between the sexes in the age of peak velocity is about two years, while the differences in the appearance of pubic hair is about nine months. The first appearance of breasts in girls precedes the increase in the size of the testes in boys by even less of a time gap. Thus the growth spurt is placed earlier in the sequence in girls than it is in boys. The practical effects of this are that in girls the first event of puberty is often an increase in height, which frequently goes unnoticed. In boys, on the other hand, peak height velocity usually occurs late in the sequence, and after pubic hair has appeared and genitalia have started to grow. Thus, as Tanner points out, boys who are late maturers can be reassured that their height spurt is still to come if genital development is not far advanced, while girls who are worried about being too tall can be informed that their height spurt is nearly over if menarche has already occurred.

Psychological effects of puberty

The changes discussed above inevitably exercise a profound effect upon the individual. The body alters radically in size and shape, and it is not surprising that many adolescents experience a period of clumsiness as they attempt to adapt to these changes. The body also alters in function, and new and sometimes worrying physical experiences such as the girl's first period, or the boy's nocturnal emissions, have to be understood. Perhaps most important of all, however, is the effect that such physical changes have upon identity. As many writers have pointed out, the development of the individual's identity requires not only the notion of being separate and different from others, but also a sense of self-consistency, and a firm knowledge of how one appears to the rest of the world (for further consideration of this issue see Chapter four). Needless to say dramatic bodily changes seriously affect these aspects of identity, and represent a considerable challenge in adaptation for even the most well-adjusted young person. It is unfortunate that many adults, having successfully forgotten much of their own adolescent anxiety, retain only a vague awareness of the psychological impact of the physical changes associated with puberty.

Experimental evidence has clearly shown that the average adolescent is not only sensitive to, but often critical of, his or her changing physical self (Clausen 1975; Davies and Furnham 1986). Thus, probably largely as a result of the importance of films and television, teenagers tend to have idealised norms for physical attractiveness, and to feel inadequate if they do not match these unrealistic criteria. Lerner and Karabenick (1974) showed that adolescents who perceived themselves as deviating physically from cultural stereotypes were likely to have impaired self-concepts, and many other studies have pointed out the important role that physical characteristics play in determining self-esteem, especially in the younger adolescent. Thus, for example, both Rosen and Ross (1968) and Simmons and Rosenberg (1975) have reported studies in which adolescents were asked what they did and did not like about themselves. Results showed that those in early adolescence used primarily physical characteristics to describe themselves, and it was these characteristics which were most often disliked. It was not until later adolescence that intellectual or social aspects of personality were widely used in self-description, but these characteristics were much more frequently liked than disliked. It is, therefore, just at the time of most rapid physical change that appearance is of critical importance for the individual, both for his or her self-esteem as well as for popularity.

Early and late development

Since individuals mature at very different rates, one girl at the age of 14 may be small, have no bust and look very much as she did during childhood, while another of the same age may look like a fully-developed adult woman, who could easily be mistaken for someone four or five years in advance of her actual chronological age. The question arises as to whether such marked physical differences have particular consequences for the individual's psychological adjustment. By and large longitudinal studies have shown that, for boys, early maturation carries with it social advantages, while late maturation can be more of a problem. In comparison with early maturers late maturing males have been found to be less relaxed, less popular, more dependent, and less attractive to both adults and peers (Jones and Bayley 1950; Mussen and Jones 1957; Clausen 1975). The picture for girls, however, is more complex, for early maturation seems to have both costs and benefits. As a number of writers have shown, girls who mature early are less popular with their peers, and more likely to show signs of inner turbulence than those who mature later (Jones and Mussen 1958; Peskin 1973). On the other hand it has also been reported that early maturation can lead to enhanced self-confidence and social prestige (Clausen 1975). Particularly important here is Faust's (1960) study which showed that early maturing girls in Grade 6 (i.e. 12-year-olds) were at a disadvantage, while early maturers in Grades 7 and 8 were seen to be at a definite social advantage. Similarly Clausen (1975) indicated that social class was significant, middle-class early maturers being at a greater advantage than their working-class peers.

The theme of the onset of puberty and its psychological consequences has been developed during the 1980s in a variety of ways. Good reviews may be found in the two special issues of the *Journal of Youth and Adolescence* already referred to in Chapter one, and in Brooks-Gunn (1987) and Petersen (1988). Two particular topics addressed by this work include, first, the meaning of puberty for the individual and for those in his or her immediate environment, and second, the factors which affect the timing of puberty. It is important to note that the lifespan developmental approach has been the inspiration for the great majority of these studies. Of significance here is the *deviance* hypothesis (Petersen and Crockett 1985) which states that early and late maturers differ from on-time maturers because of their status, being socially deviant compared to their peer group. Early maturing girls and late maturing boys would be at risk for adjustment problems because they constitute the two most deviant groups in terms of maturation. In addition Lerner's (1985) paper, in which he stresses the centrality of the reciprocal relations between the person and the environment is a further example of the conceptual model lying behind the current wave of empirical investigations of puberty.

Two studies may be selected as illustrations of this research. Brooks-Gunn and Warren (1985), already mentioned in Chapter one, utilise the on-time model to explain their findings concerning adolescent dancers. Girls in dance and non-dance schools were compared for pubertal status. Because the dance student must maintain a relatively low body weight, it was expected that being a late maturer would be more advantageous to the dancer. Results showed that more dance (55 per cent) than non-dance (29 per cent) girls were late maturers. In addition the on-time dancers (i.e. those who had already reached puberty) showed more personality and eating problems. Brooks-Gunn and Warren (1985) suggest that a goodness of fit exists between the requirements of a particular social context and a person's physical and behavioural characteristics. For the dancers, who must maintain a low body weight to perform, being on-time (and heavier) is a disadvantage. For girls for whom weight is not an issue being on-time may be a positive advantage – at least it is unlikely to be perceived in a negative manner.

Physical development

The works of Simmons, Blyth, and others may be quoted as a further example of work which studies puberty as one element of the individual's social and physical development. Blyth *et al.* (1985) report a longitudinal study exploring the effects of pubertal timing on satisfaction with body image and self-esteem in adolescent girls. Results show a more favourable body image and/or self-image if the young person approximates the cultural ideal of thinness, *and* if they are not experiencing simultaneous environmental (school transition) and physical (early puberty) changes. Blyth and Simmons (1987) expand these findings by comparing boys and girls, and showing that being off-time – i.e. out of step with your peers – has more negative effects for boys than for girls, especially at the two extreme ends of the developmental spectrum.

Studies such as these indicate a more sophisticated, theory-led approach to the understanding of adolescent issues. Results reflect accurately the complexity of the phenomena that are being studied, but raise important questions of a methodological nature. We will be considering further the relevance and impact of the lifespan developmental approach in the final chapter.

The secular trend

The term 'secular trend' has been used to describe the biological fact that over the last hundred years the rate of physical growth of children and adolescents has accelerated, leading to faster and thus earlier maturation. This trend has been particularly noticeable in the growth rates of 2- to 5-year-olds, but it has also had many implications for adolescent development. Full adult height is now achieved at a much earlier age (i.e. between 16 and 18), final adult stature and body weight have increased, and many investigators have reported that height and weight during adolescence are greater today than they have ever been. Meredith (1963), for example, found that 15-year-old American white boys were 5.25 inches taller in 1955 than they were in 1870, and Tanner (1962) reports a study of English boys attending Marlborough College who were measured at an average age of 16½ in 1873, and at that time had a mean height of 65.6 inches. Eighty years later boys of the same age in the same school were 69.1 inches tall, a gain of 4.1 inches or about 0.5 inches per decade. Muuss (1970) makes it clear, however, that it is not only height and weight that are increasing:

The knight's armour in mediaeval European castles serve as powerful illustrations of the secular trend, since the armour seems to be made to fit average ten- to twelve-year-old American boys of today. The seats in the famous La Scala opera house in Milan, Italy, which was contructed in 1776–1778, were thirteen inches wide. Thirty years ago most states outlawed seats that were less than eighteen inches wide. In 1975 comfortable seats will need to be twenty-four inches wide. The feet of the American male at the present time grow one third of an inch every generation, which means an upward change of one shoe size per generation. Today the shoes worn by the average male are 9–10B, while his grandfather in all probability wore a size 7 shoe.

(Muuss 1970: 170)

The maturation of the reproductive system is also affected by the secular trend. Tanner (1978) estimates that in average populations in western Europe there has been a downward trend in the age of menarche of about four months per decade since 1850. He and his co-workers have collected together much of the available data, which is summarised in Figure 2.7. It will be seen that the mean age of menarche has continued to drop in most countries up to 1970, although this decline does seem to have slowed down in Norway and in some parts of Great Britain (Poppleton and Brown 1966). It remains to be seen whether similar results will be obtained in other countries, or whether the secular trend has reappeared in the 1980s in Great Britain and Norway.

In spite of these two recent exceptions to the rule, the secular trend is a remarkable phenomenon, and various explanations have been advanced to explain it. One view is that girls growing up in the tropics reach puberty earlier than those living in milder climates. Although a number of writers have advanced this theory, reliable evidence does not show climate to have any direct influence on maturational rates. Figures reported by Eveleth and Tanner (1977) concerning the mean age of menarche in the years 1960–75 in a wide range of countries all over the globe illustrate this well. To take but a few examples at random, the mean age of menarche in Burma is reported as being 13.2, in Mexico 12.8, in London 13.0, in Oslo 13.2, in Uganda 13.4, and in the U.S.A. 12.8. These figures provide no evidence for the effects of climate. Another explanation sometimes put forward is that some relentless evolutionary trend is at work. However, neither Tanner nor Conger and Petersen (1984) accept this view. These writers are firmly of the belief that we must look to the social changes inherent in present-day society if we are to find a reasonable explanation for these phenomena. In particular they take the view that improved nutrition, as well as better health care, housing and

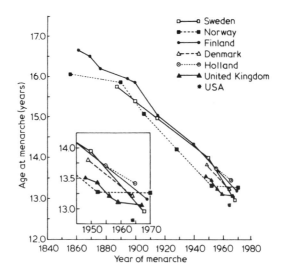

Source: J. M. Tanner (1978) *Foetus into Man*, Open Books.

Figure 2.7 Secular trend in age at menarche, 1860–1970.

social conditions generally, are the primary causes underlying the secular trend.

Supporting evidence for this may be drawn from three sources. In the first place it is clear that within individual countries those who have benefited most from improvements in health care, nutrition, and living conditions, namely working-class children, are the ones who have also shown the most accelerated rates of growth. Second, there is reliable evidence to indicate that during periods of nutritional deprivation (i.e. during World War II in European countries) rates of growth did not accelerate and the age of menarche was significantly retarded (Tanner 1962). Finally, the results of the work of Eveleth and Tanner (1977), already discussed above, also casts light on this question. For example, where comparisons are available between rural and urban populations in the same country, age of menarche is considerably later in rural areas (12.8 in urban Madras, as compared with 14.2 in rural Madras). In addition delayed menarche was only found in primitive cultures or in situations of deprivation (15.5 and 18.0 in New Guinea, 14.9 among black urban South Africans, 13.8 among Eskimos). Such findings provide a basis for the point of view espoused by Tanner (1978) and by Conger and Petersen (1984) and seem, at least at present, hard to dispute.

No discussion of the secular trend would be complete without a consideration of the question: How long will it continue? While, on the one hand, there are those who have fantasies of girls in the year 22040 reaching puberty by the age of 4 (Muuss 1970), on the other, writers such as Tanner believe that physical development can only be accelerated within the ultimate biological limits for a given population. Tanner himself (1970) suggests that the biological limit for European populations may be represented by an average menarchial age of 12.25 years. While this may seem to some an unduly conservative estimate, perhaps the problem should be considered in the same light as that of the breaking of athletic records. While men and women will undoubtedly continue to reduce the time taken to run a mile, the amount by which the record is broken each time will gradually decrease. Thus it may be that while the twentieth century has seen a reduction in the age of menarche by four months per decade, possibly in the next century the reduction will average one month per decade or even less. It is surely reasonable to assume that the continuation of the secular trend will be primarily dependent on the degree to which standards of living continue to improve.

Chapter three

Thinking and reasoning

Cognitive development in adolescence is one of the areas of maturation which is least apparent to observers. It has no external and visible correlate, as with physical maturation, nor is it manifested in any tangible alteration in behaviour, and yet changes in this sphere are occurring all the time. Furthermore, changes in intellectual function have implications for a wide range of behaviours and attitudes. Such changes render possible the move towards independence of both thought and action, they enable the young person to develop a time perspective which includes the future, they facilitate progress towards maturity in relationships, and finally, they underlie the individual's ability to participate in society as worker, voter, responsible group member, and so on. This chapter will begin by considering the views of Piaget, for it was he who first drew attention to the importance of the intellectual development which follows puberty. Some attention will also be paid to the burgeoning field of social cognition, to Elkind's notions of egocentrism, and to the development of moral and political thought in adolescence.

Formal operations

The work of Jean Piaget, the Swiss psychologist, is the most obvious starting place for a consideration of cognitive development during the teenage years. It was he who first pointed out that a qualitative change in the nature of mental ability, rather than any simple increase in cognitive skill, is to be expected at or around puberty, and he argued that it is at this point in development that formal operational thought finally becomes possible (Inhelder and Piaget 1958).

A full description of Piaget's stages of cognitive growth is beyond the scope of this book, but may be found in any standard text on child development. For our purposes the crucial distinction is that which Piaget draws between concrete and formal operations. During the stage of *concrete operations* (approximately between the ages of 7 and 11) the child's thought may be termed 'relational'. Gradually he or she begins to master notions of classes, relations, and quantities. Conservation and seriation become possible, and the development of these skills enables the individual to formulate hypotheses and explanations about concrete events. These cognitive operations are seen by the child simply as mental tools, the products of which are on a par with perceptual phenomena. In other words, the child at this stage seems unable to differentiate clearly between what is perceptually given and what is mentally constructed. When the child formulates an hypothesis it originates from the data, not from within the person, and if new contradictory data are presented he or she does not change the hypothesis, but rather prefers to alter the data or to rationalise these in one way or another.

With the appearance of *formal operations* a number of important capabilities become available to the young person. Perhaps the most significant of these is the ability to construct 'contrary-to-fact' propositions. This change has been described as a shift of emphasis in adolescent thought from the 'real' to the 'possible', and it facilitates a hypothetico-deductive approach to problem solving and to the understanding of propositional logic. It also enables the individual to think about mental constructs as objects which can be manipulated, and to come to terms with notions of probability and belief.

This fundamental difference in approach between the young child and the adolescent has been neatly demonstrated in a study by Elkind (1966). Two groups of subjects, children of 8 to 9 years and adolescents between 13 and 14, were presented with a concept–formation problem, involving pictures of wheeled and non-wheeled tools and wheeled and non-wheeled vehicles. The pictures were presented in pairs with each pair including both a wheeled and non-wheeled object. In each case the child was asked to choose one member of the pair. Choosing a wheeled object always made a light go on whereas choosing a non-wheeled object did not. The problem for the subject was to determine the kind of picture that would make the signal light go on every time. Differences in the manner in which adolescents and younger children handled the task were clearly illustrated. Only half of the younger children were able to arrive at the notion that it was the choice of a wheeled object that made the light go on. Furthermore, it took those children who did suceed almost all of the allotted seventy-two trials to arrive at a correct solution. On the other hand, all of the adolescents solved the problem, and many did so in as few as ten trials. The tendency of adolescents to raise alternative hypotheses successively, test each against the facts, and discard those that prove wrong was apparent in their spontaneous verbalisations during the experiment (for example, 'maybe it's transportation ... no, it must be something else, I'll try ...'). In this fashion they quickly solved the problem. The younger children however appeared to become fixated on an initial hypothesis that was strongly suggested by the data (for example, tool versus non-tool or vehicle versus non-vehicle). They then clung to this hypothesis even though they continued to fail on most tests. Although the adolescents might also have considered such likely hypotheses initially, they quickly discarded them when they were not substantiated by subsequent evidence. It appeared that an important part of the younger child's greater inflexibility was an inability to differentiate the hypothesis from reality. Having once adopted an hypothesis it became 'true' and the child then felt no need to test it further. Indeed, according to Elkind, he or she seemed unaware of the hypothetical quality of the strategy, and seemed to feel that it was imposed from without rather than constructed from within. This particular piece of research represents an excellent illustration of Piaget's view that it is the adolescent's awareness of possibility that enables him or her to distinguish thought from reality.

Elkind's study is concerned with one aspect of formal operational thought. Inhelder and Piaget (1958) have developed an ingenious set of tests for the investigation of many different aspects of logical thinking, and some of these have been widely used by other research workers. One such test is known as the Pendulum Problem. Here the task involves discovering which factor or combination of factors determined the rate of swing of the pendulum. The task is illustrated in Figure 3.1, and depends for its solution once again on the ability of the individual to test alternative hypotheses successively. Another well-known problem is that of the Rings, bearing directly on the concept of proportionality. The experiment is described as follows:

> Rings of varying diameters are placed between a light source and a screen. The size of their shadows is directly proportional to the diameters and inversely proportional to the distance between them and the light source. Specifically, we ask the subject to find two shadows which cover each other exactly, using two unequal sizes of ring. To do so he need only place

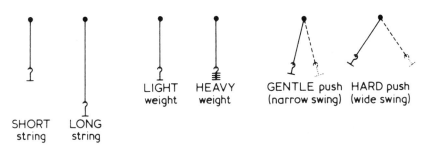

SHORT   LONG
string   string

LIGHT   HEAVY
weight   weight

GENTLE push   HARD push
(narrow swing) (wide swing)

Source: Original research for M. Shayer (1979) *Science Reasoning Tasks*, NFER.

Figure 3.1 The Pendulum Problem. The task is to determine which factor
or combination of factors determines the rate of swing of the
pendulum.

the larger one further from the light, in proportion to its size,
and there will be compensation between distance and diameters.

(Dulit 1972: 290)

Clearly, formal operational thought cannot be tested using a single
problem or task. Any investigator must use a range of tests, and
attempt to construct some overall measure of the individual's
ability to tackle problems of logical thought in a number of areas.
In relation to this it is important to bear in mind that the
development of formal thinking is certainly not an all-or-none
affair, with the individual moving overnight from one stage to
another. The change occurs slowly, and there may even be some
shifting back and forth, as suggested by Turiel (1974), before the
new mode of thought is firmly established. Furthermore, it is
almost certain that the adolescent will adopt formal modes of
thinking in one area before another. Thus, for example, someone
interested in arts subjects may use formal operational thinking in
the area of verbal reasoning well before he or she is able to utilise
such skills in scientific problem solving.

In addition to these points recent research indicates that in all
probability Piaget was a little too optimistic when he expressed the
view that the majority of adolescents could be expected to develop
formal operational thought by 12 or 13 years of age. While studies
do not entirely agree on the exact proportions reaching various
stages at different age levels, there is a general consensus that up
to the age of 16 only a minority reach the most advanced level of
formal thought. In Great Britain studies by Shayer *et al.* (1976,
1978) using a number of scientifically oriented tasks – including the

Pendulum Problem – in a standardised procedure on over 1,000 young people, have shown that slightly less than 30 per cent of 16-year-olds reach the stage of early formal thought and only 10 per cent reach the level of advanced formal thinking. These findings are illustrated in Figure 3.2. Research carried out in Australia by Connell *et al.* (1975) amplifies these results. In this study a verbal reasoning task was used, and again with a large group of teenagers evidence showed that only 44 per cent had reached the stage of formal thought by 16. No distinction was made here between early and late stages of this type of thinking. Studies such as these indicate that intelligence is associated with the development of formal thought, but it is not sufficient to explain the fact that by school-leaving age a good proportion of adolescents are still at the level of concrete operational thought. In her wide-ranging review of the area Neimark (1975) quotes a number of studies which show that even in adulthood substantial minorities are failing to attain formal operational thought. As Piaget himself acknowledges in one of his later articles (1972), such findings must inevitably lead to a radical re-formulation of our notions of adult cognitive ability in western society.

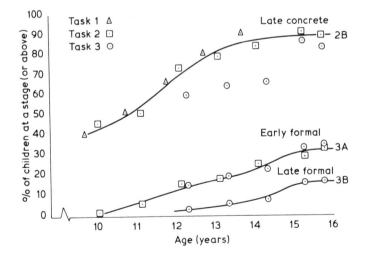

Source: M. Shayer and H. Wylam (1978) *British Journal of Educational Psychology* 48.

Figure 3.2 Proportion of boys at different Piagetian stages as assessed by three tasks.

We have already noted that intelligence is likely to play a role in the development of this level of thinking. Yet this variable is not sufficient to explain why formal operations appear in one child at 12, and in another at 16. Inhelder and Piaget (1958) paid remarkably little attention to this problem, contenting themselves simply with some speculation about the relation between intellectual and social development. They appear to suggest that as social pressures operate on the individual, encouraging him or her towards maturity and independence, so intellectual skills develop, enabling the young person to cope with the new demands of a more adult life. This is hardly a very satisfactory explanation, although it may indeed turn out that social and intellectual maturation are correlated.

Although there have been isolated attempts to unravel this problem – Kohen-Raz (1974) looked at the role of pubertal status, Cloutier and Goldschmid (1976) investigated personality factors, while Flexer and Roberge (1983) examined cognitive style – by and large the issue has faded into the background, particularly since the 1970s.

There appear to be two interrelated reasons for this. On the one hand some fairly wide-ranging criticism of the notion of formal operational thought has appeared in the literature (see, for example, Keating 1980), much of which has centred on the methodological difficulties of testing for the presence of formal operations. Major studies of cognitive development, such as the one carried out by Neimark (1975), have also been criticised for methodological failings, and Piagetian concerns have undoubtedly become less popular among the academic community as a result. A second reason for this state of affairs is the increasing popularity of topics relating to social cognition. Here methodological problems are not so obvious, and the field has generated enormous interest, diverting energy away from strictly cognitive issues. It is to these topics that we now turn.

Social cognition

In spite of the fact that Piaget may be temporarily out of favour it cannot be denied that almost all those interested in the development of adolescent thought have used Piaget's work as a starting point. David Elkind is one writer who leads us in to the field of social cognition, and who at the same time provides a good example of the way in which it is possible to elaborate on the work of Piaget. In his development of the notion of egocentrism in adolescence, Elkind (1967) has extended our notion of the reasoning of young people in an important way. He argues that while the attainment of formal operational thinking frees the individual in many respects from childhood egocentrism, paradoxically at the same time it entangles him or her in a new version of the same thing. This is because the achievement of formal operational thought allows the adolescent to think not only about his own thought, but also about the thought of other people.

It is this capacity to take account of other people's thinking, argues Elkind, which is the basis of adolescent egocentrism. Essentially the individual finds it extremely difficult to differentiate between what others are thinking about and his or her own preoccupations. He or she assumes that if they are obsessed by a thought or a problem then other people must also be obsessed by the same thing. The example given by Elkind is that of the adolescent's appearance. To a large extent teenagers are preoccupied with the way they look to others, and they make the assumption that others must be as involved as they are with the same subject. Elkind ties this type of egocentrism in with a concept of what he calls 'the imaginary audience'. Because of egocentrism the adolescent is, either in actual or fantasised social situations, anticipating the reactions of others. However, these reactions are based on a premise that others are as admiring or critical of them as they are of themselves. Thus the teenager is continually constructing and reacting to an 'imaginary audience', a fact which, according to Elkind, expains a lot of adolescent behaviour – the self-consciousness, the wish for privacy, the long hours spent in front of a mirror. All these and many other aspects of teenage behaviour, it is argued, may be related to the 'imaginary audience'.

There is one other significant aspect of adolescent egocentrism, seen as an example of over-differentiation of feelings, which Elkind calls the 'personal fable'. Possibly because the adolescent believes he or she is of importance to so many people (the imaginary audience) they come to see themselves and their feelings as very special, even unique. A belief in the unique nature of the individual's misery and suffering is, of course, a familiar theme in literature, and Elkind suggests that it underlies the young person's construction of a 'personal fable'. In essence this is the individual's story about himself, the story he tells himself, and it may well include fantasies of omnipotence and immortality. It is not a true story, but it serves a valuable purpose, and is exemplified in some of the most famous adolescent diaries. In this sort of material one can get closest to a belief in the universal significance of the adolescent experience, and it is out of this belief that the 'personal fable' is created. Elkind argues that these two foundations of adolescent egocentrism – the imaginary audience and the personal fable – are useful explanations of some aspects of adolescent cognitive behaviour, and may be helpful in the treatment of disturbed teenagers. One example he gives is that of adolescent offenders. Here it is often of central importance to help the individual differentiate between the real and the imagined audience which, as Elkind points out, often boils down to discrimination between real and imaginary parents.

In recent years a number of studies have explored the nature of egocentrism from an empirical point of view. Both Elkind and Bowen (1979) and Enright *et al.* (1980) have developed scales for the measurement of various aspects of egocentrism. In broad terms results from these studies do support the view that egocentrism declines from early to late adolescence. However, findings are not clear-cut, and a number of issues remain unresolved. An intriguing study by Riley *et al.* (1984) exemplifies this. The authors set out to answer two questions. First, are egocentrism and the appearance of formal operational thought related? Second, are there social factors, for example family support, that might affect the extent of egocentric thought? Results showed both these lines of enquiry to be important and fruitful. Findings indicated clearly that contrary to Elkind's prediction the appearance of formal thinking was associated with a reduction of self-consciousness. Furthermore, relationships with parents do affect egocentrism, in that emotionally supportive parents diminish the likelihood of high states of self-consciousness and, at least in girls, paternal rejection heightens self-conscious behaviour. The study thus illustrates the unresolved nature of a number of aspects of egocentrism, as well as the clear link between social context and cognitive development.

Studies of egocentrism may be considered as one aspect of the general interest in social cognition. Books such as those by Flavell (1977), Damon (1978), Serafica (1982), and Higgins *et al.* (1983) all attest to the fascination generated by this field of enquiry. Of course not all those concerned with social cognition have been interested in adolescence. It is probable that the writer who has done most to apply the social-cognitive perspective to the adolescent field is Robert Selman. In his view social cognition is concerned with the processes by which children and adolescents conceptualise and learn to understand others: their thoughts, their wishes, their feelings, their attitudes to others, and, of course, their social behaviour. Social cognition involves role-taking, perspective-taking, empathy, moral reasoning, interpersonal problem-solving, and self-knowledge. Selman makes an important distinction between role-taking and social perspective-taking when he argues that the former involves the question of what social or psychological information may look like from the position of the other person. Social perspective-taking more generally involves an 'understanding of how human points of view are related and coordinated with one another' (Selman 1980: 22).

Selman's most important contribution is his proposal of a stage theory of social cognition. In the most general terms Selman (1976, 1977, 1980) identifies four developmental levels of social perspective-taking. These are:

Stage 1: the differential or subjective perspective-taking stage (ages 5–9)

Here children are beginning to realise that other people can have a social perspective which is different from their own.

Stage 2: self-reflective thinking, or reciprocal perspective-taking (ages 7–12)

At this stage the child realises not only that other people have their own perspective, but that they may actually be giving thought to the child's own perspective. Thus the crucial cognitive advance here is the ability to take into account the perspective of another individual.

Stage 3: third person, or mutual perspective-taking (ages 10–15)

The perspective-taking skills of early adolescence lead to the capacity for a more complex type of social cognition. The young person moves beyond simply taking the other person's perspective (in a back and forth manner) and is able to see all parties from a more generalised third-person perspective.

Stage 4: in-depth societal perspective-taking (age 15+)

During this stage the individual may move to a still higher and more abstract level of interpersonal perspective-taking which involves co-ordinating the perspectives of society with those of the individual and the group.

We have only space here for a brief description of the outline of Selman's stage theory. It is, however, a good example of the way in which those interested in cognition have shifted their perspective. It is important also because theoretical notions of this sort underpin the applied concerns of many psychologists today. Thus for example, Adams (1983), Bell *et al.* (1985), and Leyva and Furth (1986) all describe work on the nature of social competence during adolescence. Here researchers are grappling with the origins of social development, the factors which affect social skills, and the implications of having greater or lesser social competence in both family and institutional settings. Further examples of the way in which theories of social cognition have directly influenced work with young people may be found in Coleman (1987). In this publication, which reviews methods of working with troubled adolescents, a number of contributions reflect the influence of Elkind, Selman, and others. Such approaches have enabled us to understand better those who function poorly in social situations and those who, for whatever reason, are disadvantaged in their relationships with both adults and peers. Opportunities for the development of new treatment stategies have become available as a result of these theories, and fresh ways of conceptualising the poorly integrated or immature young person have developed as a result of the growth of social cognition.

Moral thought

Moral thought is, of course, one aspect of social cognition, yet it does have an identity which is in some respects distinct from the concerns we have been discussing, and for that reason it is considered in a separate section here. As with David Elkind and others, once again Piaget's notions have formed the springboard for later thinking where moral development is concerned. Although there have been a number of different theories put forward to explain the development of concepts of morality in young people (see Weinreich-Haste 1979, for review) the 'cognitive-developmental' approach of Piaget and Kohlberg is undoubtedly more relevant to adolescence than any other. In his work on the moral judgement of the child Piaget (1932) described two major stages of moral thinking. The first, which he called *moral realism*, refers to a period during which young children make judgements on an objective basis, for example by estimating the amount of damage which has been caused. Thus a child who breaks twelve cups is considered more blameworthy than one who only breaks one cup, regardless of the circumstances. The second stage, applying usually to those between the ages of 8 and 12, has been described as that of the *morality of co-operation*, or the *morality of reciprocity*. During this stage, Piaget believed, decisions concerning morality were usually made on a subjective basis, and often depended on an estimate of intention rather than consequence. Kohlberg (1964, 1969) has elaborated Piaget's scheme into one which has six different stages. This method has been to present hypothetical situations containing moral dilemmas to young people of different ages, and to classify their responses according to a stage theory of moral development. A typical situation, now well known as a result of extensive use by many research workers, is the following:

> In Europe a woman was very near death from a very bad disease, a special kind of cancer. There was one drug that doctors thought might save her. It was a form of radium that a druggist in the same town had recently discovered. The drug was expensive to make, but the druggist was charging ten times what the drug cost him to make. He paid 200 dollars for the radium, and charged 2,000 dollars for a small dose of the drug. The sick woman's husband, Heinz, went to everyone he knew to borrow the money, but he could only get together 1,000 dollars, which is half of what it cost. He told the druggist that his wife was dying, and asked him to sell it cheaper, or let him pay later. But the druggist said 'No, I discovered the drug, and I'm going to make money from it.' So Heinz got desperate and broke into the man's store to steal the drug for his wife.

Question: Should the husband have done that?

Based on responses to questions of this sort Kohlberg has described the following stages of moral development:

Pre-conventional
Stage 1   'Punishment–obedience orientation.' Behaviours that are punished are perceived as bad.
Stage 2   'Instrumental hedonism.' Here the child conforms in order to obtain rewards, have favours returned, etc.

Conventional
Stage 3   'Orientation to interpersonal relationships.' Good behaviour is that which pleases or helps others and is approved by them.
Stage 4   'Maintenance of social order.' Good behaviour consists of doing one's duty, having respect for authority, and maintaining the social order for its own sake.

Post-conventional
Stage 5   'Social contract and/or conscious orientation.' At the beginning of this stage moral behaviour tends to be thought of in terms of general rights and standards agreed upon by society as a whole, but at later moments there is

an increasing orientation towards internal decisions of conscience.

Stage 6 'The universal ethical principle orientation.' At this stage there is an attempt to formulate and be guided by abstract ethical principles (for example, The Golden Rule, Kant's Categorical Imperative).

Some of Kohlberg's most interesting work has involved the study of moral development in different cultures. As may be seen in Figures 3.3a and 3.3b, an almost identical sequence appears to occur in three widely different cultures, the variation between the cultures being found in the rate of development, and the fact that in the more primitive societies post-conventional stages of thinking are very rarely used.

Kohlberg's findings raise a number of questions. In the first place it may be asked whether there is any relation between Kohlberg's stages and those of Piaget. Kohlberg himself (Kohlberg and Gilligan 1971) has proposed that while the pre-conventional stages are equivalent to concrete operations, both conventional and post-conventional modes occur once the individual has reached the stage of formal operational thought. Later studies (Tomlinson-Keasey and Keasey 1974; Langford and George 1975) have cast some doubt on this, however, and it now seems most likely that the attainment of formal operational thought is necessary only for post-conventional reasoning. In fact the attainment of an appropriate cognitive stage is probably a necessary but not sufficient condition for the attainment of the corresponding moral stage.

Kohlberg's theory of moral development has raised contentious issues (for review see Conger and Petersen 1984). In particular the methodological problems associated with the testing and scoring of the moral dilemmas have worried a number of critics, and as a result of this an alternative form of assessment has been devised by James Rest (1973). This method, known as the Defining Issues Test (DIT), is based on the same theoretical perspective, but uses a multiple-choice format, and can be objectively scored. Interestingly results from studies using DIT are very similar to those based on the use of Kohlberg's own method. Another matter which has aroused considerable debate has to do with the development of moral education based on Kohlberg's theory. After all, as many people have pointed out, it is one thing to illuminate the developmental stages of moral thought in young people, but it is quite another to design training courses aimed at accelerating moral development as defined by Kohlberg.

The problem with such an enterprise is that it involves the

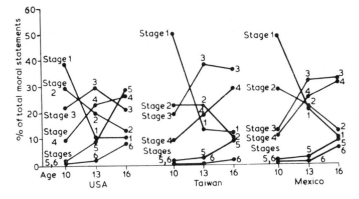

Source: L. Kohlberg and T. F. Gilligan (1971) *Deadalus*, Fall, p. 100.

Figure 3.3a Middle-class urban boys in the U.S.A., Taiwan, and Mexico. At age 10 the stages are used according to difficulty. At age 13, stage 3 is most used by all three groups. At age 16, US boys have reversed the order of age 10 stages (with the exception of 6). In Taiwan and Mexico, conventional (3–4) stages prevail at age 16, with stage 5 little used.

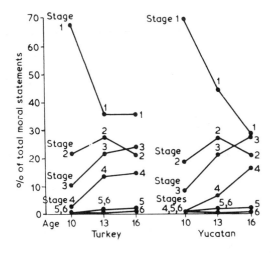

Source: L. Kohlberg and T. F. Gilligan (1971) *Daedalus*, Fall, p. 100.

Figure 3.3b Two isolated villages, one in Turkey, the other in Yucatan, show similar patterns in moral thinking. There is no reversal of order, and pre-conventional (1–2) does not gain a clear ascendancy over conventional stages at age 16.

psychologist in moving from the realm of supposedly value-free scientific enquiry into the realm of value judgement, value definition, and the teaching of a particular set of values in the classroom. It is not surprising that such an enterprise has aroused considerable opposition. Values too are at the heart of Carol Gilligan's (1982) criticism of Kohlberg's theory. In brief Gilligan argues that the essence of morality for women is not the same as the essence of morality for men, and that Kohlberg's stages are fundamentally flawed because they are based on a male concept of morality. Gilligan takes the view that the very traits that have traditionally defined 'goodness' for women, their care for and sensitivity to others, their responsibility towards others, are traits that are not especially valued by men. Indeed morality is defined in interpersonal terms at stage 3 in Kohlberg's scheme, while at stage 4 relationships are subordinated to rules, and at stages 5 and 6 rules are subordinated to universal principles of justice. Gilligan's criticisms are telling and it is to be hoped that they will stimulate others to look more closely at the interplay of values and cognition inherent in theories of moral development.

The growth of political ideas

As in the case of moral judgement, the young person's political ideas are likely to be significantly influenced by his or her level of cognitive development. In recent years a number of writers have become interested in the shift which takes place during the adolescent years, from a lack of political thought to, in many cases, an intense involvement in this area of life. How does this occur, and what are the processes involved? At what age do adolescents begin to show an increasing grasp of political concepts, and what stages do they go through before they achieve maturity of political judgement? One of the most important early studies was that undertaken by Adelson and O'Neill (1966). They approached the problem of the growth of political ideas in an imaginative way by posing for young people of different ages the following problem:

> Imagine that a thousand men and women, dissatisfied with the way things are going in their own country, decide to purchase and move to an island in the Pacific; once there they must devise laws and modes of government.
>
> (Adelson and O'Neill 1966)

They then explored the adolescent's approach to a variety of relevant issues. They asked questions about how a government would be formed, what would its purpose be, would there be a need for laws and political parties, how would you protect minorities, and so on. The investigators proposed different laws, and explored typical problems of public policy. The major results may be discussed under two headings – the change in modes of thinking, and the decline of authoritarianism with age. As far as the first is concerned, there was a marked shift in thinking from the concrete to the abstract, a finding which ties in well with the work discussed earlier in this chapter. Thus, for example, when asked: 'What is the purpose of laws?' one 12-year-old replied: 'If we had no laws people could go around killing people.' In contrast, a 16-year-old replied: 'To ensure safety, and to enforce the government.' Another commented: 'They are basically guide-lines for people. I mean like, this is wrong and this is right, and to help them understand' (Adelson 1971).

The second major shift observed was a decline in authoritarian solutions to political questions. The typical young adolescent (12 or 13 years old) appeared unable to appreciate that problems can have more than one solution, and that individual behaviour or political acts are not necessarily absolutely right or wrong, good or bad. The concept of moral relativism was not yet available for the making of political judgements. When confronted with law-breaking or even mild forms of social deviance, the young person's solution was characteristically:

> simply to raise the ante: more police, stiffer fines, longer gaol sentences, and if need be, executions. To a large and varied set of questions on crime and punishment, they consistently proposed one form of solution: punish, and if that does not suffice, punish harder.... At this age the child will not ordinarily concede that wrongdoing may be a symptom of something deeper, or that it may be inhibited by indirect means. The idea of reform and rehabilitation through humane methods is mentioned by only a small minority at the outset of adolescence.
>
> (Adelson 1971: 1023)

In contrast, the 14- or 15-year-old is much more aware of the different sides of any argument, and is usually able to take a relativistic point of view. Thinking begins to be more tentative, more critical and more pragmatic.

> Confronting a proposal for a law or for a change in social policy, he scrutinizes it to determine whether there is more to it than meets the eye. Whose interests are served, and whose are

damaged? He now understands that law and policy must accommodate competing interests and values, that ends must be balanced against means, that the short-term good must be appraised against latent or long-term or indirect outcome.

(Adelson 1971: 1026)

Adelson and his colleagues have extended their work to look at national differences. As part of the study mentioned above they compared American, British, and German young people and found that German adolescents were more likely than their American or British counterparts to stress a need for 'order, clarity, and direction', and this led them to look towards a single strong benevolent leader who could be relied upon to provide guidance and prevent anarchy and chaos. American adolescents were the most concerned of the three groups with the necessity to achieve a proper balance between the rights of the individual and those of the community as a whole. Like British teenagers, but unlike those living in Germany, American adolescents displayed some ambivalence towards authority; while they admired success, an underlying resentment that all was not equal in a society which claimed to be egalitarian could be detected in their views. According to the results of this study the British adolescents appeared most complex of all. Conger and Petersen (1984) summarised the findings which relate to young people in Great Britain as follows :

Part of the British adolescents' ambivalence about authority appears to stem from the suspicion that the government leaders themselves may not be above trying to obtain an overly large 'slice of the pie'. In sum, British adolescents emerge on the one hand as the most devoted to 'rugged individualism', the most tolerant of eccentricities and individual differences, and the most dedicated to the preservation of personal liberty. On the other hand, they also emerged as the most self-oriented and least concerned, despite support of welfare concepts, with the community as a whole – a tendency characterised by Britishers themselves in the familiar slogan 'I'm alright Jack', indicating that as long as one's own interests are being served, there is little motivation for broader social concern.

(Conger and Petersen 1984: 579)

While a few other studies have been carried out in this field (for example, Crain and Crain 1974), the topic of political socialisation has been relatively neglected. In the past few years however a new interest in political knowledge and awareness of young people has developed in the United Kingdom. Furnham and Gunter (1983) drew attention to the variables which affect the extent of political knowledge, while Banks and Ullah (1987) investigated voting behaviour and political attitudes among employed and unemployed young people. Such studies contribute an important dimension to the field of political socialisation, as does a recently published book by Furnham and Gunter (1988), which draws on a sample of over 2,000 British adolescents, and presents a wide-ranging review of social attitudes to key issues of the day, including politics and government, crime and law enforcement, work and unemployment, and Britain's relationships with other countries.

This chapter began by stating that cognitive growth is less apparent to observers than most aspects of maturation. Yet fundamental changes do occur in young people's cognitive ability between the ages of 11 and 18, changes which are no less significant than those which take place during the earlier stages of childhood. In this chapter we have examined the nature of formal operational thought, and have noted that this is achieved by considerably fewer teenagers than Piaget at first believed. However, the recent focus on social cognition has highlighted other aspects of intellectual development occurring in almost all young people, at the same time illuminating an important link between social behaviour and cognitive maturation. Finally we have seen how our knowledge of the development of both moral and political concepts has been influenced by Piaget's early work, and how each of these areas interrelates with other aspects of cognition.

Chapter four

Self-concept development

Introduction

As far as self-concept is concerned, adolescence is usually thought to be a time of both change and consolidation. There are a number of reasons for this. In the first place the major physical changes (see Chapter two) which occur carry with them a change in body image and thus in the sense of self. Second, intellectual growth during adolescence makes possible a more complex and sophisticated self-concept. Third, some development of the self-concept seems probable as a result of increasing emotional independence, and the approach of fundamental decisions relating to occupation, values, sexual behaviour, friendship choices, and so on. Finally, the transitional nature of the adolescent period, and in particular the role changes experienced at this time, would seem likely to be associated with some modifications of self-concept.

The ways in which young people understand and perceive themselves, their own agency and personality, and their various social situations have a powerful effect on their subsequent reactions to various life events. The essential dilemma for the individual adolescent in wishing to be fully integrated and accepted in society is between 'playing appropriate roles' and 'selfhood': On one hand, it is important to be able to play appropriate roles in a variety of social settings and to follow the prescribed rules for these situations. On the other hand, it is equally important to be able to maintain elements of individuality or selfhood. The denial of self can lead to depersonalisation. The relative freedom for the individual from 'rule regulated' behaviour is to be achieved through stylistic variations of role and role structures and through the choice and selection of alternative social and environmental contexts in which to provide appropriate levels of variety and opportunity.

In the process of socialisation, the various adults (e.g. parents, teachers, youth leaders) with whom young people will interact are important as role models and social agents, but so too are the functions of selfhood, perceived competence, and identity for the individual adolescent, together with the need to make sense of his or her social world and his or her place in it.

In this chapter, therefore, we will briefly review evidence available concerning the adolescent self-concept. In particular we will look at the topic of self-concept development and the factors which may be expected to affect this. Thus topics to be explored include:

(a)   Factors associated with self-concept development.
(b)   Self-esteem in adolescence.
(c)   Some theoretical approaches to identity status.
(d)   Problem behaviour and self-identity.

Before launching into the chapter it is necessary to say something about terminology: the term *self-concept* subsumes within it the notion of *self-image* (the individual's description of the self) as well as that of *self-esteem* (the individual's evaluation of the self); the term *identity* is taken here to have essentially the same meaning as *self-concept* and these will be used interchangeably within this chapter. Allied to these concepts of self, *body-concept* is a global term embracing a diversity of information pertaining to mental representations of the body gathered from a number of different viewpoints. The learning component involved and the multi-stimulus determinants of such a concept are reflected in Witkin's definition of *body image*:

> The systematic impression an individual has of his body, cognitive and affective, conscious and unconscious formed in the process of growing up.
>
> (Witkin 1965)

To Witkin, this impression arises out of the totality of experiences involving his or her own body and the bodies of others. The relationship of *body-concept* to what has been designated the concept of *self* is reflected in Argyle's comment:

> Body image may in certain respects overlap the various usages of concepts like ego, self and self-phenomenon relating to attitudes towards the body, it has wider implications which cross over into other personality areas.
>
> (Argyle 1969: 358)

Factors associated with self-concept development

Self-concept and social background

It would seem reasonable to assume that the self-concept development of young people will vary in relation to a number of factors in
relation to social background. In an earlier study by Engel (1959),
some 20 per cent of the sample were shown to have a negative self-
image on first testing and it was this group which had the greatest
level of instability of the self-image over the two-year period of the
project. In addition, those with a negative self-image also had
higher maladjustment scores on various personality tests. This was
an important study for a number of reasons. In the first place it
indicated that a relatively small proportion of the total population
are likely to show a disturbance of the self-concept. Second, it
demonstrated that a negative self-image is related to other aspects
of personality difficulty. Third, it underlined the fact that questions of change and disturbance are linked, and that very probably
a lack of disturbance goes hand-in-hand with a relatively stable
self-concept. Finally, it served to draw attention to the necessity of
considering other variables which may be associated with self-
concept development.

Rosenberg's (1965) classic study represented one important
contribution in this respect. He was able to show that low self-
esteem, characteristic of 20–30 per cent of the sample studied, was
associated with a variety of factors. The research was concerned
with older adolescents, the sample including approximately 5,000
17- and 18-year-olds in randomly selected schools in New York.
Self-esteem was measured by a ten-item self-report scale (i.e. the
degree to which the subjects agreed or disagreed with statements
such as 'I feel I am a person of worth, at least on an equal place
with others'.) Low self-esteem was shown to be related to depression, anxiety, and poor school performance. Both low and high
self-esteem adolescents were similar in wishing for success on
leaving school, but the low self-esteem group were more likely to
feel they would never attain such success, to prefer a job which
they knew was beyond their grasp, and to feel that they did not
have the resources necessary for success. The adolescents who
were high in self-esteem were significantly more likely than those
with low self-esteem to consider the following qualities as personal
assets: self-confidence, hard work, leadership potential, and the
ability to make a good impression. Low self-esteem adolescents
were characterised by a sense of incompetence in social relationships, they felt socially isolated, and believed that other people
neither understood nor respected them, and were not able to trust

them. Finally, the feeling that their parents took an interest in their affairs was significantly more apparent in those with high self-esteem.

Thus self-esteem is closely related both to general social adjustment and to stability of the self-concept. On the whole, the higher the individual's self-esteem the better adjusted and the more stable in self-concept he or she is likely to be. Adolescents do not all develop in the same way, and we can assume that those with a negative self-image are less likely to have stable self-concepts than those whose self-images are generally positive. Furthermore, there are obviously many variables, such as family background and cultural context, which play their part in determining at least some aspects of the self-concept. It is not at all clear whether the alterations in self-concept which do occur in adolescence are any different from those taking place during other transitional stages in the life cycle. Further, only a relatively small proportion of the total adolescent population are likely to have a negative self-image or to have very low self-esteem, and if such disturbance increases at any stage during the teenage years it is more probable that it will do so in early rather than late adolescence.

It is around the time of puberty that there is the greatest likelihood of some form of disturbance in the self-concept. Writers such as Erikson (1968) and Marcia (1967) have suggested that without a crisis of some sort no real resolution of the identity issue is possible. We can be fairly confident in arguing for the contrary view. This is not to deny the fact that a minority of young people do have serious identity problems, the significance of which should not in any way be minimised. It seems probable, however, that for the majority of adolescents the most viable course will be to avoid any sudden identity crisis, adapting very gradually over a period of years to the changes in identity experienced by them.

Offer *et al.* (1984) have shown that there appears to be no increase in disturbance of self-image during early adolescence. They refer to their work as providing insights into 'current contradictions in adolescent theory'. In an earlier book (Offer *et al.* 1981) they reported on a major piece of research using the Offer Self Image Questionnaire, which emphasised two important points.

One is the stress that is placed on normality in adolescence: 'The results reveal that normal adolescents are not in the throes of turmoil. The vast majority function well, enjoy good relationships with their families and friends, and accept the values of the larger society.' The other important aspect of the book is the authors' reference to the myth of a deviant adolescent world:

Throughout the ages adults have created a 'generation gap' by systematically distorting the adolescent experience. This has clearly been a disservice to normal teenagers, since distortion forestalls effective communication. But it is also a disservice to deviant and disturbed teenagers, since they are denied needed help by adults who blithely assert that 'adolescents are just going through a stage'.

(Offer *et al.* 1981)

Sex role identity

The term 'sex role' is commonly used to refer to a set of standards or prescriptions which describe appropriate masculine and feminine behaviour in a particular culture. Thus from very early childhood individuals learn what is and what is not acceptable behaviour from each of the sexes. This learning may not necessarily take place in an explicit fashion, but will more often be absorbed by the child as one aspect of the general guidelines which exist in his or her environment. As a result of socialisation he or she will come to appreciate that such standards exercise both subtle and not so subtle influences on how men and women act in society, and recently considerable interest has been expressed in the way these socialisation processes operate. Attention has been focused on the role of the mass media, on children's books, on school teachers' behaviour, expectations for the two sexes, and so on.

As far as sex role identity is concerned, this may be taken to represent the degree to which the individual believes he or she has matched the prescribed sex role. In other words, sex role identity concerns the extent to which a person feels that his or her behaviour is consistent with the standards which operate in the culture to determine male or female behaviour in general. Such concepts may usefully be distinguished from notions of 'gender' and 'gender identity', which are usually taken to refer more directly to body image and awareness of male and female sexuality (Douvan 1979). It has been pointed out by some writers (for example, Bee 1975) that while gender identity is likely to be learnt very early, usually before the age of 5, the development of sex role identity occurs later in childhood, and will probably only become an issue of real significance as the individual enters adolescence.

The fact that sex role identity becomes problematic during the teenage years appears to be generally accepted by all who have commented on this topic. Why should this be so? In the first place it is argued that before puberty a considerable amount of leeway is permitted in our society as far as appropriate sexual behaviour is concerned. Thus girls can, if they wish, act as 'tomboys' without inviting too much disapproval, while even boys can get away with quiet, reflective activities and a lack of interest in sport up to the age of about 10 or 11. Following puberty, however, two pressures are brought to bear on the individual. First, parents, teachers, and others see future adulthood approaching, and wish to ensure successful adjustment for the young person as he or she grows up. Second, the peer group comes to exercise increasing influence in determining the behaviours which are acceptable. Both groups underline sex role standards, and indicate in no uncertain manner the penalties which follow if the adolescent deviates too radically from the norm. However, changes in the wider social context exemplified by such pop stars as Boy George can blur the clarity of sex role identities and make them problematic for some adolescents.

Douvan (1979) pointed out that for boys the major discontinuity occurs in the pre-school years where a discrepancy exists between passive, dependent babyhood, and the independence and self-assertiveness that is expected of the male in his early contacts with peers and the school situation. For girls, however, this discontinuity is seen in its most extreme form during adolescence. During these years females face, according to Douvan, the following situation:

> Socialised through childhood in a double system – in which the girl is allowed dependency but is also encouraged and supported through school to be independent, individualistic, competitive and achieving – she now finds that at adolescence she must abandon or disguise these individual competitive traits if she is to be acceptably feminine. Adults, and especially her peer group, expect her to shift from direct achievement to vicarious achievement, and to take as her major goals becoming a wife and mother. ... She is asked to give up established ways of being and behaving, ways practised throughout the primary school years. Abandoning established patterns represents her critical discontinuity.
>
> (Douvan 1979: 90)

These patterns of identity have their antecedents just prior to the adolescent years. Hendry and Percy (1981) found that by the upper stages of the primary school girls saw boys of their own age typically playing football, and this, with playing space invaders, was the way boys most often saw themselves. On the other hand, quite a few boys saw girls as likely to play with dolls whereas no girl mentioned this for her own sex. Many girls said a typical

11-year-old girl would choose to go out with boys or go to a disco, but equally popular were going out with friends or parents, shopping and swimming, or ice-skating. Teenage stereotypes were fairly firmly fixed in their minds: teenagers were portrayed by both sexes as punks (i.e. followers of the youth culture of the day), socially active, and choosing to go with boy or girlfriends socially to discos.

Sharpe (1977) has reported that subjects in school were preferred by girls for form (e.g. art) rather than for content: girls become unassertive underachievers around puberty. Paradoxically, girls have a social fear of success as well as a fear of failure, believing that boys dislike cleverer girls.

> They are very tuned in to the things that will bring social approval and quickly pick up cues from inside and outside the school. Whether they accept or reject (as many do) the advice, treatment and curriculum of their teachers they still absorb the form and the sex-differentiated assumptions that these contain.
>
> (Sharpe 1977: 152)

The girls interviewed by Sharpe were from different backgrounds, yet most expected to learn domestic skills in school and were taught these skills by women while for the most part such courses as science were taught to them by men. They were further oriented toward a traditional female path by not being allowed the freedom to wear trousers to school and they were influenced by the media to take an avid interest in fashion trends, in making themselves attractive to boys. Many of the girls quoted acquiesce to the pressure thrust upon them to look 'sexy' (a word one girl used) and view their goals in life as being housekeeper and mother.

The two major sources of socialisation – home and school – are backed up by media interpretations of femininity, so that, as Shaw (1976) wrote: 'Female futures are defined in essentially domestic terms ... stereotyping which our educational system does little to undermine.' Delamont (1984) has also considered the important impact of sex roles, and particularly, sex role inequalities in educational settings in the United Kingdom. It is clear, therefore, that within the socialisation process of adolescence the school creates stresses and ambivalences for young women in that they are caught up in the dilemma of achieving their academic potential, and at the same time fulfilling and conforming to a stereotypic sex role image of femininity to ensure popularity with their peers.

Both Wells (1980) and Keyes and Coleman (1983) have discussed the relationship between personal adjustment and sex role identity conflicts in adolescence. In Keyes and Coleman's study, though no sex differences were found for measures of personal adjustment, females appeared to experience more conflict over sex role issues. Males also evidenced conflict, however, and there was not a uniform female disadvantage. No relationship for either sex was found between high academic ambition and less adequate adjustment. Individuals of both sexes who experienced the highest levels of sex role conflict also experienced more problems in personal adjustment, but only when the conflict reflected a perception of the self as deficient in instrumental, 'masculine', attributes in comparison with perceived societal expectations. It is interesting to note, therefore, the general comparability of findings for the two sexes. Both males and females evidenced conflicts over sex role issues and both males and females who perceived themselves to be inferior to their ideal selves and to societal expectations were likely to have the lowest levels of self-esteem, the highest levels of psychological malaise, and the lowest academic ambition. Such results should be of value to theorists in the field of sex role research, and suggest ways in which theory must be expanded to include potentially similar conflicts faced by adolescents, of both sexes. Archer (1984) has also discussed the interacting influences of psychological adjustment and sex role conflicts in both sexes.

The developmental literature suggests that an increase in self-image disparity (i.e. real-self vs. ideal-self conflict) is a normal growth phenomenon and may be related to overall developmental level or intelligence (Katz and Zigler 1967; Phillips and Zigler 1980).

Data from a sample of young people aged 12 to 18 years old were analysed by Streitmatter (1985) to examine the differences in gender role perceptions across age groups. A series of multivariate correlational analyses were employed to examine the relationship between gender, age, and self-reported perceptions of gender identity. The results of the study indicated indirect support for Erikson's speculations about resolution of identity crisis. The youngest respondents showed the greatest disparity between male and female role perceptions. The older subjects, those in adolescence, displayed greater ambiguity toward gender roles, while the oldest respondents, approaching adulthood, indicated a stronger perceived gender identity.

The pattern found by Streitmatter indicated that male and female gender identification prior to adolescence is fairly distinct. Entry into adolescence seems to cloud the issue. This pattern indicated decreasing differentiation from 12 and 13 to 14 years and from 14 to 15 years. However, 15- to 16-year-old comparisons reflected increasing differentiation. Apparently, the gender identifications which are adopted in childhood are reconsidered and reformulated during adolescence (this finding is similar to that of Montemayor and Eisen 1977).

As part of Coleman's (1974) research a sentence-completion test was given to large numbers of teenagers at four age levels. Some of the sentence stems concerned relationships with parents, as for example: 'When a boy is with his parents . . .' or, for a girl, 'When a girl is with her parents . . .' Results showed that in the 15-year-old group a similar proportion of boys and girls completed this sentence with a theme reflecting conflict between themselves and their parents. However, when these responses were analysed for content a remarkable difference between the sexes emerged. Whereas boys expressed conflict with their parents in behavioural terms, drawing attention to restrictions and limitations which they felt their parents imposed on them, the girls hardly referred to this problem at all. For them it was their sense of self which was at stake, and difficulties with their parents reflected issues of identity rather than of behaviour. Thus, adolescent girls may have more difficulties than boys in accepting or coming to terms with their own identity in the context of parental relationships.

Self-esteem in adolescence

Of all dimensions of the self-image in adolescence, self-esteem has perhaps been the most studied (Wylie 1961, 1974; Damon and Hart 1982), probably as a reflection of the great importance of self-esteem maintenance to overall well-being (Allport 1961; Murphy 1947; Rosenberg 1979). If the self-image is classified as an attitude toward the self, then self-esteem involves an evaluative dimension. Global self-esteem has been described by Rosenberg (1979) as the overall negative or positive attitude toward self.

The sources for self-esteem development rest primarily in reflected appraisals and social comparisons. Young people compare their competencies to those of their peers in order to discern their level of worth. Recent research indicates that social comparison is a developmental phenomenon, with children beginning to engage in comparisons at about 6 or 7 years of age (Ruble *et al.* 1980) and this intensifies during early adolescence (Scanlan 1982).

Many 'self' theorists have cast self-esteem into a hierarchy of dimensions (Epstein 1973; Harter 1983). Specifically, a global self-esteem tops the hierarchy, under which several specific dimensions of self are contained. Coopersmith (1967), Epstein (1973), and Harter (1983) all delineated four dimensions underlying global self-esteem:

1. Competence, or success in meeting achievement demands.
2. Social acceptance, or attention, worthiness, and positive reinforcement received from significant others.
3. Control, or feelings of internal responsibility for outcomes.
4. Virtue, or adherence to moral and ethical standards.

In addition to the four dimensions subsumed under global self-esteem, each of these dimensions can be divided further into situational specific categories. For example, competence can be split into cognitive, social, and physical sub-areas, and social acceptance can include peers and adults.

Affect is considered to be central in formulations of self-esteem (Harter 1983; Rosenberg 1979). The importance of affect as it pertains to self lies in its predictable effect on future motivated behaviour (Diener and Dweck 1978; Dweck and Elliott 1984). For example, Diener and Dweck (1978) found that children who attributed mistakes to lack of ability expressed negative affect toward self in relation to that task and no longer wanted to participate.

Harter (1983) implored that: 'affect should be given centre stage' when considering the study of motivated behaviour. The salience of an activity to an individual will determine the degree to which success or failure affects one's self-esteem. Coined by Rosenberg (1979) as 'psychological centrality', the importance that an individual attaches to a particular domain or activity will affect the individual's self-esteem. For example, an adolescent's low perceived competence in physical skills and activities may not have a negative effect on total self-esteem because he or she does not value physical competence as important for being successful. Rosenberg (1979) noted that components of the self-concept are of unequal centrality to the individual's concerns: 'Thus, the individual strives to excel at that which he values and to value that at which he excels.'

A cross-sectional survey of nearly 2,000 school children by Simmons and Rosenberg (1975) identified early adolescents as experiencing the most difficulty with self-esteem. Their results, although a little difficult to interpret because they included a number of different measures of self-esteem, seemed to indicate a major change between the years of 12 and 14. In their view:

the early adolescent has become distinctly more self-conscious; his picture of himself has become more shaky and unstable, his global self-esteem has declined slightly, his attitudes towards several specific characteristics which he values highly have become less positive; and he has increasingly come to believe that parents, teachers and peers of the same sex view him less favourably.

(Simmons *et al.* 1973: 558)

However, there is some controversy over the fate of self-esteem in the transition between childhood and early adolescence. While some studies show no age differences (Yamamoto *et al.* 1969; Attenborough and Zdep 1973; Coleman 1974), others indicate negative changes near or upon entry to adolescence, that is, at age 12–13 years compared to earlier years (Piers and Harris 1964; Katz and Zigler 1967; Jorgensen and Howell 1969; Trowbridge 1972; Harter 1983). These studies of self-esteem vary in their methodology. The longitudinal studies that show a rise in self-esteem during adolescence are large scale and may provide more reliable insights (O'Malley and Bachman 1983). However, many of the studies comparing children to early adolescents are not as compelling. All are cross-sectional; some have small samples (Piers and Harris 1964; Katz and Zigler 1967; Bohan 1973); and only a few indicated that they used random sampling (Katz and Zigler 1967; Attenborough and Zdep 1973).

Nevertheless, Harter (1983) has stated that children aged 4 to 7 years do not appear to possess a concept of general self-worth but rather seem able to evaluate specific behaviours only. Adolescents, on the other hand, appear to be comfortable with the idea of a general self-evaluation. If Harter is correct, then the question of interest involves the age-range at which such a concept usually emerges. However, Damon and Hart (1982) and Harter (1983) both noted that younger children's cognitive views of self may differ from those of adolescents simply because the same measure of self-esteem may not be appropriate at both age-periods.

Entry to a new period in the life-course may challenge the self-image, particularly individuals' self-evaluations, as they attempt new tasks in which they can succeed or fail, as they alter their self-values and the areas which are important for overall self-esteem, and as they confront new significant others against whom they rate themselves and about whose judgements they care. According to Elkind (1967), cognitive processes also contribute to adolescent socialisation. Adolescents become cognisant that others are formulating opinions of them, but they may be unable to differentiate their own self-preoccupations from the thoughts of this imaginary audience (adolescent 'egocentrism'). They concentrate on their own faults and believe that these faults are as evident to others as to themselves (see Chapter two).

Self-concept is a complex phenomenon, and although a number of its aspects have already been discussed, there may yet be further dimensions which have not so far been considered. One example which falls into this category is the distinction between present and future self. Douvan and Adelson first drew attention to this distinction when they wrote: 'The normal adolescent holds, we think, two conceptions of himself – what he is and what he will be – and the way in which he integrates the future image into his current life will indicate a good deal about his current adolescent integration' (Douvan and Adelson 1966: 23).

Coleman *et al.* (1977) devised a sentence-completion test specifically aimed at differentiating between present and future self-image. The subjects were working-class boys in an urban area, and results showed that, while the proportions of each age group expressing a negative present self-image remained the same, the numbers expressing negative sentiments concerning their future self-image increased markedly with age. Fears and anxieties about themselves as they grew older appeared to be very much more common in those about to leave school, and phrases such as 'dreary', 'dead', 'depressing', and 'a dreaded age' were in common usage among 16-year-olds to describe their future.

Miller and Coleman (1980) established that concepts of the self in the future are likely to be affected by a number of variables. Boys were shown to express greater anxiety about the future than girls, and social class as well as the imminence of leaving school also appear to play their part. The important point to note is that the self-concept has a number of dimensions, one of which is a notion of the self in the future (see Figure 4.1). It may well be that for adolescents in particular this component is associated with more stress than it would be for those in other age groups.

Because of the complexities of modern society, children reach physical adulthood before many of them are capable of functioning well in adult social roles. The disjunction between physical capabilities and socially approved independence and power, and the concurrent status-ambiguities can be stressful for the self-image of the adolescent.

Yet many investigators claim that for most youngsters the adolescent years are not marked by stress or turmoil (Offer *et al.* 1981; Haan 1977; Petersen and Taylor 1980; Savin-Williams and Demo 1983). In fact reviews of large-scale longitudinal studies

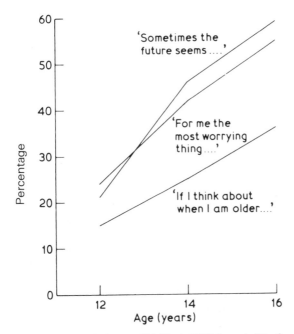

Source: J. C. Coleman, J. Herzberg, and M. Morris (1977) *Journal of Youth and Adolescence* 6.

Figure 4.1 Proportions of each age group expressing negative responses to sentence-stems related to *the self in the future*.

report a consistent rise, not a drop, in self-esteem as children move from early to late adolescence (McCarthy and Hoge 1982; O'Malley and Bachman 1983).

A question also arises as to whether young women differ from young men in terms of their self-esteem in adolescence. Once again, there is controversy in the literature. Wylie (1979) and Maccoby and Jacklin (1974) in their reviews of pre-college-age adolescents reported no global self-image differences by gender. However, significantly lower female self-esteem is indicated in nationally representative samples by O'Malley and Bachman (1979) and Conger *et al.* (1977). The studies of early and middle adolescents reviewed by Macoby and Jacklin (1974) did not, for the most part, involve the individual's own view of his or her self-esteem, and the studies of adolescents which Wylie reviews were not based on large random samples with the full social class structure represented.

On the other hand, random sample surveys in two large cities by Simmons and Rosenberg (1975) and Bush *et al.* (1977) showed that both pre-adolescent and adolescent girls scored lower than boys on self-esteem as well as on many more specific aspects of self-evaluation – particularly aspects of body image. The apparent greater vulnerability of girls at entry to adolescence may be explained in part with the help of the self-image principles emphasised by Rosenberg (1979).

Rosenberg emphasised the importance of the *reflected self* and of *social comparison* in determining self-esteem, as well as the importance of doing well in the areas one *values* (the principle of 'psychological centrality'). It is possible to suggest that in adolescence girls show an increased tendency over boys to place high value on body image and same sex popularity. Thus, girls might be placed in increased jeopardy (1) because they value peer opinion more ('the reflected self') especially in the transition to secondary school and (2) because they value body image more at a time when their body is changing dramatically and social comparisons along this dimension become more problematic. The fact that girls care intensely about body image at a time when they may be particularly dissatisfied with their own changing physique helps to explain their lower global self-esteem.

In new and uncomfortable situations the adolescent may feel what Rosenberg has called 'recurrent transient depersonalisation' (Rosenberg 1979). This self-detachment or feeling of depersonalisation may in turn negatively affect feelings of self-efficacy and thus self-esteem. Further, in many new important situations and role relationships, the adolescent might see him/herself as generally ineffective. In other words, the inability to perform easily in a variety of important new contexts and roles may generalise to a low evaluation of self. Consequently, self-esteem may drop. Within the principle of psychological centrality, Rosenberg (1979) hypothesised that specific self-evaluations have a greater impact upon global self-esteem if these evaluations are in areas about which the individual cares a great deal. This can be exemplified by the evidence on the effects of schooling on adolescents' self-esteem. A number of studies have shown how various elements of the school system can combine to differentiate pupils in terms of their attitudes towards school, their scholastic success, and their self-images where the criteria of success are mainly academic ones (Hargreaves 1967; Willis 1977). Adolescents' self-concepts will contain certain reflections of their teachers' expectations (Rosenthal and Jacobson 1968). Thus, when pupils 'receive' perceptions of their teachers' evaluations, setting up matching self-estimations in these pupils, then a process of teacher-bias arises from the perceptual impressions, 'halo effect', and labelling of pupils during normal classroom interactions. Pupils respond to this labelling process by aligning their behaviour to 'success' or 'failure' labels. Subsequent reinforcement of these patterns affect adolescents' self-esteem, and eventually teachers cease to be 'significant others' for some young people so that 'anti-school' sub-cultures emerge supported by the peer group. Yet, Hargreaves (1982) has argued that: 'The school curriculum must endow all pupils with a sense of their own competencies.' While Ryrie (1981) wrote: 'the basic reason why the varied potential of young people is not developed in our schools is that skills and abilities other than academic and cognitive ones are not sufficiently valued and respected.'

Clearly, the processes which remove concern for achievement in the school setting from its psychologically central position within the self-esteem hierarchy of some adolescents has far-reaching consequences for both the individual and society.

Nevertheless, in general, adolescence does not appear associated with a decrease in self-esteem for the majority of children. In fact, there is some evidence of a general rise in self-esteem. Yet, adolescence does appear to have negative effects for the self-esteem of some young people under certain circumstances such as in educational settings or in family relationships. Further, girls are more likely to show negative effects on entry to adolescence than boys, especially if change is marked by sharpness and discontinuity and occurs at too young an age, or coincides with too many other changes in the young person's life (Simmons and Rosenberg 1975). Thus, if change comes too suddenly – that is, if there is too much discontinuity with prior experience – or if change is too early given the young person's cognitive and emotional states, or if it occurs in too many areas of life at once, then the individual will experience great discomfort. Such young people will not feel at one with themselves nor at home in their social environments.

If the adolescent is comfortable in some environments, life-arenas, and role-relationships, then discomfort in another arena can be tolerated and mastered. Teenagers are less able to cope if *at one and the same time* they are uncomfortable with their bodies, due to physical changes; with family, due to changes in the family constellation; with home, because of a move; with school, due to great discontinuity in the nature of the school environment; with peers, because of disruption of peer networks and changes in peer expectations and peer evaluation criteria; and because of the emergence of opposite sex relationships as an important arena for success. There needs to be some arena of life or some set of role-relationships with which the individual adolescent can feel relaxed and comfortable, to which he or she can withdraw and have the self reinvigorated. More on this subject, together with a discussion of Coleman's focal model of adolescent development, will be found in the final chapter.

With maturation most adolescents begin to feel more competent and efficacious (Damon and Hart 1982; Selman 1980). Feelings of self-efficacy may, therefore, work to produce higher self-esteem even though other factors (such as the threat of unemployment as the school-leaving age approaches) may begin, at the same time, to attack self-esteem. Feelings of greater control and power relative to the social and physical environment have positive effects on self-esteem. Further, adolescents may also improve their interpersonal skills with age and may be more capable of selecting peers and contexts that do enhance their self-esteem. Tome and Bariaud's (1987) study is an important one in this context, especially since it provides a European perspective on the development of the self-concept, and underlines the role of time perspective in personal maturation.

The entry into and exit from adolescence both involve major changes. Yet there has not been a great deal of work on the effect of various types of exit from adolescence on self-esteem (Offer and Offer 1975; Bachman and O'Malley 1977; Mortimer and Finch 1984; Offer and Sabshin 1984). Nevertheless, identity theorists such as Erikson (1968) have dealt with issues involving preparation for exit from adolescence, including occupational choice, close intimate friendships, and adult identity, and we turn our attention to these theoretical approaches to identity in the next section.

Some theoretical approaches to identity status

Identity and identity crisis

A key figure in writing about identity and identity crisis was Erikson. Erikson (1968) viewed life as a series of stages, each having a particular developmental task of a psychological nature associated with it. In infancy, for example, the task is to establish a sense of *basic trust*, and to combat *mistrust*. The maternal relationship is here considered to be crucial in creating a foundation upon which the infant may build later trusting relationships. As far as adolescence is concerned, the task involves the establishment of a *coherent identity*, and the defeat of a sense of *identity diffusion*. Erikson believed that the search for identity becomes especially

	1	2	3	4	5	6	7	8
VIII								INTEGRITY vs. DESPAIR
VII							GENERATIVITY vs. STAGNATION	
VI						INTIMACY vs. ISOLATION		
V	Temporal Perspective vs. Time Confusion	Self-Certainty vs. Self-Consciousness	Role Experimentation vs. Role Fixation	Apprenticeship vs. Work Paralysis	IDENTITY vs. IDENTITY CONFUSION	Sexual Polarization vs. Bisexual Confusion	Leader- and Followership vs. Authority Confusion	Ideological Commitment vs. Confusion of Values
IV				INDUSTRY vs. INFERIORITY	Task Identification vs. Sense of Futility			
III			INITIATIVE vs. GUILT		Anticipation of Roles vs. Role Inhibition			
II		AUTONOMY vs. SHAME, DOUBT			Will to Be Oneself vs. Self-Doubt			
I	TRUST vs. MISTRUST				Mutual Recognition vs. Autistic Isolation			

Source: Erik Erikson (1968) *Identity: youth and crisis*, © W. W. Norton, New York. Reproduced by permission.

Figure 4.2 Erikson's Diagram.

acute at this stage as a result of a number of factors. Thus, Erikson laid some stress on the phenomenon of rapid biological and social change during adolescence, and pointed especially to the importance for the individual of having to take major decisions at this time in almost all areas of life. In many of his writings Erikson either stated or implied that some form of crisis is necessary for the young person to resolve the identity issue and to defeat identity diffusion. Identity diffusion, according to Erikson, has four major components.

In the first place, there is the problem of *intimacy*. Here the individual may fear commitment or involvement in close interpersonal relationships because of the possible loss of his or her own identity. This fear can lead to stereotyped, formalised relationships, to isolation, or the young person may, as Erikson put it, 'in repeated hectic attempts and dismal failures, seek intimacy with the most improbable partners' (Erikson 1968: 167). Second, there is the possibility of a diffusion of *time perspective*. Here, the adolescent finds it impossible to plan for the future, or to retain any sense of time. This problem is thought to be associated with anxieties about change and becoming adult, and often: 'consists of a decided disbelief in the possibility that time may bring change and yet also of a violent fear that it might' (ibid.: 169).

Next, there is a diffusion of *industry*, in which the young person finds it difficult to harness his or her resources in a realistic way in work or study. Both of these activities represent commitment and as a defence against this the individual may either find it impossible to concentrate, or may frenetically engage in one single activity to the exclusion of all others. Finally, Erikson discussed the choice of a *negative identity*. By this is meant the young person's selection of an identity exactly the opposite to that preferred by parents or other important adults:

> The loss of a sense of identity is often expressed in a scornful and snobbish hostility towards the role offered as proper and desirable in one's family or immediate community. Any aspect of the required role or all of it – be it masculinity or femininity, nationality or class membership – can become the main focus of the young person's acid disdain.
>
> (Ibid.: 172)

These four elements, therefore, constitute the main features of identity diffusion, although clearly not all will be present in any one individual who experiences an identity crisis. In addition to such concepts, one other notion needs to be mentioned as an integral feature of Erikson's theory, that of psycho-social moratorium. This means a period during which decisions are left in abeyance. It is argued that society allows, even encourages, a time of life when the young person may delay major identity choices and experiment with roles in order to discover the sort of person he or she wishes to be; while such a stage may lead to disorientation or disturbance it has, according to Erikson, a healthy function. As he said:'Much of this apparent confusion thus must be considered social play – the true genetic successor to childhood play' (Erikson 1968: 164).

Inherent in Erikson's conceptualisation of the identity formation process is the integration of biological endowment, significant identifications, and ego defences with roles offered by one's society; it is in their interaction and mutual regulation that a sense of inner identity can evolve. The means by which youth come into relationship with society are primarily through occupational, ideological, and sexual roles, and it is largely via these avenues that the process of identity formation during adolescence has been explored.

The real problem with Erikson's theory lies in the fact that he has never been specific about the extent of adolescent identity crisis. His use of terms such as 'normative crisis' and 'the psychopathology of everyday adolescence' implies that all young people may be expected to experience some such crisis, yet nowhere does Erikson tackle quantitative issues. He prefers to deal in the qualitative aspects of identity development, and it has been left to others to translate his ideas into a form in which they can be tested empirically.

Marcia (1966) has used Erikson's conceptual dimensions of crisis and commitment to define four identity statuses. The four stages, or identity statuses, as they are called, are as follows:

1 *Identity diffusion.* Here the individual has not yet experienced an identity crisis, nor has he or she made any commitment to a vocation or set of beliefs. There is also no indication that he or she is actively trying to make a commitment.
2 *Identity foreclosure.* In this status the individual has not experienced a crisis but nevertheless is committed in his or her goals and beliefs, largely as a result of choices made by others.
3 *Moratorium.* An individual in this category is in a state of crisis, and is actively searching among alternatives in an attempt to arrive at a choice of identity.
4 *Identity achievement.* At this stage the individual is considered

to have experienced a crisis, but to have resolved it on his or her own terms, and now to be firmly committed to an occupation, an ideology, and social roles.

The identity achievement, moratorium, foreclosure, and diffusion stances identify those attempting to resolve or avoid the identity work of adolescence in greater detail. Identity achievement and foreclosure individuals share a commitment to adult roles; however, the former have synthesised important childhood identification figures into an original product while the latter have bypassed such development work by adopting prefabricated identities from such earlier heroes. Likewise, moratorium and diffusion youths share a lack of commitment; however, that lack is instrumental to the former in the process of identity synthesis, while for the latter it represents an inability to 'take hold' of some kind of adult identity.

In Marcia's view these four identity statuses may be seen as a developmental sequence, but not necessarily in the sense that one is the prerequisite of the others. Only moratorium appears to be essential for identity achievement, since the searching and exploring which characterises it must precede a resolution of the identity problem. In Marcia's original research (1966) he found that as students moved through the four years of college the proportion of those in the identity diffusion category declined, while the number of identity achievement subjects steadily increased.

Marcia also showed that those young people who had reached identity achievement were more resistant to stress on a concept attainment task, and were less vulnerable in their self-esteem when provided with negative information about themselves. Results of a further study (Marcia 1967) indicated that this group had higher self-esteem in general than those in the other three categories. Toder and Marcia (1973), in an investigation of college women, reported that those who had reached identity achievement were least likely to conform to social pressure, while those in the identity diffusion group were most likely to conform when in a group situation. In a series of studies Waterman and colleagues (Waterman and Waterman 1971, 1972; Waterman *et al.* 1974) looked more closely at the changes in identity status during the four college years. They found that in the first six months of the first year about half the population studied changed their identity status in some fashion, and this was true even of a substantial number who initially appeared in the identity achievement category. Such a result seems to cast doubt on the whole process of categorisation, but when the students were tested again at the end of the four-year college period more stability was apparent. Results from this study showed that by and large those who had reached identity achievement at the end of the first year maintained that status throughout college, being joined on the way by others, so that by the end of the fourth year approximately 45 per cent were in the identity achievement category. Furthermore, very few students remained in the moratorium category, although about one-third remained in the identity diffusion group, much the same number as at the very beginning of the study.

Work of this type has come in for criticism on a number of counts. Matteson (1977), for example, believed that the four categories are conceptually different, moratorium referring to a process, and the other three representing outcomes. Matteson raised a number of other methodological queries, and argued in addition that it is wrong to treat an identity crisis as a single event. As he says:

> There is considerable evidence that adolescents undergo a series of crises and that at one particular time, one content area may be stable while another area of life decisions is very much in crisis. A separate analysis of each content area of the interview is needed.
>
> (Matteson 1977: 354–5)

From Marcia's work it can be suggested that those in the identity achievement category are more likely to be better adjusted in a range of social situations. We may also assume that the number of young people falling into this category increases between the ages of 17 and 21, although we certainly cannot infer that individuals can be assigned to these statuses with any confidence during their first year in college. It is disappointing to note, however, that on the whole this work has provided relatively little insight into the extent of the adolescent identity crisis. In the first place this is because the approach has been used almost exclusively with American college students, and hardly at all with other groups or with younger teenagers. The second reason for this unsatisfying result is that, as Matteson had indicated, the categories themselves are in many ways inadequate for the resolution of a large number of issues relating to adolescent identity.

Nevertheless, a range of research instruments and studies has developed over the years. Erikson's early ideas emerged primarily from his clinical experiences and ethnographic observations. As his writings have gained attention, more empirically minded researchers have begun to operationalise key concepts and test various aspects of Erikson's theory of personality development – particularly those associated with identity formation during adolescence (Adams *et al.* 1979; Grotevant *et al.* 1982; Marcia 1966; Matteson 1974; Rasmussen 1964; Simmons 1970). Despite the variety of research instruments that have emerged to measure many of Erikson's concepts, most have resulted in the categorisation of individuals, either in bipolar rating terms (identity vs. diffusion) or in terms of the identity-status system devised by Marcia (1966).

While Marcia's initial interview has been revised and elaborated to permit separate ratings of exploration and commitment in four major areas – occupation, values, politics, and sex roles (e.g. Matteson 1977) and while the content areas have been expanded to include interpersonal aspects of social identity namely, the dimensions of friendship and dating (e.g. Grotevant *et al.* 1982) along with the original occupational, political, and religious content, the categorical identity-status measurement system has been largely retained.

Even with the strength of interview assessments in capturing and conveying the diversity of human growth and experience, problems exist that include lengthy administration and scoring time as well as the potential for scoring and coding errors. Adams *et al.* (1979) and Grotevant and Adams (1984) have concentrated their efforts on the development of self-report instruments designed to be easily and quickly administered, and based less directly on coder inferences of interviewees responses and more directly on self-reporting by research subjects. Recently, Melgosa (1987) has developed a paper and pencil measure which he has called an Occupational Identity Scale.

To add to the complexity of approaches, a study by Craig-Bray and Adams (1986) carried out convergent–divergent validity and reliability estimates for clinical interview and self-report measures of ego identity. These were obtained using an extended version of the Ego Identity Interview (Grotevant *et al.* 1982) and the extended version of the Objective Measure of Ego Identity Status (Grotevant and Adams 1984). The findings suggested that the two measures may be (a) assessing relatively distinct forms of ego identity, or (b) that the ego-identity construct as measured by the process (exploration) and outcome (commitment) dimensions needs further theoretical examination.

Results from Kroger's (1986) investigation demonstrated some differences in the developmental patterns by which various identity domains are negotiated. While movement into rather than away from the achievement status appeared for both sexes on occupation and politics and on sex role values for women, no significant changes appeared in the domain of religion. Domain issues seem to be addressed sequentially rather than concurrently. By late adolescence, only one-third to one-half of subjects had reached the achievement status in any given domain. Considerable scope for identity development would seem to exist in the years beyond adolescence. Few sex differences emerged. While women were more likely than men to shift into the achieved state on sex roles, results generally indicated greater similarities than differences in identity development for late adolescent men and women. Closer scrutiny of identity components as suggested by Kroger should allow the clinical researcher an even more refined means by which to assess both the salience of identity elements and general stability of identity status resolutions in late adolescence.

Attribution theory

While social representatives are a product of social influence processes (Moscovici 1976; Mugny 1982) there is little empirical work on the social representations held by adolescents. Attribution theory was originally proposed by Kelley (1967) to describe how an individual used different types of information (consistency consensus and distinctiveness) to come to conclusions about the cause or origin of an event. Kelley argued that, in the main, people perform a rational analysis of variance on data to understand whether a phenomenon should be considered to be caused by the actor, entity, or circumstances involved.

There has been little developmental study of attribution processes despite repeated calls for it (Fincham 1983). There have been two developmental studies with young children: one on sex differences in attributions for success (Löchel 1983); the other on moral judgement in relation to the development of causal schemes (Fincham 1982). Changes in adolescence have not been particularly explored. It would seem an important area to examine in relation to what is known of cognitive changes in adolescence and *vis-à-vis* changes in social roles.

Jaspars (1985) has explored the nature of social attribution, suggesting that explanations, particularly of social phenomena, are not the product of rational inference but prefabricated by the requirements of group memberships and ideology. To this extent, attributions are immutably tied to social representations (Moscovici and Hewstone 1983). Thus, when young people explain events they should not be expected to be free of their situational and cultural constraints. In fact, studies of the attributions made about unemployment (Furnham 1982; Breakwell 1986) show they are highly dependent upon political affiliation, work values, and occupational status. Attributions for socially important issues are shaped by social influence processes. But it would also be fair to say that they have 'knock-on' effects for identity processes. Attributions may support or challenge self-definition and evaluation. For instance, the unemployed young person who attributes unemployment to laziness or stupidity is, in effect, resorting to self-blame, and the loss of self-esteem consequent upon life on the dole may be tied to acceptance of such an attribution.

Self-agency and locus of control

There is a strong movement currently in psychology which rejects the notion of the self-concept or identity as the passive product of socialisation. It proposes that people have the capacity to engage in purposive, goal-oriented, if rule-bound, action. Harré (1984), in his exploration of intentionality, rationality, emotion, and meaning, and Shotter, in his work on social accountability and selfhood, typify the movement in Britain. He posited that: 'Reality is constituted for us by the ways in which we render our activities accountable to one another in our daily social lives' (Shotter 1985).

In this, he echoed Gergen and Davis (1985) in emphasising the active social construction of the person through interaction. The person possesses agency, the power to create a social being which is not solely the product of the processes of social influence. Researchers using the notion are concerned to employ focused introspection, account gathering and negotiation, and action research. For instance, Honess (1984) has used focused introspection and repertory grid techniques to examine the changes in coping strategies and identity development in a longitudinal study of school leavers. But there is very little empirical work on the development of agency in adolescence.

The major problem clearly lies in operationalising the concept of 'agency'. A number of indirect routes through to it have been attempted. Two are worth briefly describing: self-efficacy and locus of control.

Gecas and Schwalbe (1983), in the symbolic interaction tradition, postulated that human beings are characterised by intentional and creative action. They suggested that the self-concept is based upon the person's own understanding of his or her actions in the world, especially efficacious actions. Thus, self-esteem is said to be generated by action judged effective by the actor.

Efficacious action as a basis for self-esteem is different in principle from esteem which is based on the perceived opinion of others or derived from the occupation of a particular position in the social structure. Franks and Marolla (1976) call the former 'inner self-esteem' and the latter 'outer self-esteem'. Inner self-esteem derives directly from the experience of oneself as an agent who can make things happen in the world and of effectively realising one's intentions, regardless of obstacles.

Our perceptions of the controllability of events in the world is crucially dependent on the particular nature of the causal antecedents that are held to be important, and especially whether such antecedents are controllable or not. This idea has found empirical expression in Rotter's (1966) internal–external locus of control measure, which attempts to discriminate between people who have a passive world view, and who regard important events as being essentially independent of their actions, and those who believe that, in the main, such events are within their locus of control. The idea of locus of control suggests that people differ in how far they anticipate reinforcement to be internally or externally controlled. These differences are relatively stable, such that some people habitually regard their fate to be in their own hands, others continually consider themselves to be the playthings of chance or other people. Rotter's theory asserts that internality–externality in locus of control is acquired in childhood as a consequence of parental treatment. It would be intriguing to examine how far, in adolescence, when the influence of parents wanes, orientation towards control can be changed by other influences at work or in education.

Studies of locus of control in young children and adolescents are limited. Crandall *et al.* (1965) looked at children's beliefs in their own control of reinforcement in situations of academic achievement. Considering various social aspects of adolescence, Leming (1974) discovered no locus of control differences between politically active and non-politically motivated teenagers, while Farley and Sewell (1975) found that female delinquents had lower achievement motivation and a more external locus of control than non-delinquents.

In an investigation of locus of control and the use of contraception among unmarried black adolescents Hendricks and Fullilove (1983) showed that black adolescent fathers were more likely to have external locus of control, not to be churchgoers, and not to believe in the use of birth control!

Adams and Shea (1979) in an investigation of self-identity reported that identity achievement adolescents were more advanced than diffusion (i.e. uncommitted) young people in ego stage development and in their level of internality.

It will be clear from this discussion that Erikson's notions have stimulated a wide range of research investigations. It has to be stated, however, that while there can be no doubt that identity problems do exist among a proportion of teenagers, not one single study has provided support for Erikson's view of the 'normative crisis'. There is simply no evidence to suggest that the great majority of adolescents experience a serious crisis of identity, and most studies seem to conclude that only 25–35 per cent of the total population of teenagers at any age level could be said to have a disturbance in this area, and it is around the time of puberty that the greatest likelihood of disturbance in self-concept is possible. Nevertheless, there are a number of problem behaviours which impinge on the adolescents' self-concept in the transition to adulthood, and these are considered in the following section.

Problem behaviour and self-identity

Several kinds of behaviour thought to be problematic increase over the adolescent period. Research has focused especially on drug and alcohol use, cigarette smoking, sexual behaviour, and delinquency (Jessor and Jessor 1977). Most of these behaviours would not be alarming if seen in adults, but are perceived as inappropriate for young people in the process of growing up. Of course, excessive involvement in these activities can be problematic at any age. Silbereisen and colleagues (Silbereisen *et al.* 1986, 1987) have proposed that a number of so-called anti-social activities are in fact purposive, self-regulating, and aimed at coping with aspects of adolescent development. They can play a constructive developmental role, at least over the short term (Kaplan 1980; Silbereisen *et al.* 1987). Early sexual activity and even early childbearing may have a similar function (Petersen *et al.* 1987). Nevertheless, the negative consequences of these behaviours can be noted over a longer period of time (Furstenberg *et al.* 1987).

Given the need for adolescents to maintain or enhance self-esteem, they are likely to develop strategies for dealing with threatening situations. For example, Covington and Beery (1977) found that young people with low self-esteem adopted strategies such as avoiding group participation, not trying hard, or setting unrealistic goals to create a situation whereby they could preserve what little sense of self-worth they possessed. In terms of attribution theory, the child who experiences success in light of low self-esteem will be likely to ascribe the outcome to some capricious factor as opposed to personal causation. In essence, the young person discounts information such as ability attributions for success that are not congruent with self-views of competence. Over time, adolescents with low self-esteem tend to adopt failure-prone strategies and attribute unsuccessful outcomes to lack of ability and successes to environmental causes beyond their control (Diener and Dweck 1978; Dweck and Elliott 1984; Martens *et al.* 1981).

Unemployment and self

In order to understand how any movement of the individual adolescent in the social context or any social change gains the power to threaten identity, it is necessary to examine social and personal meanings. For example, being unemployed attacks self-esteem because of the social representation of unemployed youth developed historically over time. It also attacks self-esteem for other reasons (loss of income and social status), but even these are dependent upon the social context to become meaningful. Other examples of threat such as marginality or ethnic minority group membership can be cited. These represent threats not only because they abrogate continuity and self-esteem but also because social influences append specific meanings to them (Althusser 1985; Donald and Hall 1986; Eccleshall *et al.* 1984).

There have been a series of studies by both psychologists and sociologists of the transition from school into work and, more latterly, unemployment and Youth Training Schemes (Ashton and Field 1976; Griffin 1985). These have centred upon the way societally imposed roles and obligations, social networks, and public rhetoric shape economic aspirations, expectations, and actions. The literature on gender differences in schooling and labour market participation supports the conclusions of these studies (McRobbie 1978; Deem 1980; Pollert 1981). For instance, unemployment can attack self-esteem and upset psychological stability (Warr 1983) but its impact is mediated and moderated by situational variables (Breakwell *et al.* 1984) and by the passage of time and the availability of psycho-social supports (Trew and Kilpatrick 1984; Hendry and Raymond 1986). Shamir (1986) argued that unemployment is associated with diminished well-being among individuals with low self-esteem, but is less damaging to the well-being of individuals with high self-esteem. Thus self-esteem moderates the relationships between employment status and depressive affect, morale, and anxiety.

Delinquency and self

Kaplan (1980) has stated that children turn to delinquency after a history of devaluing social feedback which has produced negative self-esteem. Delinquent behaviour is then adopted because it inflates self-esteem through behavioural rewards and psychological defences which allow the delinquent to reject general social feedback and to raise his self-perceptions. As a general principle, Kaplan has asserted that individuals who have experienced fewer devaluing experiences will require less self-enhancement. Related to the specifics of self-enhancement, Kaplan proposed three psychological defences associated with self-enhancement: denial of personal responsibility for actions, reduction of aspirations, and the disguising of deficiencies. Thus, according to Kaplan, delinquents employ psychological defences to enhance self-esteem and to retain endorsement of socially accepted values. Denial and rejection of general social feedback and incongruencies between behaviour and self-perceptions appear to be the primary defences, and such claims are supported in a study by Zieman and Benson (1983).

Theoretical approaches to delinquency can be crudely classified into those which are individual-centred and those which are socially-centred. An even cruder dichotomy is to suggest that psychologists tend to use the first approach and sociologists the second. Explanations and theories about delinquents provide useful, if partial, insights into delinquency. No one theory is complete. The purely sociological explanation of delinquency in terms of environment is only partly true, because only a small percentage of adolescents in any area join gangs or commit crimes. Psychological theories in terms of pathologically disturbed behaviour are also incomplete. McFall and his colleagues (Freedman *et al.* 1978; Gaffney and McFall 1981) are among the few investigators who have conducted a thorough and systematic analysis of the skill deficits in a group of adolescent juvenile delinquents. These researchers developed the Adolescent Problem Inventory (API: Freedman *et al.* 1978) for adolescent males and the Problem Inventory for Adolescent Girls (PIAG: Gaffney and McFall 1981) for adolescent females. These instruments empirically identified those situations that are most problematic for delinquent adolescent boys and girls. McFall and his colleagues compared the performance of a matched group of delinquent and non-delinquent adolescents on both inventories. Both instruments successfully discriminated the non-delinquent from the delinquent groups, suggesting that social-skill deficits are a correlate of delinquency.

Again, this approach only offers a limited explanation of the phenomenon. Glueck's multi-dimensional interpretation (1959), a 'dynamic interplay' of somatic, socio-cultural, and psychoanalytic factors, perhaps offers a general framework for (theoretically) understanding juvenile delinquency, suggesting its place within a coherent pattern of identity and lifestyle followed by a number of adolescents.

The significance of juvenile gangs (defined as groups with a relatively constant membership and structure) would seem to be far less in Britain than elsewhere, although clearly some do exist (O'Hagan 1976). One major participant observational study by Patrick (1973) revealed a number of important insights: many of the active gang members were still schoolboys; part of the attraction to the gang setting was excitement and aggression. Patrick's fellow gang members' self-concepts reflected realisation that they were educational, social, and occupational failures, well and truly 'at the bottom of the heap'. There was a fatalism towards their educational, occupational, and social failure. The deep frustrations they experienced as a result gave rise to aggression which had to have an outlet in sex and violence. Disillusionment had set in during school days. Focal concerns for Patrick's Glasgow gang (which possessed little camaraderie, or kindness, or solidarity) were hardness (being 'gemme'), drink, drugs, status, 'patter', and 'chat', clothes and sex. They called themselves 'slummies' (slum-dwellers) and celebrated 'hardness'. Their self- and group-identities were clear-cut and consistent.

White (1971) and also Mungham and Pearson (1976) have portrayed the urban gang in English cities in similar terms of identity-seeking excitement, exhibiting high aggression, showing strong needs for 'territory'. Such patterns need to be seen within the broader context of cities where there are working-class cultures of heavy drinking, violence, and superficial personal relationships: 'Fiddling at work; stealing from wealthy institutions and shops is allowed; toughness and masculinity are central, and vandalism is seen as attacks on property not particularly belonging to anyone' (Wilmott 1966).

Associated with this, working-class boys who are involved with specific youth sub-cultures are often placed in the contradictory situation of attracting attention and having to deal with any resultant challenge. Various fashion styles, used to display self-identity, are worn to attract attention, but 'battle scars' and other insignia are presented to indicate masculine aggression and dominance.

The 'warring' symbols within working-class territories have

implications for race relations. Pride in the local territory can become an expression of conservation, with the protection of the neighbourhood flaring into prejudice and racism. It can even manifest itself in the defence of its 'turf' by violence around the local soccer stadium (Brake 1980). Supporting professional football teams provide an obvious context for identity fellowship and excitement. Traces of 'oppositional' activity in behaviour are to be found in the expressive role of football supporter as against a passive acceptance of the role of spectator. Here, traditional working-class concerns of neighbourhood and territory, group and local identity, loyalty and rivalry, desire for participation and group solidarity, masculine aggression and heavy drinking, may be linked with participation in acts of violence around soccer (Marsh *et al.* 1983). With a backcloth of economic recession – unemployment, political and social class divisions – where young working-class people are a particularly vulnerable group, football's professionalisation has caused the creation of spectacular theatre, and the mass media's reaction to football support has been to 'sensationalise'. The social controls of such groups of supporters are clearly and radically different from those that are predominant in society – the identity encouraged is of tough aggressive masculinity.

Some adolescents seek out such a comradely socal milieu in which to pursue excitement and find occasions for establishing a 'reputation' (cf. Emler 1984). Brake (1985) has stressed that male sub-cultures are primarily an 'exploration' of masculinity. In working-class male sub-cultures the 'macho', aggressive image of masculinity, which strongly reinforces gender identity, is presented as a resistance to a collectively experienced sense of failure or rejection: however, not all men are involved in this aspect of masculinity and the 'culture of masculinity'. Male sub-cultures, such as the 'bikers' in Willis (1978), demonstrate a culture of masculinity which reinforces their particular male identity. Those who fail to meet this expectation are excluded from groups which stress other kinds of 'masculinity'. Similarly, while cultures of masculinity cut across class locations there are differences *between* classes. The physically aggressive, 'macho' form of masculinity in some working-class male youth sub-cultures (Willis 1978) is expressed in a similar way (although more socially legitimated) in the rugby-playing 'macho' competitive culture of the male middle class (Sheard and Dunning 1973).

As McRobbie and Garber (1976) pointed out, the position of working-class young women is structurally different to that of young working-class men. The common sense assumption, upon which much of the interaction between young men and young women is apparently founded, demarcate clear boundaries for 'acceptable' masculine and feminine behaviour and responses. The boundaries, however, are not derived simply from the shared assumptions of everyday life. They are structural in the sense that images of sexuality become institutionalised and legitimated within the policy responses of agencies such as schools, youth clubs, and commercial leisure providers. It is here that images translate into ideologies and form part of the social management of sexuality. It is at these levels – ideological and political – that the experiences of young women and men are structured differently and provide an institutionalised process of reinforcement to assumptions which are commonly held.

Ethnic minorities and identity

As an extension of these ideas presented above, Werthman and Piviavin (1967) also noted the importance of territory, with gang members being possessive of the local neighbourhood, and the police being seen as enemies enforcing a law supported and produced by an external power structure which suppresses minorities, and promotes racism.

Conger's (1977) review of research on this topic indicated that, particularly in America, the greatly increased acceptance of blacks and other minority groups in the last decade, in conjunction with the rise of black power and black consciousness, had undoubtedly had a beneficial effect on the self-esteem of adolescents belonging to minority groups. However, Rosenberg (1975) made an important point when he distinguished between those belonging to minority groups who are well integrated and who function in a supportive environment, and those who exist in a 'dissonant' or hostile context. To support the argument he reported a study of self-esteem among black students attending integrated and segregated schools in the USA. The results illustrate his point. At all ages – in elementary school, junior high school, and senior high school – those black children who attended segregated schools had higher self-esteem than those attending schools which were racially mixed.

Hall *et al.* (1978) argued that the whole culture of the school attacks the self-concept and culture of black pupils, and Cottle (1978) described the bitterness felt by young British blacks sensitive to the fact that white adults would not physically come into contact with them – for example, during physical education lessons or even within classroom confrontations. Linked to this, Weinreich (1979) in the U.K. has attempted to study identity diffusion among adolescents coming from immigrant communities. His method involved the use of the repertory grid technique and results showed immigrant girls, especially those from Pakistani families, to have the highest levels of identity diffusion. Louden (1980) has also commented on the 'marginal' self-images of minority group adolescents in Britain.

Further tensions may be created by the disintegration of traditional working-class values, while immigrant sub-cultural values remained effective. Robins and Cohen (1978) have argued that a threat is created by the socio-cultural cohesion and identity shown by immigrant teenagers especially when combined with the breakdown of a stable sub-cultural identity among young working-class whites.

The police may also play their part in race divisions:

> The police have increasingly taken on the guise of aliens confronted by a culture they do not understand and so for which they feel contempt. But the contempt is mutual. For the streets of Brixton, once paved with hope, are now filled with the frustration, hopelessness and desperate pride of rebels and gangsters.
>
> (Dodd 1978: 78)

The clash of cultures, and of self- and group-identities is an issue which needs to be addressed in examining social integration in modern society.

Drugs and self

Our society relies upon drugs of various kinds to help individuals in their day-to-day living to withstand strains, stresses, and anxieties with equanimity. Society itself has become a 'drug culture'! Modern medicine has made drugs highly legitimate, as something to be taken casually and not only during moments of pain or of acute and certified stress. From this viewpoint, adolescents, far from being in revolt against an older generation, seem to acknowledge how influential the older generation are as behavioural models and wish to identify with them.

If psychological problems related to self-identity, dependency needs, control of aggression, early social or emotional deprivation, or lack of interpersonal relationships, do predate drug usage, the drugs can be seen as a help with personal problems. To these factors can be added drug taking for curiosity, for kicks, for fun, or for giving individuals greater insights and perceptual variations.

Hence, drug taking is a socio-cultural phenomenon related to attitudes within society, sub-cultural values, and adolescents' self-concept.

An achievement-based society valuing success through education and wealth creates frustrations for the so-called failures and for the rejected, and adolescents may be highly sensitive to these nuances. Differing values and meanings are involved in the 'interaction' between adolescents and the drugs they take. Davis and Muroz (1970) for example, revealed the importance of social-class based meaning systems in structuring lifestyles. They argued that the differential patterns of drug usage which they discovered reflected: 'The basic contrast in expressive styles extant in the class structure. Put crudely, LSD equals self-exploration/self-improvement equals middle class; while methadrine equals body stimulation/release of aggressive impulses equals working class.'

However, social class differences in drug usage have lessened across the years. Young (1971) has pointed out the important influence of various 'drug sub-cultures in 'supporting' the adolescent drug user. While McKeganey and Boddy (1987) noted there were certain aspects related to drugs that could be seen as socially unifying in collecting a diverse range of individuals around a common set of concerns and thus furthering their collective identity. Whilst the fact of this is likely to be of some importance in describing drug abuse in a wide range of settings, it may be something that is particularly influential as far as young people are concerned since they are a group very much involved in the process of forming their own identity in contradistinction to that of parents, friends, and so on.

Another aspect of drug abuse which has attracted much media attention is glue-sniffing. Two reasons why glue-sniffing may be attractive to adolescents is that it has a pleasant 'bouquet', and it is cheaper to buy than alcohol. Glue-sniffing is more accurately described as solvent-sniffing, since aerosol sprays, dry-cleaning fluids, nail varnish remover, and petrol all give off volatile hydrocarbons which can cause intoxication (Watson 1980). Inhaling solvents has a similar effect to drinking alcohol – both can induce a state of euphoria and well-being. Nevertheless, solvents (apparently) are no more likely to induce violent behaviour than any other intoxicant since they have no specific pharmacological effect of making people violent. Like alcohols, solvents might release violence that was already there within the adolescent. King *et al.* (1981) have referred to the more immediate and dangerous toxic effects of glue-sniffing on the central nervous system, brain, kidneys, liver, and heart caused by toluene, the main solvent used in commercially available contact adhesives in Britain. Beyond such toxic effects deaths can occur due to accidents during intoxication such as suffocation when children or adolescents place glue-filled plastic bags over their heads, or sniffing other dangerous substances like butane gas lighter fuel, dry-cleaning fluids, and petrol.

It is difficult to suggest that there are particular sub-groups of adolescents who are more likely to be involved in glue-sniffing than others. At an individual level, it can be hypothesised that there may be three types of adolescents who sniff glue: the solitary user, perhaps initially handling glue in building model aeroplanes; the child who sniffs out of curiosity within a group of peers; and the child with severe emotional problems. This last category is probably a very small one. Here the whole personality could disintegrate under the effects of 'glue'! This sort of adolescent might use other drugs and would probably be destined for early drug addiction.

While solvent abuse must surely be accepted as an integral part of the wider aspect of drug abuse, it is essential to keep firmly in mind the fact that most children and young people will never at any time, in any circumstances, experiment with such substances. It is also reassuring to reflect that for the most part those who do so will regard it more in the light of a passing phase, something to be tried and tested as part of an exploration of developing self-identity (hopefully to be found wanting) rather than as a pernicious prank which could lead in time to damage or death.

This raises questions regarding adolescents' knowledge of drugs and their effects. An anonymous questionnaire survey by Wright and Pearl (1986) on knowledge and experience of drug abuse among fourth-year pupils in three Wolverhampton secondary schools in 1969, 1979, and 1984 showed that adolescents had some familiarity with the names of drugs but considerable ignorance and misunderstanding about how the drugs were taken and their dangers. The proportion of pupils who knew someone taking illicit drugs almost doubled over the period of the study from 15 per cent in 1969 to 28 per cent in 1984, and the proportion of those who had been offered illicit drugs almost trebled, from 5 per cent in 1969 to 14 per cent in 1984. Wright and Pearl suggested that television remains the most important source of information about drugs; whilst peer group and social pressures continue to be the most important reasons for young people's initial involvement in the drug scene.

The link between drugs and alcohol has been explored by Plant and Stuart (1984). The data indicated that at least casual experimentation with illicit drugs was by no means uncommon amongst young people and that such experimentation was often associated with the use of alcohol and tobacco. Their results identified clearly a sub-group of young men and women who appeared to be 'at risk' in relation to their levels of substance use.

Once more, a constellation of effects can be noted around a period of the lifespan where the young person strives to develop a clear-cut personal and social identity. Alcohol (like certain other drugs) helps to reduce tension and anxiety, provides pleasant personal and social experiences, and can offer pseudo-resolutions to personal conflicts. Curiosity, the influences of peers, a desire to appear grown up and the identification with adult models are further influences on adolescent drinking patterns.

So, the value of alcohol to the adolescent is of a symbolic and not merely of a functional nature (i.e. usually drink is taken because of a desire to create a self-image of toughness and maturity or as a perceived means of attaining attractiveness and sociability often specifically with respect to the opposite sex). The majority of youngsters interviewed by Scarlett (1975) regularly used alcohol, and of these 50 per cent were under age at the time. Most crucial of the complex reasons for alcohol consumption seemed to be adult models (consumption of alcohol was seen as being symbolic of self-entering adult status) and the fact that both pubs and discotheques sell alcohol and are often the only places of entertainment in certain neighbourhoods. Fogelman (1976) reported that many teenagers admitted to under-age drinking, and Davies (1978) stated that a not insignificant number of 14-year-olds drink in public houses. The 'blue-print' of under-age drinkers was that they probably also smoked, went to discotheques and youth clubs, but seldom to church (Davies 1978). The smoking habits of young people described by Plant and Stuart (1982) were equally striking, with 30 per cent of the males being smokers compared with 37 per cent of females. Another factor involved in young people's use of substances of various kinds may be the effects of the mass media in projecting 'desirable' adult social stereotypes associated with drinking and smoking. (Percentages for adolescent smoking and drinking from Balding's research are presented in Figure 4.3.)

A point to be considered, therefore, is that different forces may be at work in the genesis of the various types of anti-social behaviour. This was clearly illustrated in a study carried out in the U.S.A. by Kandel *et al.* (1978), in which they distinguished between parent influence, peer influence, the adolescent's attitudes, and his or her involvement in other deviant activities as

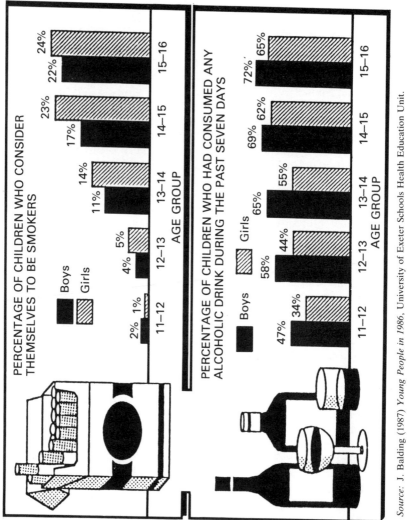

PERCENTAGE OF CHILDREN WHO CONSIDER THEMSELVES TO BE SMOKERS

Boys   Girls

AGE GROUP

11–12: 2%, 1%
12–13: 4%, 5%
13–14: 11%, 14%
14–15: 17%, 23%
15–16: 22%, 24%

PERCENTAGE OF CHILDREN WHO HAD CONSUMED ANY ALCOHOLIC DRINK DURING THE PAST SEVEN DAYS

Boys   Girls

AGE GROUP

11–12: 47%, 34%
12–13: 58%, 44%
13–14: 65%, 55%
14–15: 69%, 62%
15–16: 72%, 65%

Source: J. Balding (1987) *Young People in 1986*, University of Exeter Schools Health Education Unit.

Figure 4.3 Percentages of young people admitting to smoking or drinking behaviour.

factors which could predict drug or alcohol use. They were able to show that although other variables played their part, it was parental behaviour which was the most critical factor in leading the young person into early experiments with alcohol. Where drug use was concerned, however, no one factor stood out; the teenager's attitudes, poor parent–child relationships, the influence of one best friend, and involvement in other deviant activities all contributed to the total picture.

Plant (1979) reported that parents of young drugtakers he studied were vehemently opposed to the use of marijuana, though they themselves were heavy drinkers or smokers, or were individuals who made considerable use of barbiturates, tranquillisers, or other prescribed drugs. Thus it is impossible to say that the influences at work in the home did not play their part in their children's anti-social behaviour.

The research carried out by Davies and Stacey (1972) and Aitken (1978) in Strathclyde on the drinking behaviour of young people illustrates such a process. This research showed, first, that a remarkably high proportion (82 per cent) started drinking within the home setting, a finding which accords well with the views of Akers (1970) and Kandel *et al.* (1978). However, the remaining 18 per cent reported that their drinking started outside the home, in parks, playgrounds, and clubs, and in the company of their peers. Those in this group turned out to be the heaviest drinkers, to have poor relationships with their parents, and to have hostile attitudes to authority figures and to the older generation in general. Thus anti-social behaviour went hand in hand with alienation from the family and from the world of adults.

Hence, it is necessary to suggest that the importance of drinking and drug taking in the teenage years may be that they link to other adolescent pursuits which involve peers, yet perhaps paradoxically reflect attempts to act 'like adults' in the developmental search for a self-identity.

Concluding remarks

We have seen in this chapter that self-concept is an elusive concept – a series of complex structures and processes developed across the adolescent years, and involving roles, rules, statuses, self-agency and identity.

Erikson (1968) indicated that identity consists of three sub-constructs: a self, an ego, and formal operational abilities. The self is the content of one's thoughts as the person reflects on one's own body image, personality, or social roles. According to Erikson, when an individual possesses an identity, the self will include 'a conscious sense of individual uniqueness' and a sense of 'solidarity with a group's ideals'. Gallatin (1975) elaborated on this notion and characterised self as the person's awareness of how he or she is like all other people, like some other people and like no other person.

Because there is so much change during adolescence, and these changes require effective coping on the part of the individual, the processes involved in this period of the lifespan are also likely to be ones needed to respond to challenges throughout life. Furthermore, it could be hypothesised that adolescence differs from earlier years in the nature of the challenges encountered and in the capacity of the individual to respond effectively to these challenges. If this is correct, adolescence will be the first phase of life requiring, and presumably stimulating, mature patterns of functioning and the development of a clear-cut personal and social identity that persist throughout life. Conversely, failure to cope effectively with the challenges of adolescence may represent deficiencies in the individual's self-concept which will have negative consequences for subsequent development.

Chapter five

The family

One of the central themes of adolescent development is the attainment of independence, often represented symbolically in art and literature by the moment of 'departure' from home. However, for most young people today independence is not gained at one specific moment by the grand gesture of saying goodbye to one's parents and setting off to seek one's fortune in the wide world. Independence is much more likely to mean freedom within the family to make day-to-day decisions, emotional freedom to make new relationships, and personal freedom to take responsibility for one's self in such things as educaton, political beliefs, and future career. There are many forces which interact in propelling an individual towards this state of maturity. Naturally both physical and intellectual maturation encourage the adolescent toward greater autonomy. In addition to these factors there are, undoubtedly, psychological forces within the individual as well as social forces in the environment which have the same goal. In the psychoanalytic view, considered in Chapter one, the process of seeking independence represents the need to break off the infantile ties with the parents, thus making new mature sexual relationships possible. From the perspective of the sociologist, however, more emphasis will be placed on the changes in role and status which lead to a re-definition of the individual's place in the social structure. Whatever the explanation, it is certainly true that the achievement of independence is an integral feature of adolescent development, and that the role of the adults involved is an especially important one.

In understanding this process it is necessary to appreciate that the young person's movement toward adulthood is far from straightforward. As has been mentioned earlier, while independence at times appears to be a rewarding goal, there are also moments when it is a worrying, even frightening prospect. Child-like dependence can be safe and comforting at no matter what age, if, for example, one is facing problems or difficulties alone, and it is essential to realise that no individual achieves adult independence without a number of backward glances. It is this ambivalence which underlies the typically contradictory behaviour of adolescents, behaviour which is so often the despair of adults. Thus there is nothing adults find more frustrating than having to deal with a teenager who is at one moment complaining of having parents who are always interfering (for example, giving advice) and the next bitterly protesting that no one takes any interest in him or her (for example, not giving advice).

However, it is equally important to acknowledge that parents themselves usually hold conflicting attitudes towards their teenage children. On the one hand they may wish young people to be independent, to make their own decisions, and to cease making childish demands, whilst, on the other, they may at the same time be frightened of the consequences of independence (especially the sexual consequences), and sometimes jealous of the opportunities and idealism of youth. In addition it should not be forgotten that the adolescent years often coincide with the difficulties of middle age for parents. Adjusting to unfulfilled hopes, preparation for retirement, declining physical health, marital difficulties, and so on, may all increase family stress, and add further to the problems faced by young people in finding a route to independence which is not too fraught with conflict.

The question 'how much conflict' is one which has intrigued and puzzled almost all who have attempted to understand the adolescent process, and it will be considered in this chapter as part of the more general issue of the so-called 'generation gap'. In addition a number of other common themes run through the literature, and in this chapter some attention will be paid to the topics of the exercise of power and decision making within the family, to the part played by parents as role models, and finally to the effects of divorce and family breakdown on adolescent development. It should be noted that the so-called 'parent–peer' issue, that is, the question of the relative influence of parents and peers upon young people, will be dealt with in Chapter six.

The 'generation gap'

The concept of a generation gap has a long history in psychology. It is also continuously popular with television, the press, and other media for it has a certain sensational quality about it. In this respect it has strong affinities with other concepts such as 'storm and stress' and 'identity crisis'. There is no clear consensus as to the exact meaning of the phrase, but most agree that it implies at least two things: a discrepancy or divergence of viewpoint between adults and teenagers and, partly as a result of this, a degree of conflict between the generations. In fact some writers (e.g. J. S. Coleman 1961) have gone so far as to describe a completely separate youth culture, isolated to a large extent from the adult world, and possessing its own norms and values. More recent writing, such as Brake (1985), perpetuates the idea of a youth sub-culture, while in the same year a book for parents of teenagers was published with the actual title *The Generation Gap* (McCormack 1985) giving further currency to the idea of a divide between young and old in our society.

In fact, however, a wide variety of studies have provided evidence of generally positive relationships between adolescents and their parents. Douvan and Adelson in their book *The Adolescent Experience* (1966), were among the first to illustrate this point. They reported the results of interviews with over 3,000 teenagers across the U.S.A. The results indicated a general picture of minor conflicts between parent and adolescent, focusing especially on issues such as make-up, dating, leisure activities, music and so on. As far as major values were concerned, however, very little difference emerged. On issues of morality, political or religious beliefs, and sexual attitudes, the divergence of opinion was minimal. In fact the vast majority of teenagers, far from despising or rejecting their parents, actually looked up to them and valued their advice.

Studies carried out in the U.K. and Europe portray a very similar picture. In Fogelman's (1976) report of the work carried out by the National Children's Bureau, entitled *Britain's Sixteen-Year-Olds*, findings on relationships within the family corroborate all that has been said so far. In this study the parents were given a list of issues on which it is commonly thought adults and young people of this age might disagree. The results indicated a situation which was, from the parents' point of view, a harmonious one. The two most commonly reported areas of disagreement – dress or hairstyle, and the time of coming in at night – are what might be expected, but even here only 10 per cent of parents said that they often disagreed about these things. The views of the parents are illustrated in Table 5.1.

The young people confirmed the attitudes of their mothers and fathers. They agreed that appearance and evening activities were sometimes issues of disagreement in the home, but otherwise they reported an atmosphere free from major conflict. It is of interest to note that about two-thirds of those with brothers and sisters said

85

Table 5.1 Disagreement between parents and study child (parents' report) (N = 11,531)

	Often %	Sometimes %	Never or hardly ever %
Choice of friends of the same sex	3	16	81
Choice of friends of opposite sex	2	9	89
Dress or hairstyle	11	35	54
Time of coming in at night or going to bed	8	26	66
Places gone to in own time	2	9	89
Doing homework	6	18	76
Smoking	6	9	85
Drinking	1	5	94

Source: K. Fogelman (1976) *Britain's Sixteen-Year-Olds*, National Children's Bureau

they quarrelled between themselves, yet 'many wrote a qualifying note to the effect that although they might often quarrel with a brother or sister, or disagree with their parents, this did not mean there was anything wrong with the underlying relationship' (Fogelman 1976: 36). Family relationships as seen by the teenagers in this very large sample of over eleven thousand individuals are illustrated in Table 5.2.

Table 5.2 Family relationships (children's report) (N = 11,045)

	Very True %	True %	Uncertain %	Untrue %	Very Untrue %
I get on well with my mother	41	45	8	4	1
I get on well with my father	35	45	13	5	2
I often quarrel with a brother or sister	23	43	10	19	5
My parents have strong views about my appearance (e.g. dress, hairstyle, etc.)	15	33	19	27	6
My parents want to know where I go in the evening	27	51	8	11	3
My parents disapprove of some of my male friends	9	19	18	37	16
My parents disapprove of some of my female friends	5	15	18	40	22

Source: K. Fogelman (1976) *Britain's Sixteen-Year-Olds*, National Children's Bureau

The work of Rutter and colleagues (1976) should also be mentioned in this context. In this wide-ranging survey of all

14-year-olds on the Isle of Wight, parents, teachers, and young people themselves were extensively interviewed. As one aspect of the study Rutter examined the degree of alienation between the generations as experienced either by the adolescents or by their parents. The results showed that in only 4 per cent of the total group did the parents feel an increase in alienation at this stage of adolescence, while amongst the young people themselves only 5 per cent reported actual rejection of their parents. A further 25 per cent expressed some degree of criticism.

This is not to deny that conflicts exist. Some excellent examples of the reality of family life have been provided in Csikszentmihalyi and Larson's book, *Being Adolescent* (1984). Theirs was a relatively small scale but intensive study, of the type that has been carried out all too rarely. By using an approach called the Experience Sampling Method, the authors encouraged seventy-five adolescents to fill in approximately thirty self-report forms completed at random moments during a one-week period. The data thus collected have provided a rich source of material on adolescent concerns and activities. In the particular context of the family, or Family Aggravations, as the authors call one of their chapters, they quote one 16-year-old's description of his feelings on Sunday morning:

> I never want to go to church, but I'll go. Finally I get a Sunday off; I don't have to work, so I can sleep a little later. But now I've got to go to church. I've got to wake up earlier than if I'd had to go to work.
>
> They always wake you up, and they're always cheerful, and you go 'oh, no!' They act cheerful, but they are really hostile if you don't want to go. Right now (in the car) I'd just asked them to turn the channel. They were listening to some opera stuff. They just ignored me; you know, because we were parking and everything. Still, they could have acknowledged me. That's why I was so upset. I went, 'Jesus Christ, at least they could answer me.'
>
> (Csikszentmihalyi and Larson 1984)

As the authors point out, not only are the parents' goals imposed on this young man in relation to the way he spends his Sunday morning, but, even more important from his point of view, they can't even be bothered to acknowledge his wishes, which felt in this instance as if they couldn't be bothered to acknowledge his existence.

Of course there are many factors which will determine the

extent of family conflict during the adolescent years. One obvious variable is age, and numerous studies have shown that conflict is likely to reach a peak at a particular age – usually around 15 for girls and somewhat later for boys (Coleman 1974; Kroger 1985).

Similarly both culture and social class will have their effects too. Lesser and Kandel (1969) showed important differences between the U.S.A. and Denmark in the way adolescent independence was handled in the two countries, while Smith (1978) reported that there were differences in the U.K. between middle-class and working-class families in general attitudes towards the younger generation.

In considering relationships between parents and teenagers one interesting focus has been on the differences between the two groups in the way these relationships are perceived. Early writers to draw attention to this issue were the Eppels, in their study of adolescent morality (1966). In summarising their work they wrote:

> The picture that has emerged of this group of young working people (15–17 years of age) is that most of them regard themselves as belonging to a generation handicapped by distorted stereotypes about their behaviour and moral standards. Many feel this so acutely that they believe whatever goodwill they manifest is at best not likely to be much appreciated and at worst may be misinterpreted to their disadvantage. The view was repeatedly expressed or implied that the behaviour of a delinquent or anti-social fringe had unfortunately been extended to characterise their whole generation.
>
> (Eppel and Eppel 1966: 213)

Belsky *et al.* (1984) summarise research which shows that neither adolescents nor parents perceive the influence of social relationships accurately. Teenagers perceive their parents to be less influential than they really are, while adults perceive that they are more influential than they actually are. Furthermore young people, in assessing the magnitude of the differences between the generations, appear to over-emphasise the extent of these differences, while conversely, parents underestimate such differences. Noller and Callan (1986) tackle the same theme, showing that parents are generally more satisfied with family cohesion and adaptability than are adolescents. None the less, it is important to note that young people were still generally satisfied with family functioning – it was just that they were not as satisfied as their parents.

How, it may be asked, can all these findings be fitted into a coherent picture? Perhaps the first thing to say is that while on the one hand the notion of a full-scale generation gap is obviously not sustained by the research evidence, on the other hand it cannot simply be dismissed as a complete fiction. One important reason for the confusion which exists lies in the difference between attitudes towards close family members, and attitudes to more general social groupings, such as 'the younger generation'. Thus, for example, teenagers may very well approve and look up to their own parents while expressing criticism of adults in general. Similarly, parents may deride 'punks', 'drop-outs', or 'soccer hooligans' while holding a favourable view of their own adolescent sons and daughters. Another fact that needs to be stressed is that there is a difference between feeling and behaviour. Adolescents may be irritated or angry with their parents as a result of day-to-day conflicts, but issues can be worked out in the home and do not necessarily lead to outright rejection or rebellion.

Furthermore, as Conger and Petersen (1984) point out, too little credit is given to the possibility that adults and young people, although disagreeing with each other about certain things, may still respect each other's views, and live in relative harmony together under the same roof. Thus there seems to be little doubt that the extreme view of the generation gap, involving the notion of a war between the generations, or the idea of a separate adolescent sub-culture, is dependent on a myth. It is the result of a stereotype which is useful to the mass media, and given currency by a small minority of disaffected young people and resentful adults. However, to deny any sort of conflict between teenagers and older members of society is equally false. Adolescents could not grow into adults unless they were able to test out the boundaries of authority, nor could they discover what they believed unless given the opportunity to push hard against the beliefs of others. The adolescent transition from dependence to independence is almost certain to involve some conflict, but its extent should not be exaggerated.

Let us conclude this section with some words of Csikszentmihalyi and Larson:

In dwelling on the dramatic instances of conflict, it is easy to overlook the constant material and psychic support that the family provides, as a matter of course, in the lives of teenagers. The family is a bit like good weather, which is usually noticed only when it fails. It is true that adolescents are positively gloomy with their families compared to how they feel with friends; on the other hand, they are radiant with the family in comparison with how they feel in solitude or in classrooms. By and large, the family seems to provide a setting of neutrality where teenagers recover in relative safety and warmth from the highs and lows of daily life.

(Csikszentmihalyi and Larson 1984: 144)

Parents as role models

Parents fulfil many different functions for the developing adolescent, and one of these functions relates to the provision of what are known as role models. Here the parents represent examples of the ways in which such things as sex roles and work roles may be interpreted, providing prototypes against which the young person will evaluate other interpretations of these roles. It is of course true that children throughout their early lives depend on their parents for primary knowledge of such role behaviour, but obviously these models become crucial during adolescence, since it is at this time that the young person begins to make his or her own role choices. Thus, for example, while both parents' attitudes to work will be pertinent all through childhood, these will become relevant in a somewhat different and more immediate way when the teenager is facing questions about what he or she is going to do after leaving school. As we have seen in Chapter one, role change is likely to be a major feature of adolescent development, and it will be evident, therefore, that the role models available to the young person at this stage in life will be of great significance.

It is important to be clear, however, that the likelihood of role decisions or choices being influenced by the parents will be determined not only by the nature of the role model, but also by the degree of identification between parent and child. The topic of identification is a large one, and will not be dealt with in any depth here. Interested readers may refer to Conger and Petersen (1984). Suffice it to say that the degree of identification, that is, the extent to which the young person incorporates as his or her own the attitudes and characteristics belonging to another person, will depend on a number of factors. Among these the degree of warmth and affection experienced by the child in the relationship with the parents will undoubtedly be of central importance. An additional factor, as we have seen in the previous section, will be the structure of the family, and the child's involvement in decision-making processes. Thus it will be apparent that in considering parents as role models we cannot ignore the question of identification. It is this characteristic of the relationship which determines the final impact of parents as models, as will become clear when examining some of the evidence which has accumulated on this topic. Before we do so, however, it should be noted that virtually all the studies to be mentioned have been carried out in the U.S.A. There is, unfortunately, a dearth of European evidence in this area, and thus caution should be exercised in drawing general conclusions from the research findings.

Let us first of all turn our attention to the development of sex roles, a topic already considered in some detail in the previous chapter. As far as boys are concerned research has indicated that adolescents whose fathers provide a moderately masculine role model, but who are also involved in the feminine caring side of family life, adjust better as adults and experience fewer conflicts between their social values and their actual behaviour. Boys whose fathers provide role models which are at either extreme – excessively masculine or predominantly feminine – appear to adjust less well. To take one example from the experimental literature, the studies by Mussen and others (Mussen 1962; Mussen *et al.* 1963, 1974) have shown that, although during adolescence those boys with strong masculine role models and stereotyped masculine behaviour seem to be the best adjusted – to be the most popular, to have high self-esteem and so on – when followed up ten years later they appeared to do less well in adulthood than men who during adolescence had more ambivalent role models and more 'feminine' interests. Thus it would seem that for boys at least a rigid adherence to stereotyped sex role behaviour may be adaptive in adolescence but not so helpful in adjustment to the demands of adult life.

If sex role development is complicated for boys, it is certainly just as problematic for girls. There are at least three reasons for this. First, sex roles are usually less clear for girls than they are for boys; second, in many circumstances higher status is accorded to masculine roles, so that girls may face confusion, as to which is more preferable; and third, women's position in society is at present passing through a period of rapid change, making it even more difficult for adolescent girls to make personal choices in line with what is or is not expected of them. Conger and Petersen's (1984) view, based on research findings, is that it is perfectly possible for girls, no matter whether they are identified with a mother who is 'traditional' and 'feminine' or with one who is more liberal, independent, and socially assertive, to adjust well as women themselves. The important point is that they do have someone positive with whom to identify, someone who has resolved her own problems of sexual identification. It appears to be those whose sex role behaviour is based on rejection of a not very loving mother, or on identification with a mother who has herself failed to resolve her own identity problem, who have difficulties in adjustment.

Such a formulation is supported by the research of Douvan and Adelson (1966). In their large-scale investigation of 3,000 girls across the U.S.A. they described three patterns of sex role development. Girls with a strong and straightforward feminine sex role identification identified strongly with their mothers, with whom, by and large, they had close relationships. Of all the groups analysed this group most often chose their mothers or some other female relative as an ideal adult. These girls were compliant in the home, and clearly obtained considerable satisfaction from the feminine role. At the opposite extreme girls with strong anti-feminine identifications were least likely to choose women at all as ideal adults. Girls in this group described poor relations at home, restrictive attitudes on the part of their parents, and strong feelings of resentment towards their mothers. Falling between these two groups was a third category, those girls who, although strongly feminine, could and did recognise attractions in the traditional masculine role. As in the case of the first group, girls of this type appeared to be modelling themselves after parents with whom they had close positive relationships. Mothers of girls in this group, however, were likely to be ambitious, highly educated, and working outside the home. They encouraged their daughters towards independence, more so than the traditional feminine group, and allowed them a much greater share in decision making within the family. As Conger and Petersen (1984) point out, these studies, along with many others, underline the advantages of growing up in a caring family where the same sex parent represents a workable and rewarding role model. Within the framework of a relatively healthy family both boys and girls whose parents are moderately flexible in their own sex roles appear to be more secure and relaxed in the development of their personal identity.

As far as parents as work role models are concerned very much less evidence is available. In general many of the same things must apply. Close positive relationships are most likely to facilitate the use of the parent as a work role model, although this does not necessarily mean taking the same type of job as the mother or father. Much more important here are the transmission of attitudes to work, and the general area of work interest. Thus the boy whose father is a doctor does not himself need to go into medicine to have seen in his father a positive role model. More important will be a job which requires further education, which has a high professional standing, and which may in some way involve caring for others. In one interesting study by Bell (1969), the effect of father as role model at the ages of 17 and 27 was investigated. Results showed that those adolescent boys whose fathers acted as the most positive (i.e. highly evaluated) role models at 17 were likely to adjust best in their future careers. However, interestingly those who, at 27, still saw fathers as the most positive role models were not likely to be functioning as well in their jobs as those who had, by this time in their careers, sought other non-family role models.

In a slightly different study by Baruch (1972), women's attitudes to work were assessed as a function of their own mother's attitudes and experiences. Here results showed that women between the ages of 19 and 22 held attitudes towards work, towards feminine competence (i.e. the ability to hold down a job), and towards the dual career pattern (the combination of motherhood and a career) which resulted directly from their mother's experiences and beliefs. Women whose mothers had not worked devalued feminine competence, and whether a woman was favourable towards the dual career pattern depended directly on whether her mother supported it or not, and if she worked, whether she believed she had suffered as a result of so doing. Thus in different ways both Bell and Baruch indicate how parents play a critical part as role models where work adjustment is concerned. More studies of this sort are badly needed, but the significance of those already carried out cannot be ignored.

A theme of recent studies has been the differential effect on boys and girls of maternal employment. The studies of Hoffman (1974, 1979) together with that of Montemayor (1982) have consistently indicated that while girls appear to benefit from having their mothers in employment, this is not necessarily so for boys. Montemayor's results, for example, indicated higher levels of conflict between boys and other family members when mothers were working than when they were not, while girls showed no such differences. Hoffman's research illustrated the positive effects of maternal employment for girls, showing girls under such circumstances to be more independent, more highly motivated, and to be generally better adjusted on social and personality measures. While there may be a number of possible explanations for such findings, the importance of role modelling is almost certainly central. For girls the identification with a working mother is of positive benefit, while for boys the altered balance in the family resulting from maternal employment, together with the increased responsibility and decreased supervision, seems likely to lead to tension and conflict.

Lastly in this section we can learn something of the function of parents by glancing briefly at the studies of the effects of parental absence. In this area once again research is more readily available in the case of boys. Thus there is an accumulation of evidence to show that boys from father-absent homes are more likely than those who have fathers living at home to encounter difficulties in a wide variety of areas (Conger and Petersen, 1984). They are, for example, more likely to score lower on traditional intelligence tests, perform less well at school, and to be less popular in their social group. Interestingly, their intellectual performance differs significantly from that of other boys, in that they are more likely to obtain higher scores in tests measuring verbal ability than in those concerned with mathematics. Such a picture is in direct contrast to the usual male pattern of better performance in mathematics, and closely resembles the typical female pattern of intellectual functioning (Karlsmith 1964). Furthermore, as is probably well known, boys from father-absent homes are more likely to drop out of school, to be impulsive in their behaviour, and to become involved in activities such as delinquency, which carries with it an aura of exaggerated toughness and masculinity. It should be noted, however, that the incidence of these difficulties, especially delinquency, is closely related to a number of other factors, such as the reason for father's absence (i.e. death or divorce), the nature of the relationship between father and son where divorce or separation has occurred, as well as more general variables such as social class. In spite of this, however, it will be clear that almost all of these differences between boys with and without fathers in the home may be seen to be directly related to the absence of an appropriate model.

While there have been many fewer studies with girls, much the same conclusions may also be drawn here. The work of Hetherington (1972) provides an excellent example. In an elaborate study, which included observations of teenage girls between the ages of 13 and 17 in a community recreation centre, interviews with the girls, and their mothers, as well as the administration of various personality tests, she was able to show only too clearly the effects of paternal absence on the behaviour of these girls. According to Hetherington these were 'manifested mainly in an inability to interact appropriately with males'. In particular the daughters of divorcees spent a large proportion of their time seeking out male company and engaging in sex-related behaviour. While on interview these girls showed no lack of preference for the female role, they were rarely observed in typical female activities. This was explained by the fact that they simply spent so much of their time hanging around the areas where male activities were carried out, such as the carpentry group, basketball court, and so on. In contrast to this group, daughters of widowed women appeared much more likely to avoid contact with male peers. These girls tended to be inhibited and lacking in confidence, and thus to manifest behaviour which was exactly the opposite of that observed in daughters of divorced parents. As Hetherington says: 'It is argued that both groups of girls were manifesting deviant behaviours in attempting to cope with their anxiety and lack of skills in relating to males' (Hetherington 1972: 324). Some of these findings are illustrated in Table 5.3.

Table 5.3   Means for daughter interview measures

Interview variable	Father absent		Father present	F	P
	Divorced	Death			
Security around male peers	2.71	2.62	3.79	4.79	0.010
Security around male adults	2.12	2.12	3.66	11.25	0.001
Heterosexual activity	4.83	2.62	3.83	12.96	0.001
Conflict with mothers	5.08	3.63	4.08	5.64	0.005
Positive attitude toward father	3.08	4.66	4.21	7.57	0.001
Father's warmth	3.33	4.50	3.87	2.82	0.060
Father's competence	3.16	4.75	4.12	6.65	0.002
Conflict with father	4.43	2.25	3.46	7.03	0.002
Relations with other adult males	3.29	3.12	4.54	5.08	0.009
Self-esteem	2.87	3.58	4.04	3.34	0.040

Source: Hetherington (1972) *Developmental Psychology* 7.

In summary we have seen that, at least based on American evidence, the function of parents as role models during adolescence is a surprisingly significant one. It is undoubtedly a popular assumption that, all things being equal, parents have a more important part to play during childhood than during adolescence. Our brief review indicates that this is far from the truth. At a time when role models are necessary to a far greater extent than ever before, it is upon parents above all that adolescents depend for knowledge and example. On their interpretation of such things as work and sex roles will be based the adolescent's adjustment to the choices with which he or she will be faced.

Authority and decision making in the family

It is generally accepted that the authority of adults in relation to the young in our society has diminished since the Second World War. A variety of social changes have contributed to this phenomenon, in particular the decline in authority of major institutions such as the Church, the changing nature of the family, and an increasing emphasis on the rights of the individual. While the late 1960s are now seen as the time of greatest permissiveness and revolt by young people, there is in fact very little evidence to show that adult authority has increased during the 1970s and 1980s. Such social changes have had a major impact on individual parents, leading to high levels of uncertainty and anxiety about whether, and how, to exercise authority in the home.

All too frequently the challenges of the adolescent generation have encouraged adults in the view that parental authority is of little value, and that parents have no place in the teenage world. However, as numerous writers have made clear, the question is not whether parental models are any longer important, it is rather what sort of parental model is most appropriate in the present situation. In a society in which ageism is a dirty word, and where there are greater expectations of equality and of opportunities to express one's views openly, how should parents behave in order to ensure that their voice is heard, and their views respected?

It is towards this question – which type of parental model will be most adaptive in our present situation – that the research of Elder (1975), Baumrind (1968), and Coleman and Coleman (1984) has been directed. In the first study Elder differentiated three types of parental control – autocratic control, in which parents generally told adolescents what to do, democratic control, in which the adolescent participated in decision making but did not have the final word, and permissive control, where the young person could make up his own mind. These levels of control were then correlated with items indicating confidence in ability to make wise decisions, and the tendency to make decisions with or without prior consideration of advice from others. Among both boys and girls the level of parental control was directly related to a tendency to let others make decisions; a feeling of confidence in self-direction was most prevalent amongst youngsters with democratic parents, and least common amongst those who had no voice in making their own decisions.

Further results of the study demonstrated that within each model parents who tried to make the exercise of parental power 'legitimate' in their children's eyes by the use of frequent explanations of their conduct were more likely to facilitate optimal development. However, the frequency of explanation undoubtedly had its greatest effect among families where parents were either permissive or autocratic. Among democratic families, where communication and relationships were already good, explanations had relatively less effect. Thus the study indicates that adolescents who are provided with experience in decision making under parental supervision, and who received explanations from parents, are most likely to be independent, to want to be like their parents, and to mix with friends who are approved by their parents. As Elder says, in a different article on the same theme: 'By maximising parent/adolescent interaction, increasing trust and the legitimacy of rules, and providing experience in self reliance, this type of relationship provides a facilitative environment for acquiring autonomy and learning adult standards of behaviour' (1968: 286).

In Baumrind's (1968) study much the same distinction is made between types of parental control. However, instead of using the word 'democratic' Baumrind prefers the term 'authoritative', for this allows her to contrast such a model with that of the 'authoritarian' parent. She argues that while the 'authoritarian parent attempts to shape, control and evaluate the behaviour of the child in accordance with a set standard of conduct', the authoritative one values and encourages the development of autonomous self will. However, unlike the permissive or neglectful parent he or she also values the assumption of responsibility and the internalisation of personal discipline. The key, therefore, in Baumrind's view is the simultaneous encouragement of autonomy and responsibility – characteristics of behaviour which in other models of parenting are valued singly, but not in combination. Thus, for example, the permissive parent would undoubtedly encourage autonomy, but would not at the same time value the taking of responsibility within the family.

The research of Coleman and Coleman (1984) extends these findings by reporting the results of an investigation into the way young people themselves perceive adult authority. In line with Elder's work the study differentiated three types of parental control – democratic, authoritarian, and permissive – and asked, first, how young people preferred conflict to be resolved. As Figure 5.1 indicates, adolescents are more likely to choose a democratic solution than any other to a conflict in the home, but it indicates also that they are quite able to discriminate between authority at home and authority in, for example, the school, where they are more likely to wish for adult control. Equally interesting are the results illustrated in Figure 5.2. These show that young people are able to discriminate not only between home and school, but also between individual issues in the home. Thus, for example, while they may prefer a more democratic resolution of conflict relating to the time of coming home at night, they are more likely for example to see a place for authoritarian resolutions of conflict over domestic chores.

It will be apparent that all three studies provide much the same

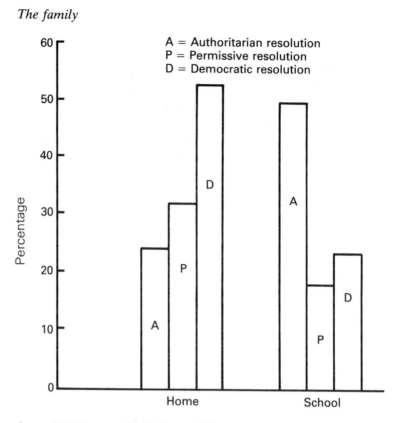

Source: J. C. Coleman and E. Z. Coleman (1984) *Journal of Adolescence* 7.

Figure 5.1 A comparison of preferred resolutions to conflicts at home and at school.

answer to the question: 'What is the most appropriate model for parents to follow in interaction with their teenage children?' In spite of today's rapidly changing fashions and uncertain values adolescents, by and large, do not seek a permissive family environment, in which they are left to get on with their own lives and make their own decisions. On the other hand it is clear that an authoritarian use of power within the family is, in most circumstances, equally inappropriate. Adolescents need direction, but most of all they need to have the opportunity of observing and living with parents who share power and influence in a democratic fashion, as well as the possibility of learning to play a part as a responsible member in the family decision-making process.

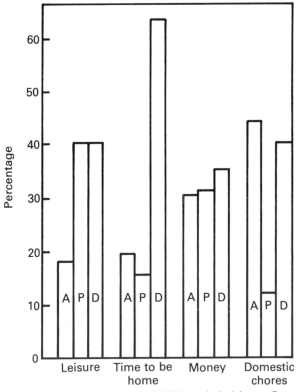

Source: J. C. Coleman and E. Z. Coleman (1984) *Journal of Adolescence* 7.

Figure 5.2 Types of resolution chosen for particular conflicts in the home. (For key see Figure 5.1.)

Divorce

It is not possible today to consider the family in relation to adolescent development without paying some attention to the question of divorce. We have, in the previous section, referred briefly to the issue of parental absence. Here we will look more closely at the effects of divorce in general. As we are all aware, the occurrence of divorce in our society has increased markedly over the last two decades, to the point that in Britain one in five young people experiences family breakdown before the age of 16, while in the U.S.A. the figure is closer to one in three. Statistics published in Burgoyne *et al.* (1987) show trends in the incidence of divorce during the last century in England and Wales (see Figure 5.3), indicating the effects of the two World Wars, but showing

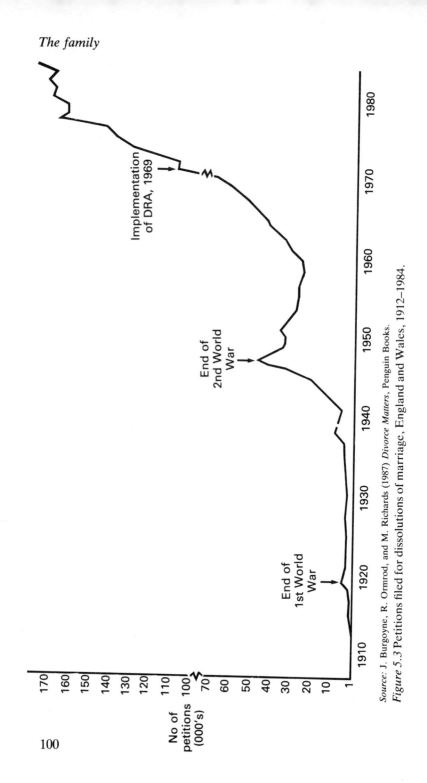

Source: J. Burgoyne, R. Ormrod, and M. Richards (1987) *Divorce Matters*, Penguin Books.

Figure 5.3 Petitions filed for dissolutions of marriage, England and Wales, 1912–1984.

indicating the effects of the two World Wars, but showing clearly the dramatic increase that has occurred since 1960. It is often argued that the U.K. Divorce Reform Act of 1969 had a major impact on the numbers of people seeking divorce in Britain, but, as the figures show, the changing pattern of behaviour preceded legislation, rather than being a consequence of it.

Not surprisingly, substantially changed attitudes to divorce underlie the bare statistics. To be a child of divorced parents no longer carries the stigma that it once did, and many varieties of family arrangement are commonplace today. However, most countries have been exceedingly slow in making the necessary legal and structural adjustments to take account of such a major shift in social behaviour. Britain in particular has so far failed dismally to come to terms with the changing needs of children and young people resulting from altered family circumstances, and we have been slow too in initiating research which will provide some answers to the critical questions concerning children's welfare where they are affected by divorce and family breakdown.

This is not to say that there has been no research at all in this field. There has, and some of it has had important results. However, relatively few studies have had adolescence as their major focus, and almost all have been beset by the methodological difficulties of needing to control for the wide variety of significant variables. The age of the child at divorce, the length of time which elapsed since the divorce, the family circumstances both before and after the divorce, the role of other siblings and adults such as grandparents, as well as many other factors, all contribute to the overall effect of divorce and, needless to say, require a very substantial empirical investigation before they can be adequately taken into account. Questions to do with divorce which have been investigated, therefore, have at this stage only been answered in the most general terms.

One example of this relates to the question of developmental level. Do children and young people have different responses to divorce according to their age and developmental status? Studies which have addressed this problem (see Kurdek 1983; and Belsky *et al.* 1984) have indicated, broadly speaking, that responses to parental divorce do vary considerably depending on age. This is not only because of cognitive capacity and the individual's increasing ability with age to make intellectual sense of the trauma, but also because of the impact of emotional maturation. As ego-centricity diminishes the child is able more easily to perceive the situation from more than one viewpoint, which in turn makes it easier to understand what is happening, and to cope with the emotions aroused. A number of studies (e.g. Wallerstein and Kelly 1980; Kurdek and Berg 1983) have hinted that older children and/or adolescents adjust better to divorce than younger children. It has been suggested that the likelihood of an internal locus of control, together with greater emotional autonomy and opportunities for social support outside the family network may all enable the adolescent to cope more readily with divorce. However, all the problems inherent in divorce research mentioned earlier apply to these findings, and they need to be treated with considerable caution.

One particular limitation of this type of research, which has been highlighted in a number of studies, concerns the fact that divorce is a process, not an event. Thus, it is not sufficient to consider the child's response, or behaviour, at one point in time, if we wish to understand the effects of divorce. The classic study of Wallerstein and Kelly (1980) made this point very clearly. They followed sixty families in California over a five-year period, and their results underline the necessity of looking at divorce from a longitudinal perspective. They found that in most children, irrespective of age, the initial response involves anger, fear, depression, and guilt. It is usually not until a year or more has elapsed that tensions diminish, and the child and parents begin to come to terms with new family arrangements. A study by Hetherington *et al.* (1978) elaborated on this picture by illustrating the way in which both mothers' and fathers' parenting practice deteriorates in the first year following divorce, but often makes a marked recovery in the second post-divorce year. Thus we can see that it makes more sense to conceptualise divorce as family readjustment, taking place over a period of time, rather than as a discrete occurrence.

A fact which will be obvious to all, and which hardly needs to be established through empirical investigation, is that children of all ages are likely to experience strong and painful emotions as a result of family breakdown. Wallerstein and Kelly (1980) and Hetherington (1980) in the U.S.A., together with Mitchell (1985) and Walczak and Burns (1984) in the U.K., have all testified to this, indicating, as we have already mentioned, that feelings of distress, rejection, anger, and unhappiness are all common experiences. In fact some writers have compared divorce to bereavement in the nature of its emotional impact on children. This is helpful in that loss is undoubtedly a component of both experiences, yet as Richards (1987) points out in some respects divorce is potentially even more damaging than bereavement. There are at least three reasons for this. First, divorce does not entail a finite point of loss, as in bereavement, but is more likely to involve continuing uncertainty and confusion. This makes it doubly difficult for any individual to come to terms with the experience. Second, in situations where a parent dies it is usual for that parent to be idealised, making it easier for the child to identify with and value the lost parent. In divorce exactly the opposite happens, with the custodial parent frequently denigrating and criticising the parent who has left the home. Third, where adults divorce, the child has to live with the feeling that his or her parents have deliberately done something against or in violation of the best interests of the child. This is rarely an issue in circumstances of bereavement. Simply stating these facts emphasises how difficult the experience of divorce must be for children, and makes it easier to understand the distressing feelings aroused.

A further important consideration which has been the focus of some attention (e.g. Belsky *et al.* 1984) is that, in the long term, it may not be the divorce itself which affects the child or adolescent most strongly, but the altered circumstances which flow from it. Thus the young person may come to live in different, frequently more straightened, economic circumstances, with poorer housing, less leisure time, and more pressure to move early into work. The young person may have to move to a different part of the country, and thus lose important social supports. The parents themselves may be more vulnerable after divorce, and less able to provide adequate parenting. In addition there may be new step-parents or other adults to make relationships with, and more stressful social situations to negotiate. All these and many other consequences may flow from divorce, making it essential when looking at this question to consider a wide range of issues and to recognise that divorce for children is so much more than the loss of a parent.

It will be obvious from what has been said in previous sections of this chapter that young people need their parents, in a variety of ways, in order to help and support them through the adolescent transitions. Let us consider some of these needs, and the way they are affected by divorce. One thing which teenagers clearly need is to have good communication with their parents. This is essential for the negotiation of independence, for decision making, for the expression of concern and involvement with the young person's life, and as part of the process of acknowledging the adolescent's changing status within the family. Yet studies of divorce have shown an extremely poor level of communication in circumstances of family breakdown. As Mitchell (1984) in her study of seventy families in Scotland found:

Few parents had explained adequately the reasons for a family to split up, two thirds of them saying that they had given their children no explanation at all. Many children had been bewildered, not knowing whether the separation was to be short or permanent and not believing parental arguments to be sufficient reason for breaking up the family. If the reason had been obvious to the parents, the children did not necessarily agree.

(Mitchell 1984: 79)

The importance of communication was illustrated in Wallerstein and Kelly's (1980) study, in which they showed that there was a direct relation between post-divorce adjustment of children, and the degree of communication between them and their parents. They also showed that young people, particularly adolescents, were clamouring for more information, and for the opportunity to be involved in decisions which they feel directly affect their lives. Not unreasonably, young people feel that they should, at the very least, be told of changes in the family which are likely to occur as a result of one parent leaving home. They expect some form of explanation, some information about where they will be living, if and when they will be seeing the other parent and so on. Furthermore, young people believe that their parents should respect and support their wishes concerning access. All too frequently, it appears, there is little consultation between children and adults about this and other fundamental aspects of post-divorce adjustment.

Teenagers have other needs too. As we have noted, parents are essential role models, and without one or other parent present it becomes that much harder to develop appropriate adult role behaviour. This is particularly true where the role model which has been lost has also in the process been devalued, a point illustrated very clearly by Hetherington's (1972) study described in the previous section. Adolescents also have a strong need for clear and well-defined boundaries, yet parents in post-divorce circumstances, themselves often confused, uncertain, and alone, are likely to find the provision of such boundaries very difficult indeed.

The picture presented in this section has emphasised the negative aspects of divorce. It is undoubtedly true that it is more difficult for single parents to meet the needs of adolescents and the introduction of step-parents into the family situation is frequently problematic, at least in the early stages. There can be no question that family breakdown is commonly a cause of considerable stress to young people, yet it would be wrong to ignore the positive aspects. Studies such as those of McLoughlin and Whitfield (1984) and

Mitchell (1985) have reported a significant number of young people describing feelings of relief that their parents had split up, and research has consistently shown that children and adolescents are better off in post-divorce families than in conflict-ridden intact families. However, preliminary indications are that this is more likely to be true where good contact and regular access is maintained with both parents, and less likely to be true where the child continues to be the centre of disagreement and to be caught up in uncomfortable conflicts of loyalty (Hetherington 1980). One cannot help but conclude that more research is urgently needed. After all, psychologists are better placed than any other professional group to provide answers to social issues of this sort. Let us hope that they will be encouraged to do so.

Chapter six

Friendship and peers

Introduction

Adolescence is a period of transition and adjustment. The young person is required to respond to the forces, both internal and external, which shape the emergent adult. The *internal* pressures involved have often been evinced as reasons for the emotional turmoil and stress experienced in the teenage years, but there is evidence that these 'storms' are more apparent than real for most adolescents. The *external* pressures on the adolescent often give rise to a high-profile youth culture seemingly opposed to the traditional lifestyle and values of the previous generation. Again, the vision of the 'opposition' of youth may be over-stated. Parental values and norms seem to be transmitted fairly steadily across the generation gap, despite the separation in appearance and activities bolstered by commercial interests. But since young people are reared in a social milieu which is quite different from that of their parents' generation, individuals have to carry with them into society the stamp of their own particular family lifestyle 'tailored' to present social requirements. In this way the rules and values of adolescent groups are influenced and altered although most adolescents create lifestyles consistent with their sub-cultural patterns. But individual adolescents may behave differently from their parents' – and sometimes their own – values because of peer group pressure, and may appear to rebel against adults' values though in a totally conformist way – by wearing almost exactly the same style of clothes and hair fashion as their friends.

If one accepts that rituals and shared meanings are part of everyday life then certain adolescent groups will develop and celebrate their own rituals. Ritual means an event or happening, arrangement, or occasion which has special meaning for the individual, for the group, and for society. Rituals all embody a fundamental social rule, namely the rule of separation (Douglas 1966).

The rituals of adolescents are embedded in certain sub-cultures, and often pop cultures. These rituals may be thought to challenge both the *status quo* and the hierarchical structure and authority of school and society (Murdock and Phelps 1973).

Milson (1972) has offered a useful typology for considering adolescents and their lifestyles and peer groups 'through their own eyes'. 'Conformists' represent the majority of young people who will absorb the dominant values of society; 'experimenters' who can be either political revolutionaries or personal revolutionaries devising a new lifestyle which allows them to 'opt out' for some time and in some way from the work ethic of an achieving society; and the 'deprived, socially rejected, and desocialised' who comprise the delinquent, disgruntled, and drifters who do not conform to society or rebel against specialism and institutionalised order. Thus, in modern society peer groupings may be vitally important to the adolescent as a context for acquiring and learning social skills and strategies. Peer groups may become more important in determining interests and influencing the behaviour and the personality of the individual, as the importance of the family in transmitting the 'appropriate' culture is diminished to some extent, even though sub-cultural values still hold sway at a general level. There appears to be a natural expansion from family relationships to affiliation into peer groups or gangs, although some time ago Cohen (1950) argued that urban working-class adolescents were most likely to develop such group allegiances.

During adolescence, individuals are exposed to new social-interaction situations and need different social-interaction skills than those required in earlier childhood (Grinder 1978). The shift from childhood to adolescence is marked by change in many aspects of social life (Damon 1983). During adolescence, peer relations become more intense and extensive, family relations are altered, and the adolescent begins to encounter many new demands and expectations in social situations. Adolescents may begin dating, working with others in a part-time job, or spending time with peers without adult supervision.

Several developmental changes serve to alter the manner in which adolescents interact with family and peers. These include more advanced cognitive, verbal, and reasoning abilities, and the changes associated with puberty. In addition, many of the developmental tasks of adolescence involve relationships and require new, and more complex, interpersonal skills (Hartup 1982).

Adolescence involves systematic changes in social development and the nature of peer relationships. The peer group increases in size and complexity (Crockett *et al.* 1984), with adolescents spending and enjoying more time with chosen friends than with classmates (Csikszentmihalyi and Larson 1984). Adolescents, relative to children, are more involved and intimate with peers, increasingly sharing their thoughts and feelings (Hartup 1983; Youniss and Smollar 1985).

The present chapter, therefore, attempts to examine various aspects of friendship and peer groups in adolescence by looking at affiliation, conformity, competency, peer pressure, sex roles, and popularity. The chapter then goes on to consider various contexts of peer group interaction such as pop culture, youth organisations, and the street corner. Finally, the influence of peers is discussed in general terms since various aspects of anti-social behaviour were dealt with in Chapter four (Self-concept development).

Peers

The word 'peer' can have a number of meanings. First, a peer group can be a small group of similarly aged, fairly close friends. Second, it can mean a group of age-mates not necessarily friends. Finally, a peer group can be a group of relative strangers sharing the same activity at a particular venue. Within this chapter either the first or second meaning will be implied in most cases. The peer group's structure contains a certain homogeneity based on age, sex, social class, or leisure activities, contexts and interests. Therefore, conformity to the group's values and activities may be necessary or the individual adolescent may experience feelings of rejection. Throughout childhood the peer group provides continuity for the individual – in play activities, in games with social rules, then mostly in leisure pursuits in adolescence – and it is only when courting behaviour (as a prelude to marriage) occurs that peer groupings disintegrate to some extent, to re-emerge later in the lifespan.

It has been suggested that the peer group is important in the individual's attempts to establish a viable identity (Erikson 1968) and as confirming experience for adolescents in their transition to a new identity (Douvan and Adelson 1966). Close friends serve especially to confirm crucial but tentative personal beliefs, and hence to validate each other's views (Duck 1973). Almost paradoxically, one set of findings (Coleman 1974) include evidence of a concern with personal loneliness and the absence of confidants among a substantial number of adolescents: 'Adolescence is generally a time of intense sociability, but it is also often a time of intense loneliness. Merely being with others does not solve the problem...' (Mussen *et al.* 1974).

Csikszentmihalyi and Larson (1984) examined the behavioural, cognitive, and affective characteristics of normal adolescents by asking them to make self-monitoring notations whenever a 'beeper' unit that each adolescent carried sounded. The beeper sounded at random intervals throughout the day and night. The investigators found that the adolescents recorded frequent shifts in mood, frequent periods of rumination over relationships and identity, and more time spent alone than with others. The prevalence of reported loneliness, shyness, and social anxiety among adolescents is of interest. Zimbardo (1977) found that over 50 per cent of a sample of seventh and eighth graders labelled themselves as overly shy, whereas Arkowitz *et al.* (1978) reported that 31 per cent of older adolescents in a survey sample indicated social interactions with members of the opposite sex as problematic. Other investigators have suggested that social anxiety, shyness, and social inhibition affect from 11.5 to 50 per cent of adolescents (Borkovec *et al.* 1974; Bryant and Trower 1974). However, less is known about the severity of these difficulties, the frequency with which relationship problems are a transient concern, and the degree to which teenagers are able to overcome social anxiety or inhibition, on their own, through increased exposure to naturally occurring social interactions.

Adolescents reporting themselves to be lonely, shy, or socially anxious appear to participate less often than their more sociable counterparts in peer activities. For example, lonely adolescents reported dating less often, spending more time alone, and participating in fewer extra-curricular activities than other teenagers (Brennan 1982). In addition, Jones (1981) reported that lonely and more sociable pupils do not differ in the *frequency* of their social interactions, but instead differ in the reported *quality* of the interactions with lonely students reporting less warmth and intimacy associated with their social contacts.

This means that acceptance by peers generally, and especially having one or more close friends, may be of crucial importance in a young person's life.

The way in which adolescents reach decisions will relate to previous social learning and role modelling (Hetherington 1972). Where levels of parental control have been carefully lessened and parents' involvement with the adolescent has been warm and friendly (Elder 1968) the adolescent may have a confident baseline from which to progress towards independence.

The desire for close friends increases as adolescents turn to their peers for support formerly provided by the family (Douvan and Adelson 1966). The adolescent tends to desire close, caring relationships with peers for the purpose of sharing mature affection, thoughts, concerns, and common interests, and to desire friends who are loyal, trustworthy, intimate, and who demonstrate potential for positive regard, admiration, and similarity (Bigelow 1977; Bigelow and La Gaipa 1975; Gallatin 1975; Grinder 1978; Rice 1978). However, as their number of acquaintances broadens, adolescents are more aware of the importance of belonging to a group; by mid-adolescence, many teenagers also strive to be accepted by members of a clique or peer group that they admire (Rice 1978).

Theories concerning the relative and shifting influence of parents and peers have been derived primarily from sociological research on the salience of peer and parent reference groups (Coleman 1961). Early findings presented a picture of a major shift from parent to peer saliency, but subsequent research has considerably revised this view. First, simultaneous parent and peer influences are not necessarily contradictory (Kandel and Lesser 1972). Second, parents' counsel is more often preferred to that of peers in important situations involving values and future decision making (Musgrove 1963; Rosenberg 1965; Smith 1976; Wan *et al.* 1969). Third, adolescents are more likely to seek help from peers when they perceive their parents as rejecting or indifferent (Iacovetta 1975; Larson 1972, 1972a; Smith 1976). In addition, Rosenberg (1979) reported that parents ranked higher than peers in interpersonal significance throughout adolescence. Burke and Weir (1978, 1979) examined adolescents' (ages 13 to 20) psychological health and its relationship to satisfaction with help from parents and peers. While adolescents were more likely to go to peers for help, *satisfaction* with help from parents was more related to their psychological health and well-being than was satisfaction with help from peers.

A study by Greenberg *et al.* (1983) examined the nature and quality of adolescents' (aged 12 to 19 years) attachments to peers and parents, and these were assessed by the Inventory of Adolescent Attachments. The relative influence on measures of self-esteem and life satisfaction of relations with peers and with parents was then investigated in a hierarchical regression model. An important finding was the absence of main effects for age on the attachment variables. Older adolescents were no more likely to report differences in utilisation or in the quality of relationships with parents or peers than were younger adolescents. Their results confirmed studies indicating that throughout high school parents are highly valued for their nurturance and counsel (Offer 1969; Smith 1976). The findings were also supportive of research on high school and college students which demonstrates that warm relationships with parents are related to high self-concept and ego identity (Marcia 1980; Mortimer and Lorence 1980). In interpreting these effects, the researchers argued that the development of ego autonomy and optimal adjustment are promoted by the development of independence in the context of warm relatedness to one's parents (Bowlby 1973; Greenberger and Sorenson 1974; Murphey *et al.* 1963). But in present-day society there is a growing family situation where sex role models may be absent through separation or divorce. In such situations the adolescent may turn to the peer group as a medium for role behaviour and for confirmation and observation of social strategies: in all this there will be age, sex, and sub-cultural differences (Bronfenbrenner 1974; Salmon 1979).

How are peer relationships distinctive in adolescence? During adolescence, peer interactions expand beyond dyadic and small-group relationships, which comprise the locus of peer relations in earlier and later stages of life, to include school or neighbourhood-based collectives commonly referred to as peer groups or 'crowds' (Hartup 1983). The prominence of crowds in adolescence has prompted theorists to ascribe numerous functions to them: social-isation into heterosexual behaviour (Dunphy 1972), facilitation of identity development (Erikson 1968), organisation of status structures (Coleman 1961), and so on.

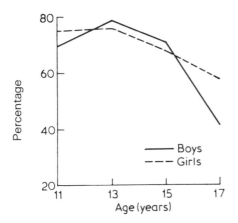

Source: J. C. Coleman (1974) *Relationships in Adolescence*, London: Routledge & Kegan Paul.

Figure 6.1 Proportions of each group expressing themes of conformity on sentence-completion test item concerning relationships within the peer group.

In a study of adolescents' perceptions of peer group affiliation, Coleman (1974) examined responses to two projective measures – an incomplete sentence ('If someone is not part of the group . . .') and a TAT story showing one individual separated from a group of peers – among 11- to 17-year-old British teenagers. Responses were coded as supporting group membership, deriding membership, 'neutral', or ambivalent. Analyses indicated that although a majority of subjects in each age group favoured group membership, the proportion of responses supporting membership traced an inverted U-shaped change with age (see Figure 6.1). The age pattern was similar for both genders, but closer scrutiny of responses showed that a higher proportion of males than females appeared to identify with the group (rather than the individual). Because the age pattern (and gender differences) corresponded to research findings on developmental changes in peer conformity (Costanzo and Shaw 1966), Coleman concluded that peer group affiliation may be primarily a manifestation of peer conformity dispositions among teenagers; belonging to a crowd is a means of conforming to peers, and as peer conformity inclinations shift across adolescence so does one's allegiance to the crowd (see Figure 6.2).

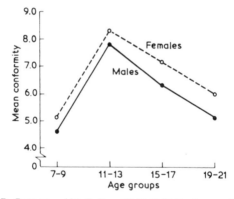

Source: P. R. Costanzo and M. E. Shaw (1966) *Child Development* 37.

Figure 6.2 Mean conformity as a function of age.

The developmental pattern Coleman noted, however, also is consistent with Dunphy's (1972) contention that peer groups serve primarily to socialise adolescents into appropriate heterosexual interests and behaviour. Based on observations and interviews with groups of Australian teenagers, Dunphy speculated that crowds evolve through several stages during adolescence. The isolated, monosexual cliques that dominate early adolescence give

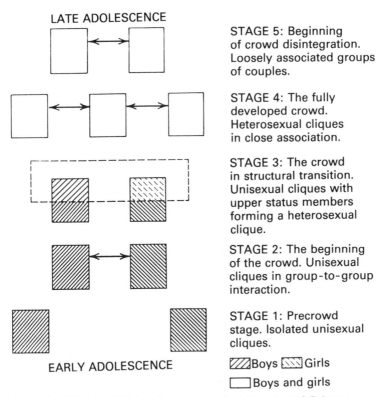

LATE ADOLESCENCE

STAGE 5: Beginning of crowd disintegration. Loosely associated groups of couples.

STAGE 4: The fully developed crowd. Heterosexual cliques in close association.

STAGE 3: The crowd in structural transition. Unisexual cliques with upper status members forming a heterosexual clique.

STAGE 2: The beginning of the crowd. Unisexual cliques in group-to-group interaction.

STAGE 1: Precrowd stage. Isolated unisexual cliques.

EARLY ADOLESCENCE

Boys   Girls
Boys and girls

Source: D. C. Dunphy (1972) *Socialisation in Australia*, Sydney: Angus & Robertson.

Figure 6.3 Stages of group development in adolescence.

way to fully developed crowds (a fusion of several male and female cliques), which disintegrate in later adolescence into relatively independent, heterosexual cliques (see Figure 6.3). Dunphy observed that the crowd's primary function was to organise social activities; more 'mature' teenagers helped their fellow crowd members learn how to interact with the opposite sex. These observations suggest that teenagers should attach more importance to crowd affiliation in middle adolescence than early or later adolescence, and should portray the crowd primarily as a source of social (or more specifically, heterosexual) activities.

Dunphy (1972) acknowledged other evidence, however, that the amount of time teenagers spend with a peer group does not follow an inverted U-shaped age trend, but declines steadily across adolescence. This developmental pattern seems to support Newman and Newman's (1976) postulates about the role of peer groups in identity formation. Based on Erikson's (1968) theory of identity development, Newman and Newman argued that the major task of early adolescence is to affiliate with a peer group that can accept one's budding sense of identity and provide supportive social relationships to offset the teenager's withdrawal from emotional dependence on parents. As a more autonomous sense of identity emerges in later adolescence, the need for strong peer group identification diminishes. Thus, one would expect the importance of peer group affiliation to decline across adolescence, and reasons for or against crowd affiliation to focus on friendship, social support, and one's sense of identity.

The functions ascribed to peer groups by Coleman (1961), by contrast, suggest that the importance attached to crowd affiliation may depend less upon age than the type of group to which a teenager belongs. Coleman focused attention on the peer group's role in determining the basis of popularity and social status. In the ten midwestern high schools in his sample most teenagers aspired to membership in their school's 'leading crowd'. Leading crowd members enjoyed greater popularity and higher self-esteem than non-members.

A study by Brown *et al.* (1986) involving 1,300 adolescents showed that the importance of crowd affiliation declined across the teenage years. Younger adolescents generally favoured group membership, emphasising the crowd's ability to provide emotional or instrumental support, foster friendships, and facilitate social interaction. Older respondents expressed dissatisfaction with the conformity demands of crowds and felt their smaller and more intimate established friendship networks obviated the need for peer group ties. The importance of crowd affiliation was not related to the strength of respondents' sense of identity but did vary significantly with their willingness to conform to peers and the centrality of their position in peer groups or the type of crowd to which they belonged.

In Brown *et al.*'s (1986) investigation respondents were asked to explain why belonging to a peer group was or was not important to them. Content analyses of open-ended responses to this question among a pilot sample of 120 adolescents (in the same schools) indicated that answers could be coded into seven categories: identity, reputation, conformity, instrumental or emotional support, friendship, source of activities, or miscellaneous responses. (Instrumental and emotional support, which were conceived as separate categories were collapsed by the researchers because very few adolescents gave responses that could be coded as instrumental support.) Table 6.1 summarises each category's specific contents.

Table 6.1   Content coded into each category of reasons for/against crowd affiliation

Category	Positive reasons	Negative reasons
Identity	Crowd is source of self-concept; helps define one's interests, abilities, personality	
Reputation	Membership builds one's reputation, image, status; increases recognition or popularity among peers; helps avoid negative reputation	Crowds have negative or undesirable image; membership damages reputation or lowers popularity among peers
Conformity vs. Individuality	Crowd fosters desirable conformity or similarity: 'Nice to fit in', 'If eveyone does it, it's okay', 'I want friends similar to myself'	Crowd impedes individuality, autonomy, self-reliance; dislike of being stereotyped; 'I don't need a crowd to tell me who I am'
Support	Crowd builds self-confidence, self-esteem; gives sense of belonging, being liked, wanted or accepted; gives someone to trust, turn to or depend on; source of feedback, advice or assistance; source of emotional security	Crowd threatens security, inhibits positive self-feelings, betrays trusts, or endangers emotional or physical well-being; crowd does not supply emotional or instrumental support, or such support is not needed
Friendship	Chance to meet new people; membership builds or maintains friendships; helps avoid loneliness; crowd is where friends are	Crowd restricts relationships; friendships are already formed; dislike of people who are in crowds (or how people act in crowds); prefer being alone
Activity	Crowd is source of activities or activity partners; crowd broadens one's range of activities; enjoy doing things in a group	Crowd restricts activities; don't need a crowd for activities or activity partners

Source: B. B. Brown *et al.* (1986) *Journal of Adolescence* 9.

Thus peer groups seem to serve multiple functions in the lives of adolescents. No single reason for or against crowd-affiliation is superordinate. In other words, rather than serving as a constant in the lives of teenagers, peer groups appear to be dynamic forces whose functions and influences shift across adolescence and vary according to characteristics of adolescents' school or community and their level of involvement in crowds. The development of values and behavioural norms can be fostered through social interaction, especially through participation in a peer group (Grinder 1978). By experiencing the values and norms of a peer group, the adolescent is able to evaluate the perspectives of others while developing his or her own values and attitudes.

Weinstein (1973) suggested that peer group relations offer multiple opportunities for witnessing the social strategies of others, seeing how far these are effective, and offering an area for learning self-presentation and accounting for one's actions. The relative equality of power relationships may facilitate the development of such social strategies (Speier 1970).

In the adolescent's emergence from the family towards independence the peer group plays an important function. Yet it appears that where decisions with implications for the future have to be taken, parents are usually the influential factor, whereas in relation to current issues and identity needs peers seem more important. Thus, while the values of parents and peers may overlap to some extent (Offer and Offer 1975), where there is less parental interest or in areas of parental uncertainty the adolescent is likely to turn to his or her peer group for help and advice with decisions. It is important, therefore, to stress that the individual *will* conform to social pressures – either from parents or peers – but the direction of this conforming behaviour will vary from one individual to another depending upon psychological resources, social background, and the particular social context surrounding the issue being faced.

These issues can be related to the teenagers' attempts to test the boundaries of authority and parental control; to combat the views of others in moving towards more independence in personal behaviour; and to holding differing views from parents, while respecting each other's opinions (Conger 1979). Clearly such means of learning independence may involve some conflict or at least a different focus of interest between the generations: but ideas of conflict should not be overstressed. Musgrove (1964) and also Eppel and Eppel (1966) have stated that adolescents have better attitudes towards adults than vice versa.

Of course, adults can play an important part in peer group interactions. Sport clubs, hobby groups, youth clubs, uniformed organisations (e.g. Scouts and Guides) all tend to be arranged for adolescents by adults, and are often closely supervised by adults. This may be significant because the degree to which adults are directly involved is likely to influence the relationships among adolescents. Adolescents' involvement in such adult-sponsored situations, though nominally voluntary, may not be genuinely self chosen. Consequently many adolescents will choose *not* to become involved in such settings (Hendry 1983). After a peak of interest in peer-orientated activities (Coleman 1979) adolescents tend to gravitate towards more exclusive dyads for courting and romance.

Peers and conversations

Special importance is attributed to friendships during adolescence. By early adolescence friendship is characterised by a sense of reciprocity and equality. Peer conversations involve more sharing, explaining, and mutual understanding, whereas adolescent–parent conversations involve parents explaining their ideas even at the expense of not understanding their children's alternative views (Hunter 1985). The influence of parents and friends upon adolescents vary according to types of activities and topics of conversation. For example, parents' influence seems to prevail in the future-oriented domains, such as choices of schools and in career plans (Kandel and Lesser 1972); friends' influence centre around current events and activities (Hunter 1985). Peer discussions can provide adolescents with opportunities to experience, contest, and verify alternative views about interpersonal relationships, which then lead to future socialisation (Youniss 1980). Adolescents find certain conversational topics – including music; the activities of friends; television, movies, and radio; and school events – higher in reinforcement value than other conversational topics (Bradlyn *et al.* 1983).

Daily meetings with friends take up a substantial portion of adolescents' free time (Crockett *et al.* 1984; Montemayor 1982). Adolescents report spending more time talking to peers than in any other activity and describe themselves as most happy when so engaged (Csikszentmihalyi *et al.* 1977).

The strong bonds between peers during adolescence relate to the unique characteristics of the adolescent's social environment. Early adolescents are not treated as children nor are they treated as adults. Sexual involvement with the opposite sex is strongly discouraged. They acquire fairly limited independence and are required to remain in school and not be employed until age 16. These conditions create a relatively stable environment of school and neighbourhood and allow a significant amount of time and energy to be devoted to peers. Further, the transition from concrete to abstract, generalised thinking allows the adolescent to better understand friends' thoughts and feelings. They become more aware of the importance of mutuality and reciprocity, which can foster stable and meaningful friendships (Berndt 1982).

Successful social interactions with other people are certainly among the most important skills that a youth must learn (Combs and Slaby 1978). For instance, talking with friends is one of the most popular ways for adolescents to spend their leisure time (Hurlock 1973), and an adolescent's conversational ability is related to socialisation and social acceptance (Damon 1983; Hartup 1982). An individual who is unable to successfully interact with others may be prone to problems in interpersonal relationships or, indirectly, to problems in school, occupational, and social activities. Thus, effective social interactions during adolescence are important for adjustment, as they are necessary for an adolescent to make friends, become part of a peer group, develop social relationships, and become an independent, socially competent individual.

Dating and social skills, such as asking an individual for a date, as well as appropriate social behaviours to exhibit on a date, are new skills that are clearly needed during adolescence. Hence, Hartup (1982) has observed that peer group influence serves important functions and contributes more to constructive socialisation than to deviance.

Social competency

Several writers (e.g. Adams *et al.* 1978; Anderson and Messick 1974; Greenberger and Sorenson 1974) have proposed that (a) individual knowledge about appropriate emotional states for specific social contexts (social knowledge), (b) ability to empathise with other persons (empathy), and (c) belief in the power of self-initiation (locus of control) are three fundamental social dimensions underlying a comprehensive definition of social competence. These three competencies are thought to be reflected in social skills which assist a person to establish and maintain positive peer relations.

Previous research using cross-sectional designs with school-aged or adolescent samples have reported general trends or relationships between age and increased empathy (e.g. Adams *et al.* 1979), social knowledge (e.g. Rothenberg 1970) and locus of control (e.g. Penk 1969; Lifshitz 1973).

In one study that examined social competence in adolescents,

Ford (1982) found that ninth and twelfth graders judged to be socially competent were able to display empathy (defined as the ability to accurately comprehend the feelings and thoughts of others). Empathy is very similar to a referential communication skill identified by Gottman *et al.* (1975) that differentiated popular from unpopular primary school children. This skill involves the ability to take the perspective of another person.

In male and female adolescents aged 14, 15, 17, and 18 years of age, the predictive relationship between social competency and peer relations, and in age differences in social competence were studied by Adams (1983). Based upon a social deficit hypothesis which would predict a positive relationship between social competency and peer popularity as a measure of positive friendship formation, linear age differences were observed in social knowledge, locus of control, and a trend in empathy.

The findings that empathic tendencies for females and locus of control for males were predictive of peer popularity support the notion that social competencies predictive of positive peer relations appear to be mediated by sex-role based competencies. Empathic abilities may enhance female adolescents' capacity to share interpersonally with others and enhance these females' peer popularity. For male adolescents, a sense of internality may focus the male's behaviour on self-initiative, which provides leadership in interpersonal relations with peers.

Authors like Montemayor and Hansom (1985), Selman (1980), Youniss (1980), and Youniss and Smollar (1985) have focused research on conflict resolution within close friendship and family relations.

A study by Leyva and Furth (1986) explored conflict resolution from a wider societal perspective. Adolescents' understanding of societal conflict and of compromise resolution in the context of peer and authority relations was investigated. Six conflict stories were prepared for three social issues. Each issue included two similar stories that were counterbalanced for presentation in peer or authority context. The adolescents – ages 11, 13, 15, and 17 – were asked to develop dialogues by continuing conversations from the stories with the aim of resolving the conflict. Responses were categorised on a 3-point scale: (1) non-compromise, (2) routine compromise, and (3) constructive compromise. In addition, one moral and one political dilemma were presented in order to relate conflict resolution to moral and political development. Within the age range investigated by the researchers a progression in mature resolution of conflictual issues was demonstrated, such that generally non-compromise solutions decreased after age 11 and constructive compromise solutions in the form of negotiation and consensus seeking increased. What were called 'routine compromises' were common to all age groups. To make a routine compromise one only needs to know a few concrete tactics ('majority vote wins', or 'split the difference'). In contrast, constructive compromises require the ability to propose and to consider multiple options, and this opens the door to negotiation and consensus seeking. The ability to consider different viewpoints critically at the same time has been related to formal logical thinking, which develops especially after the age of 12 (Kuhn *et al.* 1977; Lee 1971; Piaget 1972; Tomlinson-Keasey *et al.* 1974).

The study confirmed that compromises were more likely to be formulated in peer relations than in authority relations. In fact many adolescents, in describing conflicts in authority context, explicitly stated that the adults would win the conflict merely because they were in a power position. The peer context seemed more favourable to an equal exchange of ideas, and a situation where one's view would be heard and respected. A mature approach to conflict resolution by mutual respect and co-operation is one important function of peer relations.

Peer pressure

Peer pressure – pressure to think or behave along certain peer-prescribed guidelines – is regarded as a prominent attribute of adolescence. Peer pressure is a primary mechanism for transmitting group norms and maintaining loyalties among group members. Most studies of peer influences in adolescence have focused on a single peer group (Huba *et al.* 1979), or a specific attitude or behaviour (Collins 1974; Riester and Zucker 1968). Erikson (1968) maintained that peer group affiliations are essential to healthy identity development in adolescence. They allow teenagers to explore interests and ideologies, to test their ability to form intimate peer relationships, and to relinquish psychological dependence on parents while retaining a sense of belonging. The security and support inherent in group membership is a comforting contrast to the adolescent's uncertain sense of self.

In effect, peer pressures become the price of group membership. To the extent that peer groups differ in normative interests and activities, the content of peer pressures will vary across different groups, Yet, because all groups are oriented toward fostering identity development, certain developmental trends in peer pressures can be expected to supercede group differences, specifically, to encourage achievement of an autonomous sense of self and intimate attachment to peers (rather than to parents). Most researchers have found that early adolescents are more willing than younger age groups to conform to peer pressures (Bixenstine *et al.* 1976; Costanzo and Shaw 1966), and that they are particularly receptive to pressures concerning peer-group mores and social interactions (Berndt 1979; Brittain 1963).

Adopting the strategy of asking adolescents to report on the pressure they receive from friends, Brown (1982) discovered that adolescents reported significantly stronger peer pressure to spend time with peers and conform to peer norms than to participate in school or family activities. Pressures from friends to use drugs or have sex were lower than pressures in other life areas; in fact, many adolescents in Brown's study reported that friends actively discouraged these activities. Pressure to drink alcohol shifted from a relatively negative pressure (against drinking) in early adolescence to the highest source of peer pressure among mid-adolescent males. Pressures toward drug use and sexual activity also were stronger in later years (e.g. Clasen and Brown 1985).

Yet, many of the behaviours encompassed by Brown's misconduct scale (use of alcohol or cigarettes, sexual intercourse) become normatively acceptable activities in adulthood. Thus, as Jessor and Jessor (1979) have concluded, developmental changes in this area of peer pressure may reflect the efforts of peers to orient adolescents toward adult norms. Most important, the research evidence shows that peers are capable of discouraging as well as encouraging anti-social behaviour (Kandel 1978).

Sex roles and peers

Peer social interactions take on increasingly important roles in the socialisation process as youths grow older and are believed to make several significant contributions to the development of youths. For instance, the regulation of aggressive behaviour, sexual socialisation, the development of cognitive and social skills, and the development of moral judgement and social values are believed to be influenced by peer interactions (French and Tyne 1982; Hartup 1983).

Social interaction with peers also provides the opportunity to experience emotions and express feelings. Teenagers may experience love and caring for same-sex and other-sex peers and may develop skills for dealing with and expressing such emotions. Elkind (1983) stated that adolescents, in contrast to most adults, engage in strategic interactions to maintain or enhance their self-esteem. For instance, Elkind used the example of telephoning others. Among children and adults, this is usually done for communication, to give or get information. However, for adolescents, telephoning and being telephoned are indices of status, popularity, and peer group affiliation and therefore contribute to an adolescent's self-esteem. Additional strategic interactions include attracting and rejecting friends and demonstrating sexual appeal through acquiring dates and engaging in sexual activity.

Damon (1983) also pointed out that social interactions enhance an adolescent's sense of self, because adolescents 'stage' social interactions and exhibit an increase in self-consciousness and a sense of 'planfulness' during social interactions. Because adolescents may consciously use social interactions for enhancement of the self, social interactions often become more planned, strategic and cautious.

Adolescence brings about a tremendous increase in heterosexual interests and social relationships (Grinder 1978). There is little doubt that sexual attitudes and sex role behaviours are primarily shaped through peer interactions (Hartup 1983), and during adolescence there is much opportunity to develop and refine sexual attitudes and interests and to experiment with sexual behaviours. The skills required in dating are clearly complex behaviours that are not part of most adolescents' repertoires and are a source of significant anxiety for many adolescents (Arkowitz *et al.* 1978). In this connection, cognitive resourcefulness appears to be a salient characteristic for all socially skilled adolescents (Richard and Dodge 1982; Spivack *et al.* 1976).

Courtship is a dominant activity for many young people (Barker 1972). Adolescent heterosexual encounters begin with social events like dancing, going to a pub or cinema-going, then progressing to more exclusive dyads (Schofield 1973). Gender differences in these social patterns may begin to emerge through mid-adolescence, boys continuing activities with their chums – football, darts, fishing, drinking – whilst beginning to date girls, whereas girls begin to discard sports and youth club activities as being childish and unfeminine and graduate through groups to smaller networks attending likely social and heterosexual meeting places, and finally to 'going steady' with one boy. Older adolescents may then begin to narrow down relations to relatively close, stable, intimate friendships with the opposite sex as a prelude to living together. The pattern of these relationships can vary by social class, career commitments, religious background, and values.

The importance of boy–girl friendships in adolescence brings us to the question of sex roles and their influence on behaviour. Sex role identity is very important during adolescence. For many young people the rapid increase in sexual drive that accompanies puberty comes at a time when close social relationships and recreational activities are largely confined to members of the same sex (Conger 1979). Later, the development of the more manifest sexual characteristics of adolescents – breasts, body hair, muscles, and so on – creates the urge to experience their bodies. Often these urges are expressed in a fascination with clothes, hairstyles, and fashions of adornment.

Because peers play such an important role in the lives of most adolescents social acceptance is likely to be an urgent concern for most young people (Lerner 1969; Berscheid and Walster 1972). For example, as Fine (1977) concluded many adolescents become involved in sexual relationships not simply as the natural consequence of being 'in love' but as often amongst other reasons to gain peer approval. Cavior and Dokecki (1973) suggested that acceptance and popularity in the peer group are related to perceived attitude similarity and attractiveness.

Being liked, accepted, and finding one's identity in a group are important at any age, but may be particularly crucial during adolescence. In interpersonal relations, the effect of personal appearance seems crucial. A physically attractive individual is generally believed to possess more favourable personal qualities (Berscheid and Walster 1972; Miller 1970); he or she is viewed as having greater social power (Sigall and Aronson 1969; Sigall *et al.* 1971); and, all other things being equal, physically attractive individuals are liked better than unattractive individuals (Bryne *et al.* 1968; Walster *et al.* 1966). This suggests that physical appearance is linked to self-esteem to the extent that it influences feedback from others, and feedback can be positive or negative.

How are physical development and gender identity linked in relation to the peer group? Body shape seems to be related to social activities and leisure pursuits: adolescents who are muscular tend to be more attracted to, and more skilled in, sports than other body types (e.g. see Sugarman and Haronian 1964; Hendry 1978). Clearly physical skills and abilities are important in certain adolescent group structures, but not in others. Such groups can just as easily comprise 'conformist' youth (Hendry 1978) or street peers (Jephcott 1967). On the other hand, lean and underweight teenagers appear to experience problems of social adjustment and self-consciousness (Cole and Hall 1970; Clifford 1971), suggesting difficulties in encounters with peers. Hendry and Gillies (1978) demonstrated the social importance of physical attractiveness by pointing out the various effects of adolescents' possessing an overweight or underweight physique in certain social and educational encounters. In leisure time, underweight adolescents were less involved with the opposite sex but more involved with television viewing than others. Hence, in peer group relations, physique appeared to have some influence on social interaction and choice of friends: the influence of a particular body type, namely being underweight and thin, causing some isolation and lack of contact with the opposite sex and greater involvement with television as Coleman (1961) postulated. There is some agreement here with Cole and Hall's (1970) statement about the adjustment problems of adolescents possessing an 'inadequate' physique.

Those who are fat and overweight experience concern with self-image and have difficulties in social relationships, again posing problems in relation to group activities.

Boys and girls who are overweight are commonly considered less physically attractive and must learn to live with crude witticisms alluding to their obesity. Underweight adolescents can more readily disguise their body type with careful deployment of clothing but still usually feel self-conscious about their slender profiles. Cole and Hall (1970), for instance, reported a study of 256 adolescent boys, all of whom possessed 'inadequate' masculine physiques. The research disclosed that every one of them had some adjustment problems related to self-consciousness about feelings of physical inadequacy.

Clearly, then, one of the things which many adolescents appear to worry about is being overweight (Sauer 1966). Not only does being overweight represent a future potential health hazard but it may also affect the adolescent's social relationships, school performance and emotional adjustment (Hammar 1965). One study reported that overweight girls – in comparison with those of average physique – showed traits of passivity, withdrawal, concern with status, acceptance of dominant values, and desiring very close ties within their peer group (Monello and Mayer 1963). Stunkard and Mendelson (1967) found that of many behavioural disturbances to which overweight adolescents are subjected, two are unique to obesity; overeating and distortions of body image characterised by a feeling that the body is grotesque or should be regarded with contempt.

Of course, underweight boys and girls can be as unhappy with themselves as obese adolescents. Thin adolescent girls are often especially miserable, since our culture emphasises the slim but well-proportioned feminine figure (Clifford 1971). Boys too have their problems. The ideal masculine body image is to have broad shoulders and chest, a slim waist, and well-proportioned arms and legs. But some boys are lean, especially early in their adolescent development. They look skinny, uncoordinated, and weak. Some other boys are wide and fat, or squat. The boy with the weak-looking build may spend hours trying to improve his build. The fat adolescent who is not able to diet successfully may withdraw from normal social contacts with girls and show marked symptoms of emotional maladjustment. So much emphasis is put on having an athletic build that the boy who is not able to conform feels extremely self-conscious and isolated.

Pop culture and peers

Pop culture can consist of dancing, records, teenage magazines, fashion, and aspects of the mass media and cinema, and involvement in aspects of pop culture seems central to the leisure lives of many teenagers. In adolescence most young people experiment and explore within the framework of pop culture.

Brooke-Taylor (1970) stated that dancing is closely related to the mating procedure between the sexes, and for this reason is a popular adolescent activity. Dance forms favoured by young people maximise rhythm and sex attraction and minimise skill and set patterns. Patterson (1966) and Guppy (1970) both suggested that 'pop' dance forms appeal to the young as one of the few socially acceptable outlets for aggression. Further, pop music and dance movements serve as an important differentiating function – or at least cause diffusion from young to old (Rapoport and Rapoport 1975). The movements and dress and music emphasise excitement, colour, and sensuality.

Another aspect of pop culture is the dance hall or discotheque. Discotheques may attract their regular clientele from adolescents revealing 'compulsive sub-cultural conformities' in dress, fashion, personal mannerisms, and musical expressiveness. The admission rituals, conformity, and group cohesion, social encounters, drink/drug experimentation make the dance hall a focus of courtship, dating and sexual bargaining – a kind of market place (Roberts 1970). By contrast, mammoth pop festivals, it has been argued, contain many extensions of 'embedded' middle-class values (i.e. 'doing your own thing'; individualism; self-expression) even though they have attracted large numbers of adolescents from all walks of life (Young and Crutchley 1972; Berger *et al.* 1972). Pop concerts attract particular groups of supporters (rather like football teams) to see their favourites play.

An important point to be made is that venues such as dance halls, discotheques, or pop concerts allow young people to experiment with various roles in association with their peers (rather than with adults); and to be experiencing behaviour patterns and stimulants more usually approved for adults. Within pop culture the adolescent can achieve transitory loss of self by moving into diffuse groups or crowds of peers in which there is a high degree of anonymity, general adherence to dress patterns and hair styles, and a wide range of permissible behaviour (see Yablonsky 1967). In such settings alcohol and other drugs also enable the adolescent to use emblems of adult power, and allow evasion of self by reducing or altering consciousness.

Murdock and Phelps (1973) identified three main clusters of pop music styles, further emphasising that distinctions have to be made when discussing pop culture and adolescents. Using a sample of 15-year-old pupils, they found several distinctive features. While mainstream pop music was equally popular with middle-class and working-class adolescents, 'black music' (including reggae and soul) was predominantly followed by working-class pupils, and 'heavy rock' was preferred by middle-class teenagers.

Murdock and Phelps saw their results as indicating a tendency for middle-class teenagers, largely isolated from street culture values, to turn to certain types of pop music as a source of those values and roles undervalued by schools. Working-class adolescents were able to derive their alternative values from such street groups, and consequently pop culture was likely to be something which is part of the taken-for-granted background of group activities: interest for working-class adolescents was not likely therefore to extend beyond current hits. More recently Astley stated:

> Pop music is a symbol system used by all and sundry, not just as pleasure, leisure, politics, religion, but also used as a 'battle-ground' of the imputing of motives for actions. How are ideas about roles, choices, life, to be communicated? What is quite evident is that for good or for ill pop music is 'used' by all manner of people to convey ideas about what life is like, was like, and should be like. Wouldn't it be nice, if music was just for listening to. We certainly do have to recognise that many people, including the young are so beyond the influences of our socialist–liberal critique/frame of reference, that they will take action that will upset, offend and injure us. We have often contributed to a situation where they have been deprived of even minimal rights – let alone any real notion of citizenship – we can hardly expect them to be nice about it.
>
> Part of our crisis of pop/media/leisure is that we don't have enough of 'one man's meat and another man's poison', we are

fed endless formula pop! 'Wild Boys' aren't really being wild – at least not in the comfort of our own homes. 'Taking a walk on the wild side' indicates to me the need for us to set into motion some thorough-going deviance that sends the establishment and privileged layers in our society into a moral and cultural panic the like of which we have not seen let alone experienced for a long time.

(Astley 1985: 424)

In this connection it is interesting to consider the frequent changes in terminology and in trends – new romantics, mods, punks, futurists – all demonstrating different 'styles' (Brake 1980). As an example of these changes, as soon as 'punk rock' became accepted by the media as a descriptive term for that phenomenon, its street name changed to 'new wave'. These patterns can be related to lifestyles, and it can be argued that certain adolescents wish to avoid 'establishment' terms and to maintain a separate identity and argot (Mungham and Pearson 1976). (Further, it is important to note that these aspects of pop cultures change so rapidly that it is a difficult area for researchers to 'tune into'.)

The apparent isolation of teenagers as a distinct group in society is often validated by the pop media. The isolation of teenage subcultures becomes a major emphasis in the songs, lyrics, and magazines which are all part of a vast pop network. The culture provided by the commercial market plays a crucial role in mirroring existing attitudes and sentiments while providing an expressive field through which these attitudes can be projected. However, pop culture, in turn, fashions the tastes of its adolescent public and creates its own market from within itself, aimed at a mass base. Part of the industry's success may be due to the fact that pop culture appeals to the emotions. Popular song lyrics are intended to reflect typical adolescent sentiments, containing both emotional realism and fantasy.

The attraction of different musical styles is that different teenage groups select specific types of music which articulate aspects of their lives at a real or fantasy level (Willis 1977). Further, it has been suggested that 'pop' idols come from similar background to their adolescent fans, and are hurtled to success via an exploitative profit-oriented system:

It is no accident that the heroes of youth culture, pop singers, song writers, clothes designers and others have mostly achieved their positions without long years of study, work or sacrifice . . . youth culture is the new opium of the teenage masses.

(Sugarman 1967: 160)

127

While early success, and limited talent, may be the destiny of certain pop musicians, others have worked hard for achievement and are talented musicians.

It is interesting to note the apparent ritualisation of trends in adolescent 'pop' culture, where the influence of 'pop' heroes can sometimes lead to imitative styles in behaviour and fashion (Belson 1978). In this way the links among teenage magazines, pop music, and programme preferences in television may be a close one. Jephcott (1967) indicated the high popularity of cinema-going among teenagers, and this was explained in terms of its relative cheapness, its acceptability to parents, as a meeting place with peers, and as an amenity for courtship. In recent years, however, television and videos have to some extent replaced cinema-going in popularity among adolescents linked to visiting friends at home (Fogelman 1976).

Murdock and Phelps (1973) suggested that experimentations with hairstyles and fashion are used as identifying symbols of particular groups. Involvement with pop music can also be associated with certain fashions. Adolescents get some of their ideas for fashion from pop culture, but shop windows, friends, discos, magazines, and television are all clearly used as sources of inspiration.

The association among several manifestations of 'pop' culture – television, magazines, films – can be suggested. Sharpe (1977) has pointed out the ways in which girls are strongly influenced by the content of girls' comics and magazines. Adolescent girls have more magazines to choose from than boys, and these journals appear to reinforce stereotypic sex roles. Boys' magazines stress sports and hobbies, while girls' papers and comics deal with romance, fashion, and pop.

In support of this thesis Toynbee (1978) showed that comics for pre-adolescent girls concentrate on sports heroes, tennis stars, and budding ballerinas, but that these can give way to a variety of magazines aimed at adolescent girls which are: 'devoted entirely to boys, to get them, how to entice them, what to do with them when you've got them.' Toynbee continued by stating that in these magazines: 'Their own (i.e. girl's) ambitions have disappeared and they have settled for getting a boy who does exciting things instead.'

A prime market for consumer capitalism is popular music and culture aimed at a mass base. The launching and continuation of pop-oriented music and teenage magazines directed quite specifically at younger age groups has been accompanied by the development of commercial techniques for the creation of pop stars having both pop music and glamorous appeal.

Youth organisations and peers

Youth clubs and organisations touch the majority of young people, however temporarily, and in this way may play an important part in their social and leisure lives. Other voluntary organisations, churches, uniformed bodies, community groups, involve a number of adolescents from time to time. Further, the potential value of local authority provision has grown with the development of sports and community centres.

It should be remembered, however, that some adolescents may join 'alternative' groups, associated with oriental religions (e.g. 'Moonies') or near-delinquent activities. This can be seen as part of the 'variability' pattern of peer groupings and as reflecting the variety of sub-cultural patterns (Milson 1972).

In studying youth and community centres, one of the models which Eggleston (1976) found to be of major relevance was what he called the 'socialisation model' in which adolescents are seen to be socialised or made ready for adult society – learning and accepting approved patterns of social behaviour, knowledge, and values.

Clearly, not all young people are attracted by such institutions, and Bone (1972) has argued that acceptance patterns are related to academic attainment and social class, in that early school leavers are less likely to attend organised clubs offering sporting interests or hobbies or being a uniformed service. Jephcott (1967), Scarlett (1975), and also Hendry and Simpson (1977) have all said that the reason why many adolescents do not attend such organisations is because they are too closely linked with school organisation and structure, either because of the pattern of discipline or because school buildings are used. Many adolescents, being disenchanted, are only briefly attached to youth clubs:

> Many of the existing organisations, because they have such long histories, frequently display intense self-consciousness about their traditions and never fundamentally question their reasons for existing.... The older teenager in particular, sensing that ultimate control lies with middle-aged and older adults, seems increasingly to display dissatisfaction by avoiding what youth establishments have to offer.
>
> (Davies 1970)

West (1967) has suggested that many youth activities are not sufficiently 'with it' to attract certain adolescents. Bone (1972) has provided more details on this issue by indicating that commercial venues were preferred by adolescents for their greater lavishness and unrestrictive, undemanding provision.

Scarlett (1975) found that adolescents had mixed feelings about local authority youth clubs and centres. Some stated that they were good because they developed 'character' beyond the boundaries of school; others (although complaining about their similarity to schools in organisation, leadership and attitude – a conclusion which agrees with Jephcott's (1967) earlier investigation) admitted disliking clubs and centres because of the occurrence of violence, lack of interesting activities, or lack of organisation. For such reasons many adolescents may opt out of active participation and attend as a matter of course using the centre solely as a context for forming social relationships. They tend to receive what clubs provide in a passive way and to leave when the provision loses its appeal (Corrigan 1979; Hendry 1981).

It may be that the relatively ephemeral attachment of the early school leaver is because his social requirements can be satisfied outside formally organised groups or within commercial provision. According to Bone (1972) when members of sports-centred and interest-centred activities left it was mainly because of career demands or lack of leisure time due to study, whereas those attending casually orientated youth clubs were more likely to abandon the centre for social reasons (e.g. friends stopped going or other members were perceived as not being particularly interesting or attractive). Leadership, especially in the form of part-time leaders, has been criticised by several researchers (Scarlett 1975; Eggleston 1976). The fundamental problem in successfully running a youth centre seems to revolve around how authoritarian or democratic a leader should be. Eggleston (1976) argued that many leaders are torn between subscribing to the norms approved by the local authority and the norms of adolescent clients. Consequently their organisational approach may oscillate between a directive style with clear educational and positive goals, and a non-directive style with a flexible, less authoritarian role.

A further demonstration of the basic conformity of club attenders in the study by Hendry *et al.* (1981) was their attitudes to club leaders. Although perceptions of club leaders were mixed, they tended to be favourable rather than unfavourable, and suggest that these 'clubbable' adolescents were basically conformist and related positively towards adults with a willingness to subscribe to an acceptance of rules, regulations, and authority.

A study by Hendry and Simpson (1977) and a replication study by Hendry *et al.* (1981) on regular users of an urban sports and community centre revealed a differing pattern in terms of leisure pursuits and lifestyles. It was clear from these studies that two distinct and separate teenage groups existed with little or no contact between them: one group following sports activities, the other using the facilities as a social amenity, sitting around the community area, chatting, drinking coffee, listening to pop music.

This brings us to the important question: why do the majority of young people in the neighbourhood of the centre choose *not* to attend the sports area? Many of the community area members complained that there were too many rules surrounding the sports area, that sports area leaders were unable to mix well with young people and were unsympathetic. They agreed with the necessity of rules and were not advocating a sports area without rules. Instead, rather than subject themselves to the strict discipline and rules, they preferred not to attend, thus opting out of the organised atmosphere of sports for the relaxed, informal, less restrictive atmosphere of the community area.

An interesting observation noted by the researchers was that younger users of the sports area were less likely to be reprimanded than older members. It would appear that not only do young people come to an age when they more critically perceive rules and regulations, but that these written and unwritten rules are likely to be enforced more strictly by leaders as adolescents progress through the teenage years. It became clear during conversations with community users that their dislike of or disinterest in the sports area was often due to confrontations with sports leaders over enforcement of these unwritten rules.

One further observable feature of the sports area was that groups were already formed, creating possible difficulties for such adolescents in 'infiltrating' these activities. In other pursuits 'star' performers were seen as individual attractions with their own band of 'groupies'. For serious sports participants one obvious sign of difference was their 'uniforms' of tracksuits, specialised clothing, and equipment which may create a symbolic barrier between them and other adolescents who might want to follow sports simply for recreation and enjoyment with no great interest in the pursuit of excellence.

Together with an antipathy to organised sports and its trappings, there was also a pull towards the social amenities provided by the community area at a time when many adolescents are exploring the possibilities of relationships with the opposite sex (Coleman 1979). Several young people interviewed admitted that the main reasons for attending the centre were that: 'it was better than sitting at home', but especially that it provided an opportunity to meet other teenagers of the opposite sex.

The two groups however differed in their views of the centre, and perceived themselves as clearly different from those in the other group. Feelings of group solidarity were quite clear. They were loyal to their own area and its leaders, and revealed a need to belong, to identify, and to support their own particular group, seeing it as a mirror image and reinforcement of their own qualities and characteristics.

With regard to an investigation of a rural centre by Hendry *et al.* (1981), it was found that teenage boys in general attended the centre for the activities offered, whereas girls claimed to attend to meet established friends or to make new ones. In this there may be some conscious or unconscious subscribing to expected sex roles. Linked to this, a considerable percentage of 'non-attenders' at the senior youth club stated that they preferred commercial provision to the centre – a finding which agrees with Bone's (1972) assertion that girls are the most enthusiastic supporters of commercial leisure provision. Eggleston (1976) also believed that commercial facilities satisfied the older teenagers' need to be independent.

Alternatively, it could be argued that their allegiance had changed from the establishment to the values and norms dictated by peers. Whatever reason is more acceptable, these findings are closely aligned to Coleman's (1979) ideas that the adolescent's focus of interest changes across the teenage years.

As the adolescent grows older he or she becomes more critical, questioning, and sceptical of adult-oriented organisations, and wishes to use peers to reinforce an emergent self-image. The need to feel independent may be a vital reason why the older adolescent moves towards commercial leisure provision. Thus Eggleston (1976) believed that many problems in youth clubs might be solved by allowing a greater measure of 'shared responsibility' between leaders and members.

Those who provide structured leisure activities and who organise them may perceive these organisations differently from the clients. Adolescents may perceive these organisations as being more structured and authoritarian than do the organisers: 'Like the school itself, like the education system as a whole, like the Duke of Edinburgh Award Scheme, like the Scouts, like the Youth Service and like school based leisure, Youth Clubs describe themselves as non-authoritarian' (Corrigan 1979).

This involvement provides an opportunity for those adolescents who attend organised clubs and structured activities to associate with adults (beyond the family) on a regular basis. At the same time in pursuing more casual leisure interests they can continue to align themselves with their peers. In this way they can have a foot in both camps, so to speak, have the opportunity to experience a wide range of social roles, and perhaps are given the chance to develop a greater versatility in their social relations whilst absorbing and accepting adult attitudes and values. It has also been suggested there are dangers for the teenagers who do not involve themselves in adult organised groups: 'In turning to commercial enterprises for leisure activities, or in creating their own ... adolescents are in a vulnerable position with respect to commercial exploitation and are likely to reduce the amount of informal contact with responsible and caring adults' (Hargreaves 1972).

Anti-social behaviour and peers

In relation to social problems in general – drug abuse, alcoholism, delinquency, and hooliganism – a number of studies emphasise the role of identity processes in determining action (Marsh *et al.* 1978; Weinreich 1985; Emler 1983). The desire to identify with a peer group requires adherence to particular norms of behaviour, role performance imposes conformity and so-called anti-social action can result.

Delinquents tend to live in close promixity to one another and in similar urban conditions. On these grounds alone, the impact of peer group influences in initiating, maintaining, or perhaps restraining delinquent behaviour is obviously an important area for investigation. Spontaneous comments by youths suggest that disengagement from the influence of peer groups was an important feature in the abandonment of delinquent habits (Rutter and Giller 1983). The avoidance of delinquent friends would certainly seem to be a factor in reform (West and Farrington 1977). Most delinquent acts are committed in the company of other children; delinquency is as strongly associated with delinquency in a person's brothers and sisters as with crime in the parents (Farrington *et al.* 1975; Robins *et al.* 1975); young people living in a high-delinquency area or attending a high-delinquency school are more likely to become delinquent than similar children living in other areas or attending other schools; boys who claim delinquents as friends are more likely to admit delinquent behaviour than boys who say their friends are not delinquent (Voss 1963; Johnson 1979); the probability of a boy committing a specific delinquent act has been found to be statistically dependent upon the commission of similar acts by other members of his friendship group (Reiss and Rhodes 1964); and the number of delinquent acts committed by a boy's friends and acquaintances is predictive of his own future convictions (Farrington *et al.* 1975). Although delinquents have delinquent friends it is important to know whether such friendships existed before or after the initial delinquency. Hirschi (1969) took the view that: 'The boy's stake in conformity affects his choice of friends rather than the other way round.' Hirschi also noted that any theory of delinquency must be modified to include some notion of the effect of peer group processes, and possibly the importance of delinquency in contributing to an adolescent's self-esteem (as suggested by the potency of adult-status items such as smoking, drinking, dating, and driving a car). Elliott *et al.* (1979) concurred in this view, noting that one of the major weaknesses of social control theories has been the fact that weak bonds and lack of restraints cannot alone account for the specific form of the behaviour which results. It is necessary to add on the concept that delinquent activities have a social meaning which is rewarded in some way by the social groups in which it occurs. Johnson (1979) has also attempted an eclectic synthesis of sociological theories on the basis of a self-report delinquency study. The findings suggest that the key influences are delinquent associates, delinquent values, school experiences, and parent–child relationships.

The neighbourhood is clearly related to the kinds of peer groups formed. The fact that certain individuals will (or will not) be drawn into certain peer groups is associated in part with the uneven distribution of leisure facilities across various types of social area. This means that it may be more socially deprived groups who are most involved in the 'street culture' (Jephcott 1967; Corrigan 1976). Since such groups are most likely to be socially alienated, deviant activities may be the currency of groups established in such settings, even though these settings were officially created for other social purposes.

Fogelman (1976) indicated that many teenagers were dissatisfied outside the home with their available meeting places. That being the case, the importance of 'the street corner' as a location for social interaction is crucial to some adolescents because they lack power in all formally structured institutionalised contexts.

The street has always provided the main arena for the leisure activities of working-class youth. It is on the streets, too, where troubling aspects of their behaviour are at their most visible, and contact with the police is most likely. The boys described their main leisure activity on the streets as 'doing nothing' or 'just hanging about', yet it still offered the most potential for something exciting *to* happen:

> given nothing to do, something happens, even if it is a yawn, or
> someone setting down on somebody else's foot, or someone

turning over an old insult or an old injury and it's this in the context of 'nothing' that leads to fights – something diminutive and unimportant outside the context of 'doing nothing' yet raging and vital within that context.

(Corrigan 1979: 133)

'Doing nothing' may, however, be interpreted by external observers as 'loitering with intent' (see Figure 6.4).

The boys see trouble as something connected purely with the police, or other social control agents: one cannot get into trouble without the presence of one of these groups. At no stage do they perceive it as doing wrong or breaking rules. . . . What wrongs are they doing if they just walk around the streets and the police harass them? The reasons for the harassment lie with the police, and NOT inside any rule that the boys are breaking since for the boys the streets are a 'natural' meeting place.

(Ibid.: 139)

It has been shown (Corrigan 1976), for instance, that a regular and intense activity engaged in by a majority of working-class teenagers is the simple but absorbing task of 'passing time'. One major element in 'doing nothing' is talking – about popular (e.g. football), fanciful (e.g. exaggerated self-exploits), and cohesive experiences. The street is not seen as a lively environment, but as the place where there is a greater chance that 'something will happen'. As Patrick (1973) wrote:

Life with the gang was not all violence, sex, and petty delinquency. Far from it. One of the foremost sensations that remains with me is the feeling of unending boredom, or crushing tedium, of listening hour after hour at street corners to desultory conversation and indiscriminate grumbling.

Within research on youth sub-cultures the invisibility of young women's lives and experiences to the main action of 'the lads' has been paramount. Recent work has attempted to redress the balance in providing a feminist perspective on sub-cultures which actually starts from the experiences of young women themselves (McRobbie 1978; Griffin 1981; McRobbie and McCabe 1981; Nava and McRobbie 1984). As McRobbie and Garber (1976) pointed out, the position of working-class young women is structurally different to that of young working-class men. The common sense assumptions upon which much of the interaction between

Figure 6.4 'Doing nothing' or 'loitering with intent'? Adolescents' and adults' perceptions of the street corner.

young men and young women is apparently founded demarcate clear boundaries for 'acceptable' masculine and feminine behaviour and responses. The boundaries, however, are not derived simply from the shared assumptions of everyday life. They are structural in the sense that images of sexuality become institutionalised and legitimated within the policy responses of agencies such as schools, youth clubs, and commercial leisure providers. It is here that images translate into ideologies and form part of the social management of sexuality. It is at these levels – ideological and political – that the experiences of young women and men are structured differently and provide an institutionalised process of reinforcement to assumptions which are commonly held.

Wilson (1978) has suggested that girls involved in delinquent sub-cultures may be in rebellion against their traditional sex roles. This has important implications for present and future society. Smith (1978) found that court records revealed that in no way was female delinquency restricted to sexual misconduct, but also included the usual delinquent acts of boys of similar age.

In Smith's study, girls reacted to being labelled as 'sluts' or as 'common' or 'loose' by behaving aggressively rather than by accepting the label of promiscuity. They developed self-images as tomboys – tough, dominant, and willing to join in fights on equal terms with boys. Sharpe (1977) also noted that it is common for girls to fight each other until they are 14 or 15 years old even though they may still remain fashion conscious and 'tuned in' to feminine culture. Smith argued that a girl's 'isolated' position because of 'masculine' aggressive behaviour led to more fighting, shop-lifting, and drinking, and Brake (1980) has pointed out that gangs now contain girls who are prepared to fight other girls. But as Robins and Cohen (1978) wrote: 'This aggro did nothing to alter the girls' fundamental one-down position in the local youth culture – as in other areas of their lives.'

Thus, it appears that the quest for excitement and violence, once almost exclusively belonging to working-class white male adolescent delinquent peer groups (and/or researched from a typically white, male perspective) is being infiltrated by black youths and by girls as social changes create patterns of employment crises, urban decay, changes in police roles, the rise of feminism, and multi-ethnic communities. There is little evidence yet of middle-class gangs, though unemployment may provide a social milieu for their emergence. Short (1968), for example, has described theft as a game providing tensions, excitement, and adventure for adolescent groups, and several authors (Erikson 1968) have conceptualised adolescence as a period of licence, a time for social and sexual exploration. Short held that: 'Such groups offer members a breathing space for the acquisition of confidence, as they extricate themselves from emotional dependence on their families.'

Yet they may well adopt a style of life which could be described as delinquescent. Meyerhoff and Meyerhoff (1964) interpreted the gang as meeting strongly felt needs of its members and as providing a collectively derived solution to common problems of adjustment. This is a similar argument to Murdock and Phelps's (1973) viewpoint on working-class adolescents. Yet the Meyerhoffs were describing the activities of middle-class gangs in California in their search for 'real' excitement and 'real' danger. They emphasised the non-violent nature of their 'delinquescent' leisure activities, finding personal aggression rare. The technique of smooth social relations, being the 'bread and butter' of the middle class, were used for handling trouble with authorities. Open defiance of authority was rarely evident; manipulation by the use of interpersonal skills rather than rebellion was used. Despite all this, they indulged in highly criminal activities, such as stealing cars and luxury goods, great prestige being accorded to those who could carry off a theft with the greatest amount of daring and expertise. The leaders of these gangs seemed to be well balanced, had sound social skills and could get on well with people.

Concluding remarks

As the individual adolescent begins to grow more independent of his or her family the peer group becomes an important point of reference. It supports independence, meets needs for identity and recognition, presents opportunities for achievement, and affords the opportunity of playing a variety of quasi-adult roles. Adolescents are influenced by each other in important ways, in learning social skills and strategies on their road to adulthood, and they need, simply, to associate with other teenagers in corporate activities ranging from organised sports through commercially based pursuits to delinquent acts.

In a swiftly changing society which can often be seen as somewhat constrained and impersonal, the variations of youth groups may be considered as adjustments to, and (conversely) reactions against, the dominant values in society. In the adolescent years young people have less clearly defined roles and are not always allowed full legitimate expression of their individuality. Additionally, there are economic, social, and legal restrictions preventing full participation in adult pursuits. Adults tend to have a stereotypic view of teenagers as a homogeneous group which is often described in the media as irresponsible and violent.

Certainly some adolescents exhibit pseudo-rebellion in dress and hairstyle, gain release of aggression via pop music, and experience peer activities that do not gain adult sanction. These can include vandalism, drugs, drink, and sex. But the majority are hard working, law abiding, and conformist. The social aspects of adolescence are perhaps most evident in pop culture, courting, and sexual activity, in the sense that (potentially) these peer activities can occur conjointly. Sex role identity is very important during adolescence and body shape and fashion styles are related to popularity and social acceptance. Further, pop culture, provided by a commercial market, mirrors adolescent attitudes and sentiments while providing adolescents with an expressive field through which such emotions can be projected, and allows adolescents to demonstrate their energy, their corporate fashions and styles which are, on the surface, quite different from adults'.

In our society, juvenile delinquency – ranging from acts of vandalism, alcoholism, glue-sniffing, to sexual promiscuity, and rioting – is evident perhaps mainly because of the type of achieving society we have. The proposed reasons for delinquency are many: personality disorders, decaying urban conditions, deprived homes, ethnic areas, and so on; but equally some of the reasons for seeking delinquent groups parallel reasons for becoming involved in other interests and pursuits: identity and belonging, significance in the peer group, entertainment, release from boredom and frustration, providing hedonistic fun, friendship, prowess, satisfaction, and excitement.

Chapter seven

Adolescent sexuality

No study of adolescence would be complete without some consideration of the process of sexual maturation for, as we have seen in Chapter two, it is this process which forms the physiological background to many of the social and emotional changes which occur during the teenage years. Although the significance of sexual maturation has been recognised by many, from Freud onwards, who have written on the theme of adolescence, the volume of research on this topic has hardly matched its importance. Thus while there have been a number of surveys of sexual behaviour in adolescence, these have tended to concentrate on a limited range of issues: either on attitudes to sex, on sex education, and the sources of initial sex information, or on the ages at which various types of sexual activity first occur. In contrast, hardly anything is known of the consequences for adult life of different patterns of teenage sex, and in particular the effects of early premarital sexual experience on psychological maturation. Furthermore, relatively little information is available on topics such as sexual difficulties in adolescence, young people's attitudes to sex education, the psychological consequences of abortion, the effects of the AIDS phenomenon, the problems of handicapped adolescents, and so on.

It is very much to be hoped that in future more attention will be paid to these rather more practical issues, since it is this type of information which is most needed as a result of the fundamental changes in sexual attitudes which have occurred among young people over the last two decades. So far-reaching are these changes that they have led commentators to talk of the development of a 'new sexual morality', which has significantly affected the behaviour of young people. In this chapter the origins of these changes of attitude will briefly be examined, and the results of the behaviour surveys which have been carried out will be discussed. Attention will also be paid to some of the very real practical problems faced by teenagers as they come to terms with their sexual maturity, and in the last section the issue of sex education will be considered from a number of different points of view.

The 'new sexual morality'

There are few today who would disagree with the proposition that since the end of World War II fundamental changes have occurred in the attitudes of society generally towards sexual behaviour. It is these general changes which form an essential background to an understanding of adolescent sexual development. In the adult world extra-marital sex has become widely accepted, divorce has become commonplace, there is much greater tolerance of different types of sexual behaviour, homosexuality no longer needs to be invisible, advertisements, films, and television bombard us all with sexual information, and the topic of sex is discussed openly and frequently. As part and parcel of all this, widely available contraception has had the effect of making possible a distinction between sex and procreation. These shifts in attitude, which are in some respects almost revolutionary, cannot fail to have had an effect on young people. Children growing up in a society cannot be insulated from what is happening to those of their parents' generation, and while it may be regretted by some, it is of course inevitable that such fundamental changes in adult behaviour will affect those just beginning their sexual lives.

Research evidence which is available, both in European countries and in the U.S.A., indicates that young people are changing in their attitudes to sexual behaviour in ways which are very similar to adults. Essentially, if comparisons are drawn between the attitudes of adolescents today and those of adolescents twenty or thirty years ago, there seem to be three important differences. First, young people today are more open about sexual matters; second, they see sexual behaviour as more a matter of private rather than public morality; and third, there appears to be a growing sense of the importance of sex being associated with stable, long-term relationships. Let us consider these points in turn. In the first place, young people are more open about sexual matters. This in itself is obviously a reflection of the general frankness about sex in today's society. However, it is important to note that it is also associated with a need on the part of young people for greater opportunities for the discussion of sexual problems with adults, and for a greater availability of sex education in the widest sense of the term. This is a topic to which we shall return later in the chapter.

Second, it is clear that young people believe sexual behaviour to be a matter of individual choice and belief, rather than of public morality. Thus present-day teenagers, it appears, are far less likely to condemn sexual minorities, or to make absolute judgements about what is right or wrong in individual cases. There has been a move among adolescents towards a moral stance which is more relative and less judgemental, with most believing that what is done in private is up to those concerned. Phrases such as 'doing your own thing' reflect this view, which is also associated with a rejection of the part played by official institutions, such as the Church, in determining moral values. Third, today there is undoubtedly a belief in the importance of personal relationships where sexual behaviour is concerned. A common fear among adults is that greater sexual freedom will lead to greater promiscuity, yet all the evidence points in the opposite direction. Young people of the present generation, it appears, far from sanctioning 'sex for fun', much prefer to view sexual activity as needing a framework of a relationship to give it meaning. Perhaps in this they have been influenced to some extent by the sight of their elders experiencing so much unhappiness in their own search for sexual fulfilment.

Evidence for these changes may be drawn from a wide range of sources. In the research literature Conger and Petersen (1984) have summarised surveys of American youth, Meikle *et al.* (1985) have reported from Canada, while Jones *et al.* (1985) discuss findings from various European countries. As far as the U.K. is concerned, Farrell's (1978) study remains the most far-reaching, but more recent work is summarised in Bury (1984) and Allen (1987). Even the most recent studies, however, have not yet been able to show the effects, either on attitudes or behaviour, of the AIDS phenomenon. It is still too early to know whether this will cause a substantial shift among teenagers to a more 'conservative' approach to sexual behaviour. If so this has not yet been documented, and here we will only be able to consider the evidence which is available, taking us to the mid 1980s.

How are changing attitudes reflected in behaviour?

While it seems clear that attitudes have changed radically since the 1950s, we need to consider how such changes have affected sexual behaviour. Answers to this question are provided by the results of some of the surveys already mentioned, but before considering these a word of warning is in order. By the nature of things all the evidence which is available on the sexual behaviour of young people is derived either from interviews or from self-administered questionnaires. Not unnaturally researchers investing time and effort in the design and carrying out of such projects are often loath to dwell too much on the limitations of the methods involved. However, it must be evident that data derived in such a fashion are open to question on a number of counts.

Sexual behaviour is associated with a multitude of worries and anxieties; it is a matter of preoccupation to most teenagers, it is certainly an extremely emotive topic, and most important, for many it represents a standard of evaluation against which to judge success or failure. Thus it seems highly unlikely that responses to interviews or questionnaires are going to reflect accurately real behaviour. In particular it should be borne in mind that for many boys sexual activity is a sign of achievement, and 'conquest' a matter for boasting. There is thus a strong possibility that reports of male sexual behaviour will tend to be exaggerated. On the other hand, for girls, sexual activity is not always a source of pride, and certainly in the past it may well have been true that female sexual behaviour was under-reported. Unfortunately it is extremely difficult to tell whether biases of this sort are operating, but some reservations at least need to be kept in mind in considering the available evidence.

We will first consider the evidence relating to girls, and we may begin with Kinsey (Kinsey *et al.* 1948; 1953). They found that in the U.S.A. by the age of 17 years approximately 10 per cent of females had had sexual intercourse. At the age of 20 this figure had risen to 18 per cent of the population studied. These results are put in perspective by figures published in 1980 by Zelnick and Kantner. In a meticulous study, carried out over a whole decade in North America, they showed that in 1971 26.1 per cent of 17-year-old girls had had intercourse; in 1976 this figure had risen to 42.9 per cent, and by 1979 48.5 per cent of 17-year-old girls were sexually experienced. Among 19-year-olds in 1979 69 per cent had had sexual intercourse, compared with 46.4 per cent in 1971. These figures illustrate more vividly than any commentary the changes that have occurred in teenage sexual behaviour in recent years.

In the U.K. the same sort of trend is apparent, although we only have available comparisons with the early 1960s and 1976–77. Schofield's (1965) evidence indicated that 11 per cent of 17-year-old girls were sexually experienced, a figure which rose to 23 per cent by the age of 19. In contrast, Farrell (1978) showed that by the mid 1970s 39 per cent of 17-year-old girls had had sexual intercourse, while 67 per cent of 19-year-olds were sexually active.

As far as males are concerned, Kinsey reported in the 1940s that in the U.S.A. 61 per cent had had intercourse by the age of 17, and 72 per cent by the age of 20. When they first appeared these figures were greeted with some scepticism, especially in view of the very small number of girls reporting involvement in sexual activity! Kinsey explained the large differences by pointing out that most boys obtained their experience with prostitutes. With hindsight, however, it seems possible that bias in reporting may have played its part in obscuring accuracy. These conclusions are supported to some extent by the more recent work of Zelnick and Kantner (1980) who showed that in 1979 55.7 per cent of 17-year-old boys had had sexual intercourse. This figure is more in line with the frequency of sexual activity reported by girls. Turning to Great Britain, Schofield (1965) found that 25 per cent of 17-year-old males had had intercourse, a figure which increased to 37 per cent by the age of 19. Once again these data contrast sharply with the figures reported by Farrell. In the 1970s it appears that 50 per cent of 17-year-old boys were sexually experienced, while 74 per cent of 19-year-olds had had intercourse. It is, of course, extremely difficult to assess the precise meaning of all these percentages. Even allowing for bias and some degree of inaccuracy, however, there can be little doubt that the findings reflect a marked increase in sexual activity over the years.

Conger and Petersen (1984) make a particular point of emphasising the importance of taking into account individual differences when considering figures such as these. Apart from age, sex, and nationality, variables such as social class, ethnic origin, and cultural background will obviously play their part in determining sexual behaviour, and certainly the research evidence bears this out. Thus, for example, in the U.S.A. Zelnick and Kantner (1980) demonstrated a marked difference between white and black teenagers. In 1979, 48.5 per cent of white 17-year-old girls were sexually experienced, while the figure for black girls was 73.3 per cent. For males the difference is not quite so striking, with 54.5 per cent of white 17-year-olds and 60.3 per cent black 17-year-olds reported as being sexually active at this time.

Social class is another variable of obvious importance. For example, Farrell (1978) was able to show that working-class boys in Britain were more sexually experienced than middle-class boys, and Conger and Petersen (1984) reported studies in America which found that the biggest relative changes, both in attitudes and in behaviour, have occurred among liberal white middle-class boys and girls. As we have already noted, wider social groupings, such as nationality, also play their part in determining differences. While it is difficult to find strictly comparable studies, the

Guttmacher Institute (Jones *et al.* 1985) has shown wide disparities between different countries. They reported that in the late 1970s close to 60 per cent of 17-year-old girls in Sweden were sexually experienced, while around 30 per cent fell into this group in France and the Netherlands. Great Britain, the U.S.A., and Canada were in between these two extremes.

Finally, in this section mention must be made of the alterations in contraceptive practice which have taken place in the last three decades, for nothing illustrates more clearly than this the radical nature of the changes in the whole field of sexual behaviour which have affected young people. Schofield (1965) showed that in the early 1960s over half his population of teenagers took precautions irregularly, if at all, and that of those who did the great majority used either the sheath (82 per cent) or withdrawal (31 per cent). He writes:

> Our enquiries into the use of birth control methods among teenagers have shown that many boys are not using contraceptives and most girls who are having intercourse are at risk. This does not seem to be because teenagers have difficulty in obtaining contraceptives, but because social disapproval means that many of their sexual adventures are unpremeditated and therefore adequate precautions have not been taken beforehand; many of the teenagers are aware of the risks, but in these extemporary situations sexual desire may override an awareness of the possible consequences.
>
> (Schofield 1965 : 251)

In contrast to this situation, Farrell (1978) was able to report a major change. She showed that, in the main, in the 1970s sexually active young people were using methods of birth control, and only 8 per cent said that they had never taken any precautions. This small group of teenagers was predominantly working class, and two out of every three were boys. However, according to Farrell, adolescents still appeared to be particularly at risk in the very early stages of their sexual experience, for only 54 per cent of the sample reported that they had used some method of birth control on the first occasion. Of particular interest are the changes that occur in the use of contraceptives with age and experience. The data in Table 7.1 illustrate the way in which both boys and girls shift to more reliable methods as they get older or become more experienced.

Implications of changing sexual behaviour

The evidence which has been presented so far, in spite of the methodological difficulties which may distort it to some extent,

Table 7.1 First and most recent methods of birth control used by age and
sex

Methods*	16-year-olds		19-year-olds	
	First	Most recent	First	Most recent
	%	%	%	%
Males				
Withdrawal	37	24	34	14
Sheath	57	65	57	34
Pill	2	6	7	52
Others	4	5	2	–
Number using birth control (= 100%)	49	49	137	137
% of sexually experienced young males who had never used any method	11		6	
Females				
Withdrawal	30	15	23	8
Sheath	61	45	53	22
Pill	6	36	19	67
Others	3	4	5	3
Number using birth control (= 100%)	33	33	120	120
% of sexually experienced young females who had never used any method	11		4	

*Percentages add to more than 100 because some had used more than one method (e.g.
chemicals)
Source: C. Farrell (1978) *My Mother Said*, Routledge & Kegan Paul.

makes clear that adolescent values and attitudes, as well as sexual
behaviour itself, are changing rapidly in today's society. Shifts in
attitudes and behaviour of the order we have been discussing must
inevitably have implications for adolescent development, as well
as for personal adjustment. Not only do young people have to
cope with their own maturational changes, but they also have to
come to terms with a confusing inconsistency among adult views,
and a lack of any clear standard or moral code of conduct. Such a
situation hardly makes life for the teenager any easier. It would be
reassuring if at least more adults in responsible positions showed
an interest in these difficulties, and were more often seen developing ways and means of helping young people come to terms with
problems associated with sexual behaviour. With rare exceptions,
however, the boot is all too frequently on the other foot, with
older people bemoaning the increased 'permissiveness' of the
behaviour of their adolescent sons and daughters.

As has already been noted, the major fear of most adults is that greater sexual freedom, associated in particular with the increased availability of the pill and the greater accessibility of abortion services for young people, will lead to more and more promiscuity. While promiscuity may be very difficult to define, it is the opinion of all social scientists who have investigated the reality of the situation that no such consequence has become apparent. Here is how Farrell summarised her findings:

> Although teenage sexual activity was not investigated in detail, there was little evidence of promiscuity. The majority of young people currently involved in a sexual relationship were having sex with someone they had been going out with for more than six months, and there was no evidence that the pill was encouraging casual relationships since most of the girls who were taking the pill at the time of the interview had known their partners for more than six months. . . . This overall picture of teenage use of birth control gives the lie to the image of careless and casual teenage sex often promoted by the media. Although there are gaps in birth control use particularly at the initial stages of sexual experience, the majority of teenagers held responsible attitudes to sex before marriage.
>
> (Farrell 1978: 219)

A more recent study (Tobin 1985), also carried out in the U.K., came to much the same conclusions. Tobin followed 100 sexually active teenage girls for two and a half years and showed a very high continuity rate regarding both the chosen method of contraception and the girls' original sexual partner. Only 12 per cent of the population studied had had more than two partners during the two and a half years of the investigation.

Evidence of teenage pregnancy rates is interesting too in this respect. Figures published by the Office of Population Censuses and Surveys in the U.K. show that in the period 1969–84 the numbers of pregnancies for both 13- to 15- and 15- to 19-year-olds have remained relatively steady. If anything, the figures show a declining level of teenage pregnancy since the early 1970s. Details are shown in Table 7.2.

Another factor which is often quoted as being indicative of increased promiscuity is the incidence of venereal disease. In fact however the figures once again do not support commonly prevailing mythology. As is shown in Table 7.3, the incidence of gonorrhoea – the most common venereal disease today and the only one where there are a sufficient number of cases to illustrate a trend – has fallen steadily over the period 1977–83. It is of course true that part of this decrease may result from improved diagnostic

Table 7.2   Teenage pregnancy rates in England and Wales, 1969–84

Year	Total conceptions 13- to 15-year-olds		Total conceptions 15- to 19-year-olds	
	Number	Rate*	Number	Rate*
1969	6,500	6.8	123,400	75.0
1970	7,700	7.9	134,300	82.4
1971	8,800	8.7	132,700	81.3
1972	9,600	9.3	130,400	79.2
1973	9,800	9.2	125,500	75.2
1974	9,400	8.5	118,100	69.6
1975	9,200	8.1	111,900	64.1
1976	9,200	7.9	105,600	58.7
1977	9,000	7.6	107,300	57.9
1978	9,100	7.6	114,500	60.2
1979	9,100	7.5	121,000	62.0
1980	8,600	7.2	117,200	58.7
1981	8,600	7.3	115,200	57.1
1982	9,000	7.8	113,900	56.4
1983	9,400	8.3	112,400	56.0
1984	9,600	8.6	118,200	59.9

*The rate is per 1,000 women
Source: OPCS Monitor, 3 December 1985 and 15 July 1986.

techniques and better contact tracing. None the less the figures certainly do not support the worst fears of the adult population.

The fact that promiscuity among young people has not increased to any great extent since the 1960s is of great significance, and should not go unremarked by anyone interested in the lives of teenagers. This is especially so in view of the pressures which operate in society, and which impinge on today's adolescents. Hershel Thornburg (1975) has coined the phrase 'social puberty' to describe the situation created by some of the more insidious of these pressures. In particular he draws attention to the heterosexual involvement which is thrust upon the pre-adolescent prior to physiological maturity. This occurs, he argues, as a result of the highly suggestive stimuli presented to young people, usually through the medium of television, but also in films, literature, and pop music. Sex in this context is usually portrayed with a materialistic emphasis, and is often associated with the theme of immediate gratification. It is Thornburg's contention that young people are thus almost bullied into sexual activity by the social environment, long before they are mature or have reached puberty proper. Another closely related issue is that of peer pressure. For many teenagers a conflict exists between what they believe is right and what it appears many of their friends are doing. This is a theme

Table 7.3 New cases of gonorrhoea per 100,000 population seen at hospital clinics in England 1977–83

| | 1977 | | | 1979 | | | 1981 | | | 1983 | | |
	M	F	Total	M	F	Total	M	F	Total	M	F	Total
Under 16	2.25	8.04	5.06	1.50	5.86	3.62	1.82	5.30	3.52	1.59	4.13	2.83
16–19 years	331.52	508.19	417.67	284.80	412.83	347.31	277.54	393.83	334.44	273.26	381.68	325.89

Source: F.P.I.S. Fact Sheet D5, July 1986.

already discussed in some detail in Chapter six, but it is especially acute in the area of sexual behaviour. It is just this sort of issue which needs sympathetic and informed support from adults most closely involved with young people.

In considering the difficulties faced by teenagers it should also be pointed out that the simple availability of contraceptive measures does not necessarily solve the problems associated with sexual activity. Some teenagers may, quite rightly, fear the biological consequences of the pill, while others, through shame or anxiety, may be unable to use the advisory medical services. The threat of AIDS has called into question the use of contraceptives such as the pill and the cap and, in addition, there will be those whose contraceptive method has failed, and who therefore have to face the prospect of abortion, adoption of the child, or unintended marriage. Yet, even if there was a perfect contraceptive used by all, there remains the most complex of all issues – what is right when it comes to sexual behaviour? It is to this problem that we shall undoubtedly turn to an increasing extent in the future, yet certainly today there are few obvious answers. It is for this reason that sex education ought to occupy a more and more important place in the socialisation of young people.

Before closing this section on the implications of changes in sexual behaviour some mention needs to be made of current changes in the law, for it is through the legal apparatus that the most tangible evidence can be gained of a society's shift in attitudes. In the U.K. the 1969 Family Law Reform Act, which reduced the general age of majority from 21 to 18, states that a person of 16 can give consent to surgical, medical, or dental treatment on his or her own behalf without the consent of parents being obtained. The medical age of majority is set at two years lower than the general age of majority of 18. Under the law in Britain, therefore, a person of 16 is regarded as medically adult, having the right of professional secrecy and being able to decide what information, if any, should be passed to his or her parents. As far as teenagers under 16 are concerned, it is for the individual doctor to decide whether to provide contraceptive advice and treatment.

In the U.K. this particular issue has received an unusual degree of attention over the last few years as a result of what is known as the Gillick case (F.P.I.S. 1986). In 1980 a Government Department, the D.H.S.S., issued the following statement:

There is widespread concern about counselling and treatment for children under 16. Special care is needed not to undermine parental responsibility and family stability. The Department would therefore hope that in any case where a doctor or other professional worker is approached by a person under the age of 16 for advice on these matters, the doctor, or other professional, will always seek to persuade the child to involve the parent or guardian and will proceed from the assumption that it would be most unusual to provide advice about contraception without parental consent.

It is, however, widely accepted that consultations between doctors and patients are confidential, and the Department recognises the importance which doctors and patients attach to this principle. It is a principle which applies also to the other professions concerned. To abandon this principle for children under 16 might cause some not to seek professional advice at all. They could then be exposed to the immediate risks of pregnancy and of sexually transmitted disease, as well as other long-term physical, psychological and emotional consequences which are equally a threat to stable family life. This would apply particularly to young people whose parents are, for example, unconcerned, entirely unresponsive, or grossly disturbed. Some of these young people are away from their parents and in the care of local authorities or voluntary organisations standing in loco parentis.

The Department realises that in such exceptional cases the nature of any counselling must be a matter for the doctor or other professional worker concerned and that the decision whether or not to prescribe contraception must be for the clinical judgement of a doctor.

(F.P.I.S. 1986)

Mrs Gillick challenged this statement on the grounds that it deprived her of her parental rights, and she sought an assurance that no contraceptive advice or treatment would be given to her daughters without her knowledge and consent. The Health Authority would not give such an assurance, and the case went all the way to the House of Lords, judgment being finally given in October 1985. By a 3:2 majority the Law Lords ruled that:

A girl under 16 of sufficient understanding and intelligence may have the legal capacity to give valid consent to contraceptive advice and treatment including necessary medical examinations.

Giving such advice and treatment to a girl under 16 without parental consent does not necessarily infringe parental rights.

Doctors giving such advice in good faith are not committing a criminal offence of aiding and abetting unlawful intercourse with girls under 16.

The Law Lords further ruled that the decision of a doctor to give contraceptive advice and/or treatment to under age girls should be guided by the following precepts:

1. That the girl (although under 16 years of age) will understand his advice;
2. That he cannot persuade her to inform her parents or to allow him to inform the parents that she is seeking contraceptive advice;
3. That she is very likely to begin or to continue having sexual intercourse with or without contraceptive treatment;
4. That unless she receives contraceptive advice or treatment her physical or mental health or both are likely to suffer;
5. That her best interests require him to give her contraceptive advice, treatment or both without the parental consent.

Doctors ought not, the Law Lords ruled, to regard this as a licence to disregard the wishes of parents.

At first sight it may appear that this judgment left the situation unchanged, the individual doctor still having the right to treat someone under 16 without necessarily informing the parents. For at least two reasons, however, the Gillick case has in fact made the position of the under 16s worse rather than better. First, the complexity of the case, and the legal wrangles surrounding it, have left teenagers confused and uncertain where they stand. Second, the publicity accorded to Mrs Gillick, as well as the tightening up of definitions, have left doctors with less room to manoeuvre and have caused almost all medical practitioners to exercise greater caution than before.

Quite apart from the effect of all this on teenage sexual behaviour the issue is of considerable interest because it relates to one of the key issues in adolescent psychology: at what point does an individual cease to be a child and start to become an adult. One by-product of the Gillick case was that the Law Lords were forced to consider this question – a question usually considered more appropriately answered by a psychologist rather than a lawyer. Lord Fraser addressed the question as follows:

> Parental rights to control the child existed not for the benefit of the parent but for the child. It was contrary to the ordinary experience of mankind, at least in Western Europe in the present century, to say that a child remained in fact under the complete control of his parents until he attained the definite age of majority, and that on attaining that age he suddenly acquired independence.

In practice most wise parents relaxed their control gradually as their child developed and encouraged him to become increasingly independent. Moreover, the degree of parental control actually exercised over a particular child did in practice vary considerably according to his understanding and intelligence.

It would be unrealistic for the courts not to recognise those facts. Social customs changed, and the law ought to and did in fact have regard to such changes when they were of such major importance.

(*The Times* Law Reports, 18 October 1985)

Lord Scarman agreed, adding this rider:

If the law should impose upon the process of growing up fixed limits where nature knew only a continuous process, the price would be artificiality and a lack of realism in an area where the law must be sensitive to human development and social change.

(Ibid.)

The implications of such statements are very far-reaching, not least because they contain a recognition of the limitations in the use of chronological age as a benchmark for the determination of maturity. Interestingly, a similar debate took place in the U.S.A. during the 1970s. As Hoffman (1978) pointed out, during the 1970s regional decisions across the United States had given growing support to the notion that a person may be a minor in law but mature enough to take certain decisions without parental interference. Of the essence in this notion is the view that maturity and the capability of giving 'informed consent' rather than chronological age, are the primary determining factors in deciding when a minor should have rights of privacy and access to health care. Such a view was embodied in a major constitutional ruling by the United States Supreme Court. In this case the Court was asked to rule on the constitutionality of a Missouri law which, in part, required parental consent for an abortion of a girl under 16. The Court invalidated the requirement, stating:

the State may not impose a blanket provision requiring the consent of a parent ... as a condition for abortion of an unmarried minor. The State does not have the constitutional authority to give a third party an absolute, and possibly arbitrary, veto over the decision of the physician and his patient to terminate the patient's pregnancy. Minors as well as adults are protected by the constitution and possess constitutional rights. Any independent interest the parent may have in the termination of the minor daughter's pregnancy is no more weighty than the right of privacy of the competent minor mature enough to have become pregnant.

(Hoffman 1978 : 31)

In Hoffman's view the significance of this decision can hardly be underestimated, for it reflects as clearly as any single statement can the growing acceptance in society of the right of the teenager to determine his or her own medical care, and by implication, therefore, his or her own sexual behaviour.

To summarise to this point, we have seen how changes in sexual behaviour have had implications throughout society. Of course it is impossible to determine how attitudes and behaviour interact, or to say which precedes the other. Do changes in the law, for example, encourage young people to gain sexual experience, or do these changes simply provide a legitimate framework for behaviour which is already occurring? No one can say. Undoubtedly the availability of oral contraceptives has played as big a part as any in causing the changes, but other less tangible factors in society should not be underestimated. From the point of view of the teenager we have seen that, in spite of adult fears to the contrary, there is no evidence to support the view that promiscuity or casual sex has increased among the young. However, the availability of contraception, while it may have reduced some problems, has in turn created others. Social pressures to gain sexual experience are hard to resist, and can be the cause of much personal conflict. The contraception available today is far from perfect, in spite of the myths which abound in films and literature, and many teenagers have to discover this for themselves the hard way. Finally, increased opportunities for sexual activity create moral and ethical dilemmas which are as complex and difficult to handle as any. It is because of this that good, informed sex education, which is not limited simply to the provision of biological facts, becomes so essential. It is to this issue that we now turn.

Sex education

All that has been said so far serves to underline the necessity for adequate sex education. Teenagers need the best possible preparation to enable them to cope well with their sexual development and to avoid the most obvious pitfalls. In this section we will consider some of the problems associated with sex education, and look at some of the ideas which are being used in schools to improve the traditional curriculum. Let us first, however, consider

Table 7.4 Teenagers' assessment of where they got most information
about sex, contraception, and personal relationships

	Column percentages		
	Sex	*Cont.*	*PR*
Teaching at school	63	66	35
Doctor	0	0	0
Family planning clinic/advice centre	0	2	0
Mother	15	6	19
Father	2	2	2
Both parents	5	2	11
Brother/sister	4	1	2
Friends own age/sex	29	20	29
Friends opp. sex	3	2	4
TV	0	1	2
Books	2	3	1
Other media	3	1	2
Older friends	4	3	2
Other relatives	0	0	0
Don't know	0	2	2
Base	(209)	(209)	(209)
2 answers	35%	15%	19%
1 answer	64%	84%	80%

Source: I. Allen (1987) *Education in Sex and Personal Relationships*, Policy Studies Institute.

briefly the question of where most information on sexual matters
comes from at the moment.

Many investigators have considered this question, and by and
large the results of these studies are surprisingly consistent. In the
U.S.A., for example, Thornburg (1975) showed that among a
large sample of teenagers from eleven different locations young
people estimated that they obtained about 40 per cent of all their
information from their peers, and another 40 per cent from school
literature. Only about 15 per cent was believed to come from
parents. Thornburg broke these figures down further to show that
the source of information was linked closely with the content.
Thus while 40–50 per cent of teenagers obtained information
about menstruation from their mothers, only 9 per cent obtained
information about contraception in this way.

A similar picture emerged from Allen's (1987) study of teenagers in the U.K., as can be seen in Table 7.4. However, it is
important to note that a somewhat different perspective emerges if
alternative questions are asked. Thus for example Allen included
in her study the query: 'Who do you think would give you the
most accurate information about sex/contraception/personal relationships?' From this it became apparent that approximately
33 per cent thought parents would provide the most accurate

information, 25 per cent thought the doctor or other medical services and only 15 per cent rated teachers as the most accurate. An equally interesting variation occurs when the question is 'Who would you turn to first with a question about sex/contraception/ personal relationships?' Here schools and teachers came even lower on the list as can be seen from Table 7.5.

These results show only too clearly the problems of credibility and trust inherent in the provision of sex education. In many respects Allen's (1987) study is very encouraging. While Schofield (1973) and Farrell (1978) were reporting limited opportunities for sex education in U.K. secondary schools, Allen was able to show that by the mid-1980s the situation had improved dramatically. Allen's report indicates that, by the age of 16, 98 per cent of adolescents had had some education on puberty and human reproduction, while 83 per cent had had material on sex and personal relationships, and 85 per cent on venereal disease. These figures indicate a very substantial increase over the figures reported by Farrell (1978). However, the fact that young people have relatively little faith in the information they receive from school, and the fact that so few of them would turn to teachers for information is a worrying phenomenon. The conclusion must be that while the last decade has seen a considerable expansion in the amount of sex education in schools, the task for the next decade must be to improve the quality of this education, and to provide greater opportunities for discussion and the sharing of views and opinions. It is only in this way that the credibility of sex education in schools will be enhanced.

Although there is undoubtedly room for improvement in the material available to teachers, some useful ideas have emerged concerning ways in which sex education can be made interesting and challenging to young people. Three approaches will be briefly considered here. In the first example, the Health Education Council in Great Britain have used visual material concerning relationships and social situations to provoke discussion of this type of topic. In the second case Juhasz, an American doctor, has set out a chart which takes the adolescent through a process of sexual decision making. Third, Laishley, a British social psychologist, has developed materials which encourage pupils to gain a greater understanding of themselves and of human relationships.

As sexual behaviour among young people has become a matter of social concern, teachers and others have looked for ways of incorporating into the curriculum topics which, without too much embarrassment, can become the focus of group discussion. Bodies such as the Schools Council and the Health Education Council in

Table 7.5 First person teenager would turn to with question about sex, contraception, or personal relationships

	Column percentages								
	Re sex			*Re contraception*			*Re personal relationships*		
	Total	*Boys*	*Girls*	*Total*	*Boys*	*Girls*	*Total*	*Boys*	*Girls*
Mother	41	27	54	40	22	55	42	26	56
Father	5	9	22	8	14	2	5	9	2
Parents	1	2	0	2	4	0	6	10	2
Friends same sex/age	27	25	28	19	20	18	23	20	26
Friends opp. sex/same age	5	7	3	2	4	0	3	5	1
Brother/sister	4	3	5	3	3	5	5	5	5
Teacher	5	8	3	9	12	5	4	6	3
Doctor	2	4	0	5	5	5	0	0	0
Family planning clinic	0	0	0	0	0	0	0	0	0
Older friend	1	0	2	1	0	2	1	0	2
Books only	4	7	2	4	6	2	3	7	0
School nurse	0	0	0	0	0	0	0	0	0
Don't know	3	6	0	5	7	4	5	9	2
Base	(209)	(99)	(110)	(209)	(99)	(110)	(209)	(99)	(110)

Source: I. Allen (1987) *Education in Sex and Personal Relationships*, Policy Studies Institute.

Source: P. McPhail (1977) *And How Are We Feeling Today?*, Health Education Project.

Figure 7.1 'It's no good saying anything. They always do what they want.'

Britain have produced materials which can be used with adolescents between the ages of 12 and 18. In general this material tends to consist of 'kits' of cards, stories, or situations illustrating relevant issues likely to provoke interest among the age group concerned. One example from the Health Education Project, 'Living Well' (McPhail 1977), is shown in Figure 7.1. This picture has the following set of questions attached to it:

1. Describe the attitude of the girl at the bus stop. What do you think she hopes will happen?
2. Why do you think she feels as she does?
3. Why do the women talking about her react as they do?
4. Is this sort of conflict between the young and middle-aged bound to happen? Give your reasons for thinking it is or is not.
5. Discuss with your friends how you feel about the cartoon.

A more direct, some might say too direct, approach to encouraging young people to think about sexual behaviour and its consequences is reflected in the work of an American, Ann Juhasz (1975). She believes that by focusing on the decision-making process she can force teenagers to examine and face up to what can happen as a result of sexual behaviour. In turn this, she argues, will help them acknowledge that their behaviour, and thus their

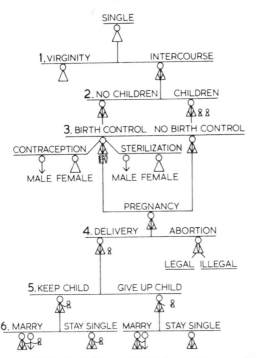

Source: A. M. Juhasz (1975) in R. E. Grinder (ed.) *Studies in Adolescence*, Collier-Macmillan.

Figure 7.2 A model for sexual decision making.

future, is within their own control – to see that they do have a choice in the matter. She presents a model for sexual decision making, illustrated in Figure 7.2, which enables the teacher or counsellor to discuss with the group the cumulative ramifications of any single decision in sexual behaviour. The six questions on which this logical chain is based are as follows:

1. Intercourse or no intercourse?
2. Children or no children?
3. Birth control or no birth control?
4. Delivery or abortion?
5. Keep the child or give it up?
6. Remain single or marry?

As Juhasz says:

> For each of the six questions in this chain, the adolescent should understand factors which could influence decisions. In addition,

for each possible choice, he or she should be aware of the
questions which will arise, the additional problems which must
be faced, and the implications of subsequent actions. In other
words a logical, systematic consideration of the knowns and
unknowns is required

(Juhasz 1975: 345).

For some this approach may simply be too cold-blooded, but what
more effective techniques are there to bring home to young people
the possible long-term consequences in their own lives of one
single act? It may be argued that the decision to have intercourse
or not is rarely a rational one, and that to consider it as part of a
logical thought process is meaningless. This may well be true, but
on the other hand the use of an effective contraceptive can, with
help, be a rational decision. If sex education aims, as it must, to
prevent unwanted pregnancy and unwanted marriage, then it is in
contexts such as this that Juhasz's shock tactics may really help,
encouraging teenagers to learn essential lessons about the consequences of their behaviour.

A rather more gentle, but no less thoughtful, approach is
exemplified in Laishley's (1979) development of a Human Relations course. Here her aim was to enable teenagers to develop a
deeper understanding of themselves and the problems they were
likely to face in everyday living. In order to do this she designed
materials which focused on four areas: person perception and
judgement of character, issues of self-knowledge, the behaviour of
individuals in groups, and personal development in relation to the
events of adolescence such as sexual maturation. She relied
heavily on participation in group discussion, and used aides such as
a 'Who am I?' questionnaire, a check list of Self and Ideal Self,
and a set of cards on which pleasant and unpleasant personality
traits were depicted to encourage self-examination. Stories and
visual material were used to illustrate common interpersonal
situations, such as 'The problem of Carla and Andrew'. Here two
teenagers were depicted who had just begun to date each other.
Both are described as feeling that they fall short in some important
respect, which they have judged by comparing themselves with
other teenagers. As it happens this 'deficit' is of no concern to their
partner, who admires the other for his or her good qualities. None
the less these anxieties hinder the relationship. The group, having
been presented with the problem, is then asked 'What should
Carla and Andrew do? Are their worries reasonable? How can
they cope with them?' and 'Is this a common problem?' Material
of this sort, while not directly relevant to factual sex education,

obviously acts as a background to the more traditional curriculum, and provides a basis for the more realistic sexual decision making discussed above.

In the last few years a variety of books have appeared which attempt to provide sexual information for adolescents in a readily accessible manner, but to place it in a wider context. Good examples of texts are Hayman (1986), Bruggen and O'Brian (1986), and Cousins (1987). The last of these, a book entitled *Make it Happy*, is an illustration of changing attitudes. When the first edition appeared, in 1979, there was uproar in the press and in Parliament about a publication which discussed homosexuality, venereal disease, abortion, and so on in such a frank manner. It was even claimed that books of this sort should be banned, or at least removed from the shelves of school libraries. Today Jane Cousins' book is probably more widely read than any other in the U.K. and, with a different climate of opinion, partly no doubt as a result of concern over AIDS, the frank and open approach of *Make it Happy* is seen as essential in order to engage the interest of young people.

Clearly the examples given above are only a selection from the many which could have been chosen for discussion. Each of them, however, reflects a shared assumption: that greater sexual freedom for young people necessitates greater responsibility on the part of adults. In particular this responsibility should lead teachers, psychologists, and others to provide the best possible preparation for the many problems and conflicts that adolescents will have to face as they mature sexually. Naturally it should not be assumed that all problems will evaporate as a result of good sex education. It remains a fact, however, that anything which prepares young people for potentially troublesome areas of their future, and does so in time to prevent difficulties, must be beneficial. Thus self-knowledge, an understanding of sexual decision making, a recognition of the consequences of sexual behaviour and a knowledge of parenthood and what it entails, are all integral aspects of the intellectual equipment needed to grow up today. The more this material can be incorporated into education, the greater the chances young people will have of avoiding crises and of retaining control over their own lives.

Chapter eight

Work, unemployment, and leisure: the transition from school to adult society

Introduction

This chapter looks at a critical period in adolescence when young people can legally leave school and officially start to enter adult society. If adolescence as a whole is often seen as a creation of the twentieth century, the curious limbo of post-school adolescence is a state created by the depressed labour market of the 1980s. Young people's passage to adulthood is inextricably linked to the world of work. Work not only provides the resources and finances to be an independent agent, to be mobile, to start making real choices, but also confers status, structures one's daily life, assembles a ready-made group of peers, and other adults with whom to interact. It further changes, perhaps for ever, the young person's attitude to, and use of, leisure.

The passage from school to work can no longer follow an assured pattern. In the middle years of this century, after the Second World War, trade union pressure and successive 'welfare' governments of all political complexions seemed to have established a continuing trend towards safer working conditions, shorter and more flexible hours, longer holidays, protection for employee's rights with regard to unfair dismissal and discrimination, protection in the event of sickness, the first moves towards the establishment of minimum wage agreements, and so on. The 'new' world of work seemed an attractive proposition for young people – relatively unproblematic in many respects, so that as much attention was focused on the 'problem' of how with all this extra cash and extra free time, young people should disport themselves in their leisure lives.

It was already clear by the late 1970s and early 1980s, however, that this model had been shattered both by the impact of an economic slump that deprived millions of their jobs, and by the restructuring of the economy shown in the decline of traditional manufacturing industry and the emergence of the silicone chip industries based on new technologies and the development of the service sector.

The impact of these changes has been felt keenly in the youth labour market, perhaps more than in other sectors. Young people have had to suffer not just the downturn in fortunes experienced by all, but also deliberate attempts to intervene and restructure the opportunities offered to them.

This chapter sets out to examine contemporary research evidence on how young people are prepared for and cope with their entry into adult society at a time of social flux. The first part of the chapter explores the preparation of young people before they leave school. What are their hopes and aspirations? Are schools capable of preparing young people for the demands they face? Should they prepare young people for unemployment as well as employment?

The second part of the chapter looks at young workers and unemployed adolescents and considers the impact of occupational trajectories on their lifestyles, their transition towards adult status, and on their personal and social development.

Employment and social change

Most dramatically, the major economic changes in Britain have produced schism. It appears that a polarisation is taking place between:

> the comfortable and the established of the middle and skilled working classes and various groups of outsiders, mostly weakly supplied with market capabilities. Included in the latter would be many of the young, a lot of unskilled and semi-skilled older workers, and a disproportionate number of black and brown Britons.
>
> (Rees 1987: 118)

Goldthorpe and Payne (1986) noted a continuing expansion of the 'service class', with a consequent continuation of opportunities for upward mobility. At the same time the rise in unemployment between their two surveys (1972; 1983) had also generated increased possibilities of 'downward mobility' out of paid employment altogether.

> There seems to be general agreement that the traditional patterns of working and leisure life will undergo profound change – are indeed already doing so to an increasing degree –

163

under the impact of technological development.... It is suggested that many young people already living will never have paid employment of the traditional kind. It is irrefutable that very many people will find themselves with vastly increased amounts of what has been regarded in the past as 'leisure'.

(Scottish Council for Community Education 1981)

School

Schooling and preparation for society

What is the role of the school in helping young people develop the skills – and preoccupations – necessary for a changing society? Is the school's role a successful one?

Some years ago Carter (1972) argued that: 'there is this substantial hard core of young people to whom the idea of remaining at school is abhorrent ... and [this is] based in a sub-culture and a social system which rejects school and all it is presumed to stand for'.

Thus, over the past twenty years or so a relatively high percentage of British adolescents have appeared eager to leave school at the earliest possible opportunity and to be indifferent or even hostile towards the values of school and the processes of schooling. Many years ago Morton-Williams and Finch (1968) painted a general picture of the contrasting qualities of 'early leavers' and the pupils staying on beyond the minimum leaving age. They described 'early leavers' as having less favourable home backgrounds, being less inclined to have academic interests, being more inclined to resent school disciplines, being less identified with school values, occupying their leisure time less satisfactorily, being more easily bored and giving their parents more cause for anxiety.

More recently a study by Hendry and McKenzie (1978) has shown that since the raising of the minimum school-leaving age to 16 years in the 1970s comprehensive schools still contain two groups of pupils having sharply different values, attitudes, and aspirations. Pupils' pro- and anti-school sub-cultures with their sharply different values, attitudes, and aspirations seem as firmly entrenched in comprehensive schools as they were in selective and non-selective schools (Hargreaves 1967; Ball 1981).

It can be suggested that such a divisive system of schooling is no longer appropriate in the changing modern world. There is an increasing awareness of the fact that both for employment and for other aspects of life in the adult world young people of all kinds require many competencies, abilities, and qualities other than the cognitive academic skills which are emphasised in schools. Thus, Ryrie (1981) questioned whether, if academically able children are given opportunities in keeping with their type of ability, the same can be said of the less academically able children. Are the varied gifts and potentials of such children – of whatever background – recognised, valued, encouraged, and developed in such a way as to allow them to grasp the opportunities of life as fully as possible? The answer would seem to be that within our schooling system they are not. He further suggested that there is good reason to believe that the basic reason why the varied potential of young people is not developed in our schools is that skills and abilities other than academic and cognitive ones are not sufficiently valued and respected. If this view is correct, he claimed, we are unlikely to achieve a more appropriate approach to the non-academic youngster, or to provide an education system that is relevant to people and society today and in the future. We should accord a greater respect, dignity, and importance to the varied and usually not-very-academic potential of many young people.

The 'inappropriate' nature of what is taught in many secondary schools is well illustrated by the aspirations and awareness of their future displayed by working-class pupils in Willis's (1977) and Corrigan's (1979) case studies. These working-class pupils saw secondary education as a 'confidence trick' and were totally disengaged from it. They behaved in the school by 'playing the system' in order to gain some personal control over the school organisation. Such opposition involved an inversion of the values held up by school authority (such as diligence, deference, and respect); these behaviour patterns became antithetical as conducted by the 'lads'. Their opposition was expressed mainly as a 'style'. Popular criticisms of education are based on the feelings of many pupils and their parents 'that school by its compulsory nature is a sentence which must be served before the real business of life can begin' (Weir and Nolan 1977). Yet, there is clear evidence that young women and men experience schooling differently, and this leads to distinct outcomes (Deem 1980). Within the curriculum this need not take the overt form of differential option choices (e.g. domestic science for girls, woodwork for boys) but it can involve '. . . a myriad of subtle ways in which the educational process brings to life and sustains sexual divisions – the process of quite literally, teaching girls to be women and boys to be men.'

Within school there are clearly female counter-school cultures just as there have been shown to be male counter-school cultures.

Whereas the *class* significance of male counter-school culture has been stressed (Willis 1977), female counter-school cultures are seen to involve negotiation around age, race, class, and *gender* relations. Resistances to schooling for young women are not solely about gender or class but are bound up with their complex development towards adulthood. It is likely that this has been further intensified with the raising of the school leaving age which leaves young adults in a system geared to childhood and based on a clear age-related authority structure (Johnson 1981).

Young women's resistances within school, however, do take on a specifically female form and cannot simply be equated to those of male youth. It challenges the school definition of a 'nice' girl which is seen to emphasise neatness, passivity, hard work, politeness, which will result in a 'good', 'suitable' job (e.g. nursery nurse, infant teacher). It is important here to see resistance not necessarily as a 'problem' (as viewed by the school) but perhaps a 'legitimate source of pressure' (Johnson 1981). McRobbie (1978) stressed the importance of 'appearance' as a form of resistance for adolescent young women. By wearing make-up, jewellery, altering the school uniform, young women often use overtly sexual modes of expression which demonstrate quite clearly that they are overstepping the boundaries of girlhood (as demanded by the school) into womanhood. However, McRobbie argued that young women's own culture then becomes the most efficient agent of social control for by resisting they reaffirm and reinforce patriarchal power relations: 'They are both saved by and locked within the culture of femininity.'

Young women's resistances are not restricted to those involving appearance. Griffin (1981) discussed a further strategy that young women use to negotiate their existence in schools. Most teachers would recognise her description of young women's silence and the 'sullen stare' in classroom encounters.

Schooling and preparation for work

Virgo (1981) claimed that it is the inability of our education system to cope with change which threatens to deny us the benefits of the new technology. A radical restructuring of this system is needed to provide lifelong learning options for the majority of the population rather than a mandarin experience which is irrelevant to the needs and inappropriate to the capabilities of all but a few. We should, therefore, shift resources from non-vocational to vocational education and promote 'lifelong education', predicated upon the individual's need to equip him or herself for the series of distinct and unrelated careers to which he or she will need to adapt in the course of working life. The period of compulsory education should concentrate on the transmission of 'basic skills' which can be identified and foreseen and which can be applied in future trades and professions not yet foreseeable. However, before specifying what political action is required to bring about the necessary reforms, Virgo closed his paper with the assertion that: 'You don't need O-levels to be a road mender, A-level maths to be a computer programmer or a degree to be a systems analyst. Too high a qualification is really a disqualification for a contented, competent employee!'

Underlying these recommendations is the belief that there are two sorts of systematic learning: 'training' which is useful and relevant, and 'education' which is a luxury few want and collectively we cannot afford. In reality, of course, we are not faced with this choice, since education and training are discrete only when the skills to be acquired are utterly trivial.

The trend of the 1980s to equate preparation for life with preparation for economic role may well be a reaction against the equally simplistic cries of the 1960s for education for leisure. Both demands rest upon a false dichotomy between work and leisure, and an unreal distinction between the prerequisites for pleasure and responsibility in the two areas of life. It can well be argued that there is a correlation between the quality of a person's work and the quality of leisure.

Jonathan (1982), in discussing life-long education, argued that: 'Preparation for life cannot be seen as a choice between "educating for leisure" or "training for work".' While Gatherer (1982) indicated that: 'New thinking on this (i.e. 16–19 year) age-group clearly indicates a movement towards strengthening the vocational element in general education and broadening vocational training to cater for the development of the whole person.' Both papers are helpful in highlighting the need for schools to readjust their curricular approaches and in suggesting possible changes in emphasis which schools might employ.

Stonier (1983) has envisaged a not-too-distant future when education would occupy 50 per cent of the workforce, as teachers and students. The British government's responses to youth employment in the 1980s sought to apply part of this remedy. They addressed an alleged mismatch between school-leavers' capabilities and occupational requirements in the service and high-technology sectors which, it is claimed, contain the best hopes for future job creation. Unless the quality of the workforce is improved, the argument runs, economic growth will be retarded, youth unemployment will remain high, and many victims will face jobless adulthoods until demographic shifts change the unemployment situation.

The link between schooling and occupation – and the qualities associated with an employee's role – have been continually stressed in works on education. Nisbet (1957) said: 'Few would deny that preparation for an occupation is one of the tasks of education ... occupation is a role which gives the individual a real and tangible place in the community.'

Coming closer to the present, views can be seen as changing somewhat, although the inherent link between the educational system and occupation is still present: 'The logic of automation ... is not that it creates armies of unskilled workers, but that it makes the unskilled redundant' (Entwistle 1970).

Clearly, education has continued to reflect an emphasis on the value and importance of work. While the modern school may additionally emphasise education for leisure, it is still preparation for leisure within the context of work. Secondary school education has been seen by many pupils, teachers, and parents, as being primarily a preparation for work (e.g. Morton-Williams and Finch 1968; Lindsay 1969; Hendry 1978). Like government vocational training schemes, this stress only helps to reinforce assumptions about the centrality of work in the human life plan, and by implication increases the individual's social and psychological dependence on it. But as Hargreaves indicated:

Very little of our secondary education is strictly vocational: schools are more orientated towards public examinations than towards jobs. Yet for those who leave school at sixteen, a job is the natural next step, one that has been awaited with eagerness for it signifies independence and adult standing.

(Hargreaves 1981: 199)

Findings of Pollock and Nicholson (1981) lend further support to the suspicion that the average (non-academic) teenager saw little benefit being derived from secondary education, although they readily acknowledged the importance of qualifications and take to college, if granted day-release, readily enough.

The evidence reported indicated both criticism and praise for the careers service and guidance teachers. It was apparent that pupils expected careers officers to be much more positive than they were prepared to be: to advise rather than counsel, and to find jobs. No doubt those who settle successfully into a career think more highly of the service than those who do not!

These are hardly surprising results since schools have rarely treated careers as a priority subject, but they operate in a work-like manner. Children become accustomed to tasks offering little intrinsic satisfaction, and to supervisors – their teachers. Perhaps most important, young people's attainments in education allow them to anticipate their future positions in the occupational hierarchy. Early selection, apparently by merit, accustoms young people with modest prospects to subordinate positions, and teaches disadvantaged youth that their destinies are commensurate with their abilities and efforts. Losers in the educational competition become apathetic and difficult to control in secondary schools' lower streams. They acknowledge school's value for individuals with different talents and prospects, but realise how little it can offer them (Birkstead 1976).

Of all the criticisms levelled by employers at school one – the lack of training in skills related to the workplace – does stand out in relation to our major economic competitors. Research undertaken by Prais (1981) on the vocational qualifications of the labour force of Britain and West Germany shows that while both countries are more or less comparable at degree level, West Germany has twice the percentage of workers with intermediate levels of technical and vocational training. Why Britain suffers such a deficiency is easy to see: in Britain just under 70 per cent of school children leave school at 16 and many of these are lost to education for ever.

Jobs accessible to young people with just basic education have declined rapidly. In 1974, 61 per cent of 16-year-olds were in employment; by 1983 only 18 per cent held jobs (Ashton and Maguire 1983).

There are two distinct providers seeking to meet the needs of young people within a society in transition. On the one hand, the education service, traditionally providing for those who remain in full-time education: on the other, the MSC providing the rest. The two services come together where educational consortia exist to cater for technical and vocational education within 16–19 initiatives.

Since the 'Great Debate' of 1976 there have been renewed attempts to promote work experience for secondary school pupils. Virtually all schools are now equipped with computers. Courses in information technology have multiplied. Many of these developments are supported under the MSC's Technical and Vocational Education Initiative (TVEI). By 1984 two-thirds of LEAs in England were involved. Simultaneously, the MSC's role in further education, as financier and arbiter of course content, was strengthened. Young people are being prepared more thoroughly for employment that has become scarcer than ever. Enrolments in part-time further education have risen. Off-the-job training, which usually means college, is mandatory on the YTS. In 1974, 47 per cent of 16-year-olds left school, obtained employment, and severed connections with education. In 1984 only 24 per cent (13 per cent unemployed, and 11 per cent in jobs) had lost contact. However, more young people are staying on at school beyond 16 years, becoming 'new sixth formers', and less than 14 per cent of school-leavers are now completely unqualified.

For those who leave school and move towards adult society schemes have replaced jobs in many early school-leavers' immediate prospects. The scheme is now extended from 12 to 24 months. Successive special measures have been subjected to detailed investigation by the MSC (Bedeman and Courtenay 1983), and independent researchers (Fiddy 1983; Varlaam 1984).

Alongside current educational developments, recent changes in youth labour markets could be nurturing 'enterprise cultures' among certain groups of young people. Some young people are pioneering their own forms of alternation – moving from education into training or employment, then back to college. Current educational trends could be creating an underclass at the bottom, and a more enterprising younger generation in the middle layers of society.

The inadequacy of familiar economic and educational remedies has inspired radical intellectual responses to unemployment, including a broader concept of work. It is pointed out that work need not be in employment. People can work on their own accounts. The rewards may be intrinsic satisfactions or self-provisioning rather than cash (Gershuny 1978).

Instead of educating young people to expect employment, therefore, it has been proposed to orient them towards self-employment, and to encourage youth co-operatives, voluntary service and community projects (Watts 1983).

These responses to unemployment would restore work to local communities wherein, it is anticipated, the inhabitants will develop lifestyles superior to consumerism (Henriksson 1983). Employment supplies the skills, social relationships, tools and, in many instances, other materials that facilitate informal enterprise. But Coleman and Husen (1985) have argued that these new educational practices are helping to create a new underclass. They claimed that, within secondary schools, a tail-end abandons hope and effort, and sometimes attendance, long before the official leaving date. The majority of young people now leave school with some qualifications, so the 'failures' are a disadvantaged minority.

Schooling and unemployment

The British government's responses to youth unemployment have addressed an alleged mismatch between school-leavers' capabilities and occupational requirements in the service and high-technology sectors which, it is claimed contain the best hopes for future job creation. Hence the case for Britain's Technical and Vocational Education Initiative, the Youth Training Scheme, and the Sixteen to Eighteen Action Plan. However, educational solutions to the disappearance of jobs for adolescents seem to be yielding diminishing returns (Bates *et al.* 1984). Young people in Britain are now being given more vocational advice, work experience, and generic skills than ever before. Traditional academic syllabuses are being widened to include up-to-date technical and vocational courses. These attempts to tighten the bonds between schooling and job requirements and to strengthen young people's vocational orientations seem problematic. Holt has argued that the vocational skills of today may well be outdated for use in future society:

> The fact about tomorrow is that it will be different from today, and will present quite new problems. New problems can be solved only by those with the personal and moral autonomy to interpret our culture – by those who have enjoyed a liberal education.
>
> (Holt 1983: 86)

The removal of the prospect of employment for many young people may encourage some adolescents to reject a narrowly academic or vocational curriculum while at school. As Hartley wrote:

> Hitherto, there was little need to formalise the hidden curriculum because its subliminal messages were, for the most part, effectively assimilated. In the main, pupils were adequately socialised by the hidden curriculum to fit into society. Now, however, it appears that pupils cannot be assumed to have acquiesced either in the formal goals of education or in their justification. When teachers justify schooling in vocational terms, the message is questioned by children who know full well that academic credentials are no guarantee of a job, and this will be especially so of low-achievers.
>
> (Hartley 1985: 96)

In offering 'hard facts' Raffe has provided us with trends in youth unemployment from the mid-1970s to the 1980s. Discussing the situation, he wrote:

> The association between qualifications and employment remains strong: Although unemployment rose among qualified school leavers, they retain their relative advantage over the unqualified.
>
> (Raffe 1983)

The pervasive influence of unemployment reaches beyond those adolescents actually out of work. In Hendry *et al.*'s (1984) study, pupils about to enter the job market seemed fully aware of the problems of finding a job, and the school's emphasis on this aspect of unemployment stressed the importance of work in the eyes of the pupils. Their reaction to the immediate future was realistic: they were aware of the problems which might lie ahead in the job market, but there was no indication that the fear of unemployment had destroyed their personal confidence. However, their knowledge of the experiences of unemployment did not appear to have come from the classroom. Very few pupils stated that there had been any discussion of life on the dole or how to cope with large amounts of free time. Further, pupils tended to see future day-to-day living and leisure patterns in terms of the sort of opportunities that only a job could provide. Many adolescents go straight from school to unemployment, and hence any sense of loss is related to expectations about the benefits of work, and to recognition of the lack of status in being unemployed. As Brown pointed out:

> 'What does he do?' remains the most illuminating question to ask about someone met for the first time. It is illuminating precisely because a man's or a woman's work, or the fact that they do not need to or cannot work, is indicative of so much else about their social situation and their likely life experiences . . . .
>
> (Brown 1978: 55)

Thus paid employment is a major factor in defining the parameters of human life. Braun (1977), Dennehy and Sullivan (1977), Hill (1978), and Pahl (1978) all agreed that the unemployed feel a sense of guilt about spending their days in idleness. In Pahl's study, school-leavers were conscious of the gap between the assumption that school is followed by work, and their awareness that in reality they may be forced to deviate from this expected progression.

While work is central in giving structure to the individual's life, it is also important as a key element in popular culture. Trade unions may agitate for increased leisure, but they will also demand the right that everyone should have employment. The idea of constructive unemployment or work outwith the traditional bounds of employment continues to be rejected for more than purely financial reasons. Both the cultural framework of western capitalism and the status or self-esteem of the individual lean heavily, though increasingly precariously, on the concept of work. This helps to explain why, even though work is frequently un-pleasant, boring, and alienating, it is still firmly held to be preferable to unemployment. Jenkins and Sherman summed up this paradox:

> Yet whether skills become outdated or not, whether people start to feel inadequate at work or not, they do feel they have to work – and not just for the money. The work ethic is so deeply engrained in British and other industrialised societies that it has acquired a value in itself even though it is widely regarded as unpleasant.
>
> (Jenkins and Sherman 1979: 2)

It has been suggested that young people without jobs tend to be those with fewest academic qualifications, and they tend to come from families of manual workers in which other people are also unemployed (Holland 1978; Raffe 1983). Reference however, can also be made to other, less easily identifiable factors. Hill *et al.* concluded:

> It is generally recognised that individuals sharing a seeming parity of circumstances and opportunities may yet achieve varying degrees of success, the differences being accounted for by highly individual factors relating to the psychologies of the persons concerned.
>
> (Hill *et al.* 1973)

It may be that some of these factors emerge while adolescents are still at school. First, Holland noted that:

> 42 per cent (of a sample of unemployed young people) had played truant at some stage during their last years at school. The young people tend to be those who vote with their feet about school as they have experienced it.
>
> (Holland 1978)

A second factor is concerned with frequent or 'chronic' job-changing – defined both by Baxter (1975) and Cherry (1976) as those who have had, on average, more than one job every six months. It has been suggested that the type of adolescent who, during times of relatively full employment, changed jobs frequently after leaving school may be particularly vulnerable to longer periods of unemployment as the overall rate of youth unemployment rises (Phillips 1973; Baxter 1975). Thus attributes formerly found to be associated with frequent job-changing may currently be associated with unemployment among young people. On this point, Carter (1966) reported that higher rates of job-changing in young people were associated with 'a refusal to accommodate to discipline', lower academic ability, and immaturity (Carter 1966). Yet pupils with favourable and positive attitudes to school, authority and work, who are rated by teachers as more co-operative and mature, and who attend school regularly and punctually may be as likely to experience similar periods of unemployment on leaving school as those whose attitudes are less favourable towards school and teachers. Lavercombe and Fleming proposed that:

> A school leaver's effectiveness in looking for jobs may be influenced by the information and skills he brings to job-hunting. School leavers may differ not only in attitudes but also in their social skills (influencing how they 'came across' at interviews) and information-seeking skills (including their grasp of job-hunting techniques).
>
> (Lavercombe and Fleming 1981: 42)

Job selection may, of course, also be influenced by relatives or friends of the family 'putting in a good word' with employers on behalf of applicants. In addition, different firms operate various selection procedures, and interpret 'acceptable and desirable attitudes' differently (Mackay 1971).

So employment – and unemployment – may have a multi-faceted impact on the life of individuals, involving such diverse matters as self-esteem and income, lifestyle, and leisure pursuits. This may be particularly important in adolescence. 'When employment is then denied to the young school leaver with his or her scroll of "qualifications" the reaction is naturally one of shock and disappointment, personal crisis and social dislocation' (Hargreaves 1981). A little further thought, however, indicates that this simple assumption is not always justified, and that the relationship between youth unemployment and self-image or self-esteem is a complex one. Closer examination sometimes demonstrates the profound ambivalence exhibited by adolescents towards work. In a different social climate Carter (1971), for instance, argued that many adolescents were not particularly interested in a future job or jobs but rather in 'the status and perquisites of a young worker', and the financial opportunities it offered to develop a rich leisure existence. Murdock and Phelps (1973) suggested that for adolescents the attempt to resolve contradictions contained in the school or work situation through the creation of meaningful styles of leisure frequently took place within the context provided by broadly-based social class sub-cultures. How are these leisure sub-cultures affected when contradictions are created not necessarily in work settings but within the context of unemployment? Schools generally do not seem to have done much in terms of helping pupils to develop the skills and attitudes necessary for a 'leisured existence', but then they are caught in a trap where to educate for leisure can be seen as a euphemism for educating for the dole queue. Hargreaves (1981) commented: 'It is quite easy to see special leisure-based courses for pupils destined for the dole queues, or educational grants, or Youth Opportunity Programmes, as modern instruments of social control.'

Watts pointed out the blurring of concepts of 'work', 'paid employment', 'leisure' and 'unemployment' is an important issue for young people in present-day society:

> The only times I liked school were the times I could play truant. Because then I could go to the local library and study at my leisure. Whereas in school the teachers are hanging over you all the time making pupils nervous. [Non-certificate boy, truanted weeks at a time, unemployed. Quoted in *Tell Them From Me*, edited by Gow and McPherson 1981.]

Schooling and leisure

The importance of leisure has become more apparent in recent years due primarily to shifts in the work–leisure balance in society and to the spectacular increase in unemployment, particularly among young people. Unemployment creates a great deal of 'free' time, but the equation of 'free' time with leisure time has been strongly disputed (Hendry *et al.* 1984). It has been suggested by Leigh (1971) that education for leisure attempts to increase both the true range of choices available and the ability of the individual to make effective and significant choices. The majority of schools attempt to provide leisure education in very similar ways, usually through a mixture of curricular and extra-curricular activities, with the addition of schemes such as the Duke of Edinburgh's Award Scheme and community service. Hence, the activities which educators often see in terms of the leisure lives of pupils are sports, games, art, music, community-based skills and practical subjects, such as woodwork, metalwork, and technical drawing, which, even though they may have a vocational bias in a narrow sense, are useful for 'do it yourself' and recreation (Basini 1975). Often these subjects are also offered to pupils in extra-curricular time.

The restricted appeal of schools in general, and their leisure education programmes in particular, has been commented on by Emmett (1971), Scarlett (1975), Roberts (1983), and Hendry (1983). In designing leisure education programmes, schools may well reject ways in which adolescents actually spend their leisure time simply because these do not conform to the school's view of how leisure should be 'profitably' used:

> Educationists who plead the new problem of leisure as an urgent reason for the development of this or that in the curriculum are expressing, whether they are frank about it or not, their disappointment with the way that people use their time.
>
> (Simpson 1 73: 279)

Thus, it has been found that of the range of extra-curricular activities which the vast majority of schools provide in order to substantiate their claim of providing leisure education, most are only actually pursued by a minority of adolescents – mainly middle-class, academically able pupils and young men rather than women (Hendry 1983). The less organised 'fun' orientation in the leisure activities of working-class adolescent males is not so well catered for within schools' leisure education programmes (see Figure 8.1). Hendry (ibid.) has argued that there is an adolescent leisure focus which *in general* shifts from adult-organised through casual to commercially oriented leisure, and these transitions occur roughly at the ages when certain major relationship issues – sex, peers, parents – come into focus (Coleman 1979).

But young women also need 'space' to develop confidence and leisure interests. This is especially true in mixed schools for the evidence clearly indicates that in all social situations males dominate space (Spender 1982; Young 1980). In co-educational schools the primary female-only space is in toilets, cloakrooms, and changing rooms. These are the areas where young women 'hang out', where they spend time together away from 'the lads' and the teachers (Griffin *et al.* 1982). It might be a positive move to open

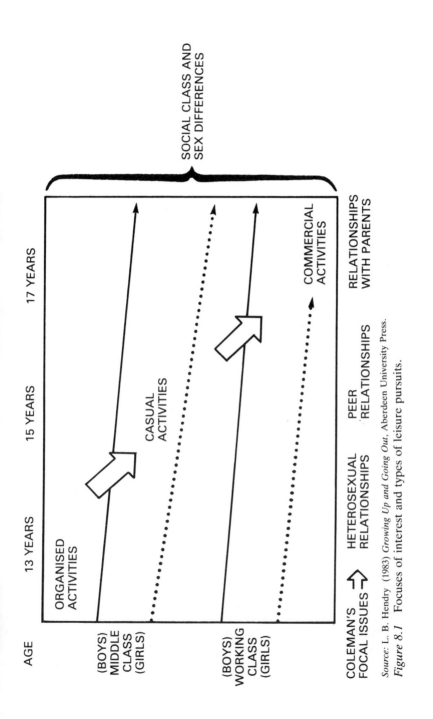

Source: L. B. Hendry (1983) *Growing Up and Going Out*, Aberdeen University Press.
Figure 8.1 Focuses of interest and types of leisure pursuits.

up leisure facilities during breaks, lunchtime, and after school to encourage young women to use the space available for their 'leisure' whether it be netball, table tennis, or chatting with a friend.

It is clear, therefore, that school influences provide important constraints and opportunities for young people's leisure. In Hendry and Marr's (1985) study all schools reported an extensive range of available extra-curricular activities. Yet, despite this range, these findings provided evidence (as do other studies) that about one-third of pupils were regularly involved in the extra-curricular life of the school, while more than half were completely non-participant.

A diversity of approach to the question of leisure education was clearly evident in the schools surveyed. Hobbies, sport, and extra-curricular activities were nevertheless seen by most schools to be self-evidently worthwhile leisure pursuits, and figured prominently with schools' leisure provision (Hendry and Marr 1985).

The majority of schools perceive non-participation to be explicable in terms of the pupils' attitudes, abilities, and so on rather than in terms of inappropriate approaches and attitudes. Mundy and Odum (1979) have proposed an 'enabling' approach that aims to develop a person's ability to think through, evaluate, and make his or her own decisions and choices regarding leisure while understanding the impact of his or her choices upon his or her own life and upon others in society. Thus, Mundy and Odum favour the learning of decision making and evaluative/social skills. Such training, they argued would allow pupils to '. . . develop a cognitive, conscious awareness of their own behaviour and beliefs . . . establish criteria for leisure issues and decisions . . . and develop skills related to enriching self-determination, pro-activity and meaningful control over their own leisure lives' (Mundy and Odum 1979). But schools have tended to concentrate on providing short-term recreational and activity skills rather than equipping pupils with such attitudes and social skills that may enable them to organise, select, and participate in chosen leisure pursuits in post-school years (see Figure 8.2).

Hence, both the formal leisure education curriculum and the extra-curriculum can alienate and disaffect a large number of adolescents (Hendry 1983). Certainly, Leigh has argued that leisure activities have been seen as a means to achieving personal and social development for some pupils, but little attention has been paid to future interests, abilities and skills:

> It is dangerous to assume that those who do take part in school clubs and societies necessarily participate very much either in

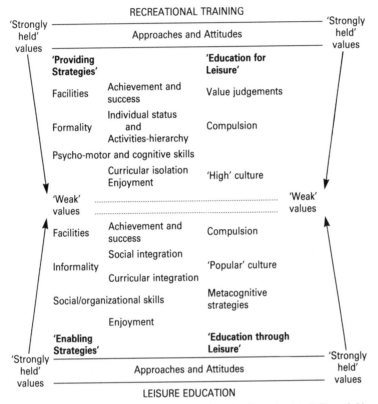

RECREATIONAL TRAINING

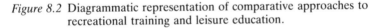

Source: L. B. Hendry (1986) 'Changing schools in a changing society', in J. Evans (ed.) *Physical Education Sport and Schooling*, London: Falmer Press.

Figure 8.2 Diagrammatic representation of comparative approaches to recreational training and leisure education.

the practical organisation of the activity with which they are concerned or in the social organisation of the group with which they are involved . . . .

(Leigh 1971: 14)

The experiences of adolescents within the school setting may have repercussions for their attitudes towards competence to cope with, and ability to adjust to, the adult world of work, or unemployment and leisure.

Young people and adult society

Starting work

School leavers over the years have complained of the failure of
the education system to equip them for the labour market (Keil
1978; Youthaid 1979; Pollock and Nicholson 1981; West and
Newton 1983). Kaneti-Barry *et al.*'s (1971) survey of over 2,000
sixth formers found that only 18 per cent had discussed their
further education courses with teachers, while universities had
provided few occupational role models for students to emulate and
evaluate, and had not encouraged much vocational exploration
(Ching 1970). Even vocational courses presume prior commitment
(Kelsall *et al.* 1972; Gothard 1982).

Yet the transition from school to work holds certain continuities
for many working-class adolescents. The informal shop-floor
culture of the factory has some marked similarities with the
counter-school culture:

> Most work – or the 'grafting' they accept they will face – is
> equilibrated by the overwhelming need for instant money, the
> assumption that all work is unpleasant and that what really
> matters is the potential particular work situations hold for self
> and particularly masculine expression, diversion and 'laffs' as
> learnt in the counter-school culture. These things are quite
> separate from the intrinsic nature of any task.
>
> (Willis 1977: 100)

Nevertheless, unqualified and unskilled adolescents may have
special work related problems because the young have always
been at risk of being jettisoned by employers at the point when
they become entitled to a full adult wage. According to Frith
(1978), ten years ago the 'job mobility' of unskilled youths
reflected both their own readiness to leave when 'fed up' and their
employers' readiness to sack them for 'disciplinary problems'. This
pattern is not dissimilar to the dilemmas involved in governmental
training schemes in the late 1980s.

Throughout the decades of full employment, job mobility was
high among young unskilled workers. Ferguson and Cunnison's
(1951) Glasgow school-leavers held an average of 2.77 different
jobs in their first three years in the work force, and in Carter's
(1962) Sheffield study 60 per cent of the young people changed
jobs during their initial six months. Maizels did not find the rate of
job changing in her London enquiry surprising. She considered
most of the jobs on offer to be unsuitable for young people:

Since few occupations allow for the full time use of talents, while a large proportion of jobs for adolescents, as adults, require little technical or other skill, any match achieved is minimal. In many cases it depends on the capacity of the individual to modify his inclinations, and to function with many of his known and unknown talents dormant.

(Maizels 1970: 275)

Maizels argued that:

the present requirements of the economic and social structure conflict with the needs of young adolescents to develop and assert their true individuality.

(Ibid.)

Hence, rather than indicating that young unskilled workers were unable to settle, their frequent job changing could be interpreted as a rational use of limited opportunities (Roberts 1981). Young people's choices and employers' decisions were inevitably provisional, though both parties seemed to have been able to cope with the uncertainty by using a variety of strategies including changing jobs (Waddington 1982). Individuals moved to obtain pay increases, to reduce travelling costs and, sometimes, simply for variety or to relieve boredom. Mobility did not appear to damage young unskilled workers' career prospects.

Media images of young people earning a wage to be spent solely in hedonistic leisure pursuits were, and are, distorted pictures of youth. It would seem that a frequent desire of young school leavers was to find 'interesting work' (Sykes 1953; Crowther Report 1959; Hale 1971).

Over the past few decades, the majority of young people travelled along well-signposted trajectories. Their home backgrounds and educational streams enabled them to anticipate their initial occupations and the types of adult employment to which these early jobs would lead, and they were realistic about their occupational prospects. On entering employment, adolescent workers needed to learn both technical and social skills, and to adjust to new daily routines. Yet problems with workmates, bosses, and coping with a longer working day were usually resolved within weeks (e.g. Palmer 1964). In most cases, when jobs were available, there was no clash between the new demands to which young workers were exposed, and the latter's aspirations and self-images (Ashton and Field 1976).

Occupational socialisation has been studied most frequently in professions such as medicine, nursing, and engineering where

181

recruitment and training progress in clear stages (Merton, Reader, and Kendall 1957; Becker and Carper 1956a and 1956b; Becker 1963; Simpson 1979), but similar on-the-job socialisation has been observed among apprentice electricians, printers, hairdressers, and business machine operators (Geer 1972; Flude 1977; Reimer 1977). As apprentices acquire craft knowledge and skills, they also develop occupational identities.

Thus some young people are socialised into occupations by positively identifying with the skills involved; while others, having built up a number of material and social benefits and perks (e.g. attractive salary, less arduous jobs, life insurance schemes, longer holidays) within their work situations are reluctant to place them at risk by leaving (Freedman 1969; Krause 1971; Mann 1973).

Even in a society with declared equal opportunities young women and young men's vocational aspirations differ. Homes and schools separate the sexes' aspirations like the labour market divides their opportunities. In general, young women's occupational horizons are more limited than young men's (Wilkins 1955; Douvan and Adelson 1966; Closs *et al.* 1977). While the sexes' aspirations are actually less divided than their actual occupational opportunities, girls are still more likely than boys to abandon first choices and lower their sights when difficulties arise. An American study of unsuccessful medical school applicants found that women are less likely to reapply and more likely to abandon medicine for less prestigious careers (Weisman *et al.* 1976).

For adolescents, smooth transitions from education to adult occupations are never guaranteed. Sometimes young people's inability to settle occupationally may be a symptom of deeper socio-psychological disturbance: work can be just one of many situations to which they are unable to adjust (Logan and Goldberg 1954; Wilkins 1955). Research has identified a minority of chronic job-changers who seem unable to settle in any occupation (Department of Employment 1970; Baxter 1975). In other instances, adolescents are unable to find occupations compatible with aspirations and self-concepts developed during childhood, and this situation can be particularly problematic at a time of economic and technological change.

The work–leisure 'package'

Hendry and Raymond (1983) revealed a number of important connections between work and leisure from the adolescents' perspective. Simon (1978) has pointed out that enthusiasm for working life tends to evaporate quickly on leaving school. This was reflected in the cynical attitude to work expressed by employed school leavers in their study. Even those in skilled jobs or learning a trade (the most popular aspiration among school pupils) felt there was little intrinsic satisfaction in working. As a source of money, as a chance to be with friends, and as an alternative to the boredom of unemployment, work was acceptable. But there was evidence that the scarcity of job opportunities meant that teenagers were more likely to suffer their present unenjoyable and uninteresting work than to risk becoming unemployed in an unsuccessful attempt to seek out a more personally satisfying job. Interviews with post-school adolescents suggested that those with a job tended to make more use of commercial leisure activities: and most of the employed group saw the value of leisure in terms of escape or relaxation from work (Parker 1983). There was some indication that those with more demanding jobs pursued more demanding leisure. Like pupils, they saw work and leisure as a package each giving the other meaning. Hence, work can provide a variety of satisfactions, including achievement, recognition, responsibility, and intrinsic pleasure. Work also imposes a time structure, and provides opportunities for social interaction and for the development of identity and self-esteem (Kelvin 1981). Jahoda (1979) listed five basic needs that are met by the structured framework of employment:

1. Work provides a true structure for the day, the week, and the year.
2. Work implies regularly shared experiences outside the family.
3. Work links the individual to goals and purposes that transcend his or her own.
4. Work defines aspects of personal status and identity.
5. Work enforces activity.

Conversely, to be unemployed, places the individual outside this accepted, taken-for-granted system. It puts in question one's capacity to carry responsibility for oneself, let alone for one's dependants. The demise of large-scale, labour-intensive, and repetitive work has far-reaching consequences in altering the relationship between work and leisure.

Being unemployed

In October 1984 Youthaid estimated that half the country's under-18s and one in four under-25s were out of work. Over half a million under-25-year-olds had been unemployed for more than six months, and there were over quarter of a million unemployed young people aged 18 and over who had *never* had a full-time job since leaving school. On the other hand, it has been suggested that with the introduction of the extended (two-year) Youth Training Scheme no one under the age of 18 years need be unemployed! Of course, Y.T.S. may be perceived by young people equally as a 'gang plank to the dole' or a 'permanent bridge to work'.

Kelvin (1981) has suggested that unemployment is becoming an acceptable aspect of young people's self-perceptions and self-identity as more and more adolescents fail to find a niche in the job market when they leave school. In connection with this, Bloxham (1984) has made a plea for the development of lifeskills within the vocational structure of Youth Training Schemes which would help young people to cope with unemployment if they cannot find work at the end of the course. Yet, there is little research evidence to suggest that the experience of Y.T.S. had helped prepare adolescents for a return to a 'leisured' existence on the dole. Further, there is a crucial unresolved conflict in that Y.T.S. encourages a vocational perception among trainees, yet it leaves them without the sure identity of being a young worker and confers no promise that this status will even be achieved in their future lives.

It must be admitted that as the Scheme becomes more established as part of the educational landscape of post-school life, the low social status of trainees may become less pronounced. However, the growing importance of the Scheme makes it imperative that research continues to monitor not only its impact on the ability of young people to find work but also on a wider network of psycho-social factors which may be necessary aspects of a truly rounded process of socialisation for adolescents in modern Britain.

A study by Hendry and Raymond (1986) showed that Y.T.S. trainees were 'caught' between their own perceptions of the Scheme and the cynicism – and sometimes scorn – of both their employed and unemployed peers. Although critical of some aspects of the Scheme, trainees were quick to refute suggestions that it implied they lacked the qualities necessary to find a 'real' job. It was perhaps not surprising that trainees displayed little regret that they had few contacts with adolescents in other employment statuses. The lack of interaction between trainees and young workers extended to leisure contacts. For trainees there was more contact with unemployed adolescents than with young workers. As Hendry and Raymond (1985) argued previously, the lack of contact between different groups of young people – unemployed, workers, and trainees – can develop narrow attitudes about work and working life.

We live in a society where much more than financial independence is at stake through lack of work. Because of the continuing emphasis placed on jobs, even within the context of high levels of unemployment, lack of work stands to equate with lack of individual identity. No age group finds this experience liberating (Martin 1983; Breakwell 1983; Kelvin *et al.* 1984).

A combination of pressures leaves many adolescents feeling that their unemployment is their own fault. They blame themselves for failing to search hard enough, or for their inability to impress employers (Breakwell 1983). Some find all social contact painful. It exposes the stigma of unemployment. One reason why illness rises among the unemployed is that a 'sick' role may be a more acceptable status (Fagin and Little 1984). However, reduced income is the main reason why unemployment depresses leisure activity. Researchers have stressed that it is difficult, probably impossible, to separate the effects of unemployment and poverty (Kelvin *et al.* 1984). Roberts (1986) has indicated that unemployed young people are precluded from participation in the activities of the post-work or leisure culture as these generally are often commercial–consumer activities and require some expenditure. Further, conversations with peers in the leisure context may revolve around work. Seabrook (1982) talked of unemployed youth as spectators rather than consumers in a market society which has expropriated, packaged, and offered for sale most areas of family and leisure life. Thus, the research evidence is clear: few young people respond pro-actively to unemployment (Fryer and Payne 1984). The experience is usually considered 'an ordeal' (Hendry *et al.* 1984); young people resent the restrictions surrounding unemployment. Compared with teenagers in jobs, the young unemployed worry more about their dress, appearance, and money (D.E.S. 1983). They are more prone to loneliness, anxiety, and self-doubt. Smith (1986) stated that evidence shows 'beyond all reasonable doubt' that unemployed individuals die earlier, especially by suicide, and suffer more physical and mental ill-health than those in work (Banks *et al.* 1984). According to one study, long-term youth unemployment is related to suicidal tendencies (Francis 1985).

Jahoda (1979; 1982) emphasised the personal demoralisation and social decay that spread during the Great Depression, and has argued that the effects of unemployment today are basically unchanged. Other writers have echoed this position, insisting that poverty, stigma, shame, and social isolation descend as harshly as ever (Sinfield 1981; Marsden 1982).

In general, unemployed youth want decent jobs or the education and training that will open up such prospects, put cash in their pockets and enable them to enjoy conventional leisure. Turner *et al.* (1983) reported that young people place even more stress than their parents on economic rewards from employment. The British working class has long regarded the contours of inequality and the labour market as 'beyond control' (Blackburn and Mann 1979). Hence, workers' renowned fatalism and stoicism. Their first response to unemployment is usually to convince themselves that the predicament is 'abnormal', and hopefully temporary.

First reactions on becoming unemployed are usually to seek personal escapes. Like unemployed adults, jobless teenagers do not merge into a solidaristic army. They are divided by race, gender, education, family backgrounds, and previous occupations. Many insist that they do not belong among 'that crowd', the dole queue regulars. It has been argued that the unemployed have not been mobilised as a political force because they are offered no ideologies linking their personal predicaments to political action (Scholzman and Verba 1980). But another reason for preferring personal rather than collective solutions is that, for the majority, the former work. The majority find it simpler and earn much greater respect by devising individual escapes than by uniting with their unemployed fellows. Clubs for the unemployed do not recruit huge memberships. The unemployed display little interest in concessionary admissions to cinemas and sports centres. They want to lose, not publicly proclaim, their unemployed status (Town 1983).

The Social World of the Young Unemployed (1987) reported that views expressed by young people 'tend towards passive acceptance' of being out of work:

> Either young people do not feel cheated because they accept the idea that one must work for one's money – and they do not, or they feel cheated because they realise that it is something they must simply come to terms with.

> (White 1987)

Young men did not have the same sense of isolation or anger felt by young women, and while many youngsters wanted to have more money to spend they did not argue for direct action to change their situation.

> Rather than unemployment creating a pool of hostile young people desirous of overthrowing society, what it seems to be creating is an ever larger pool of young people waiting for their turn to join society.

> (Ibid.)

But family pressures can be greatly increased by having a young unemployed son or daughter in the home, with constant bickering over petty issues.

Work generally kept family members quiet and out of each other's way during the day but: 'Some mothers complained of young unemployed people being underfoot all the time.'

The report said parents often wanted their offspring to demonstrate a willingness to comply with parental standards, for example by regularly handing over money for their keep.

Donovan and Oddy (1982) pointed out that the unemployed school leaver and the unemployed adult cannot be treated in homogeneous fashion because the former in unemployment suffers a denial of the traditional *rites de passage* into adulthood, while for the latter, deprivation is about a loss of established identity and status.

In a longitudinal study of school leavers, Tiggeman and Winfield (1984) reported that the self-esteem of all young people in their sample improved on leaving school with greatest increments for those securing jobs, while in another investigation Dowling and O'Brien (1981) found no diminution of work commitment in unemployed school leavers after a year on the dole. On the other hand, Jackson and Banks (1982) argued that commitment to work moderates the impact of unemployment – low work commitment on the part of unemployed youth could be construed as a realistic coping strategy enabling them to guard against diminished psychological well-being and, in particular, the effects on self-esteem of cumulative job rejection.

Feather (1982) suggested that the negative experiences of unemployment effect cognitive and affective changes relating to one's view of self. This in turn may exacerbate the negative impact of the experience itself. 'When a boy or girl personally accepts the label "unemployed" the subjective environment changes; it becomes a state of inactivity and lassitude, where personal powers cannot be adequately used or expressed' (Kitwood 1980). Equally, Fagin (1981) wrote that 'unemployment leaves scars which remain even after re-employment, in terms of irreparable damage to confidence and esteem'; and in Australia, Feather (1982) compared young employed and unemployed respondents in a cross sectional study and found that unemployed adolescents had lower esteem than those in employment. Hartley (1980) spoke of the 'atrophied self esteem' of the unemployed individual resulting in overall life dissatisfactions.

Gurney (1982) found that unemployed leavers were more likely to believe themselves powerless to change circumstances (i.e.

external focus) and may gradually make internal attributions about their predicament. Likewise, Furnham (1984) proposed that a young person's attributions about getting a job were more frequently internal rather than environmental or societal. Failure to get a job was seldom attributed to internal factors, supporting the general psychological claim that success is attributed to internal factors while failure is projected to external factors, hence protecting self-esteem.

It is when the individual adolescent begins to feel alienated and worthless that the malignancy of unemployment begins to erode confidence and stability. Feather and Barber (1983) distinguished two depressive reactions to unemployment. The first was a situation-specific reaction that accompanied failure to find work and reflected frustrated work motivation. Drawing on expectancy-valence theory they stated that negative affective reactions that are involved in failing to secure employment correspond to those that may follow any successful attempt to achieve a positively valued goal when expectations are within the realm of possibility while at the same time goal attainment is blocked by external forces. The second depressive reaction was conceived of as a set of symptoms that might follow prolonged and repeated periods of unemployment which brings with it a more general focus involving self-blame, diminished self-esteem, and reduced self-belief about changing negative situations or conditions.

Hendry *et al.* (1984) suggested that three broad, yet distinct, descriptions can be noted in adolescents' expressions of the experience of unemployment. These descriptions indicate possible variations which may exist in the way young people regard unemployment; being unemployed does not have the same meaning for each adolescent. Within their sample, unemployment, as interpreted by the researchers, was viewed as being 'vocational', 'vacational', or 'an ordeal'.

Unemployment was interpreted as 'an ordeal' – and this was the major perception – if the adolescent saw it as time which should be spent at work. Further, rejected job applications, lack of day-to-day structure, and continuing boredom had led in many cases to a feeling of apathy which affected any enthusiasm for tackling problems.

When the adolescent perceived unemployment as a long-term 'career' or in terms of a temporary escape from the constraints of work, then the experience seemed to be given a more positive meaning. By seeing the experience as a 'holiday' from the constraints of work, a few adolescents had given their period of unemployment some meaning.

Others tried to treat unemployment as much like work as possible. The formalities and obligations of 'signing on' and looking for work took on a disproportionate importance as a way of structuring time and giving the experience some kind of direction and meaning. In the same way as it was possible to identify different 'meanings' of unemployment, it was also possible to identify a variety of responses to the problem of free-time among the adolescents in the sub-sample. The variations in lifestyle, therefore, can perhaps best be identified on a continuum of fairly consistent living patterns ranging between relatively rigidly structured use of time to completely unstructured time.

In Hendry and Raymond's (1983) study pupils in schools often referred to the unemployed as 'layabouts' and 'hooligans', but there was no sense that the unemployed necessarily blamed themselves for their situation. As one pointed out, the workless state was: 'Like seven Sundays, not even seven Saturdays!' Interestingly, about one quarter of the unemployed teenage boys interviewed by Hendry and Raymond mentioned that unemployment leads to boredom, and this in turn leads to thoughts of exciting and possibly delinquent activities. There is some evidence (e.g. Murray 1978) that periods of youth unemployment can lead to the development of uncooperative and disenchanted attitudes. When this feeling of early failure is coupled with unofficial discrimination, as in the case of ethnic minorities, the consequences can be very disturbing. As one of the boys Murray interviewed explained:

Working here is better than being on the dole because when you're on the dole you have all day to yourself, you start doing daft things. Breaking and entering and things like that, because, well, for a bit of excitement and the dole money isn't all that good.

(Murray 1978)

A retrospective look at unemployment came from one girl who was involved in a Youth Opportunities Programme placement and who spoke graphically of the importance of work as a social context for making friends:

It's hard to remember what I did when I was unemployed, there was nothing definite ... I went shopping down the town, but always on my own ... it got very lonely, there was no way to meet people. There's no way of making friends when you're unemployed. I'm getting out with people in the evenings more often now that I'm working.

(Hendry and Raymond 1983: 37)

Economic and social changes portend a number of paradoxes for young people. First, the present position of youth in society has been structured by government policy. Instead of developing a potentially flexible, innovatively-minded future workforce training schemes offer low status, relatively poorly rewarded two-year 'apprenticeships' with no guarantees of full worker status on completion of training. Second, it is now law that adolescents *must* join a Youth Training Scheme to enable them to claim social benefits, yet prospective employers need not be involved in this arrangement. Hence, in some areas of the country there are insufficient places for young people to join schemes: Thus Y.T.S. opportunities are extremely restricted in some regions. Third, this situation, in turn, reduces the consumer leisure spending powers of young people, which is quite different from the expressive, and commercially viable, leisure youth sub-cultures of 'the swinging sixties'.

Denial of the work–leisure 'package'

Being unable to find work appears to frustrate many adolescents' expectations of post-school patterns of work and leisure. The frustration of the work–leisure 'package-deal' spoken of by young people may make growing up more difficult for the adolescent who cannot find a job.

The relationship between unemployment and leisure is a vital element in our understanding of how unemployment affects the individual. The time during the day when the adolescent feels he or she should be working becomes 'free time', not extended leisure time. The majority of unemployed adolescents see this free time as 'wasted time' and as an empty, unpleasant experience.

Concerns about youth unemployment often centre on the 'future-orientation' of young people and the effects of unemployment on their mental and physical welfare.

Willis (1984) believed that 'one real possibility is simply depression, disorientation, personal decline and pathology'. Discussing adolescents, Jahoda wrote:

This is the age group on whose skills, motivation to work and general outlook on the world in which they live the whole of the country will depend in the next decades. Many of them are without hope, without plans and without ambition and are gradually abandoning the habits and aspirations that family and school had tried to instil in them.

(Jahoda 1982: 91)

While Feather (1983) feared that continued unemployment might result in 'adults who will not be of help to themselves or society as a whole'.

Hence, the impact of unemployment on adolescence is clearly complex and far-reaching. Hendry *et al.* (1984) pointed out that pupils about to enter the job-market tended to view future day-to-day living and leisure patterns in terms of the opportunities that only a job could provide. They envisaged a shift away from sports, hobbies, and youth clubs towards new, more sophisticated 'adult' leisure interests. Seen together with their enthusiasm for a working life, their view of the future seemed to amount to a 'package deal' where both work and increasingly sophisticated forms of leisure would create facets of an adult lifestyle. This view of work and leisure in post-school life offering status and independence is, in their eyes, necessarily dependent on finding a job.

Like adults, unemployed teenagers are cut off from the culture of work which also curtails their leisure activities. If they continue to visit pubs and cafes they spend less. They are less likely to reduce their frequency of activity than their expenditure. When they 'go out' they usually remain close to their homes. Local discos replace city-centre nightspots. Even travelling costs are prohibitive. Yet attendance at youth clubs is perceived as a 'childish' pursuit by older adolescents.

However, unemployed young people appear better able than adults to protect their leisure. Their peer groups are more resilient (Warr 1983). Out-of-work youth spend more, not less, time with peers than when in employment. But reactions to unemployment depend upon which young people are affected (see Figure 8.3). Unqualified school-leavers from unskilled working-class homes, and young people with impressive credentials and aspiring parents do not respond in identical ways when offered (or denied) identical opportunities. Boys' peer groups are more resilient than girls'. The former are the more skilled in colonising streets and other environments to enjoy each other's company. Rather than finding it 'less of a problem', girls may be the more injured by unemployment. Unemployed ethnic minority youth appear less likely than native-born whites to accept their bad luck, and more likely to regard themselves as victims of an unjust society (Roberts 1983).

	'Good' unemployment has	'Bad' unemployment has
1. Money	more	less
2. Variety	more	less
3. Goals, Traction	more	less
4. Decision latitude	more	less
5. Skill use/development	more	less
6. Psychological threat	less	more
7. Security	more	less
8. Interpersonal contact	more	less
9. Valued social position	more	less

Source: P. Warr (1983) *Bulletin of the British Psychological Society* 36.

Figure 8.3 Characteristics of psychologically 'good' and psychologically 'bad' unemployment.

The major impact of unemployment on adolescents seems to be its ultimate effect on the transition from adolescence to adulthood. Being unable to find work appears to frustrate adolescents' expectations of post-school patterns of work and leisure. Unemployment creates a structureless time-state for some adolescents within which leisure with all its concomitant social opportunities vanishes. Unemployment, even in the short term, redefines the individual's conception of leisure time. As De Grazia (1962) wrote: 'Work is the antonym of free-time. But not of leisure. Leisure and free-time live in two different worlds . . . . Anyone can have free-time.'

Hendry and Raymond (1983) indicated that this relationship determines the attitudes school leavers have towards leisure. 'You can only have leisure when you're working – you'd enjoy yourself more in your free time if you're working.' The unemployed adolescents in their study felt that they were being excluded from the more 'adult' leisure of their employed contemporaries: 'I'm too old for youth clubs now'. 'You can't go out with your mates when they're working, they've got more money than you've got.'

Hendry *et al.* (1984) also discovered that a major consequence of unemployment was the adolescents' conception of their workless status as denying them entry into the 'package' of work and leisure which makes up 'adult' lifestyle. In addition, Coffield *et al.* (1983) noted how the young unemployed lacked the financial resources to play an active part in the culture of young workers. This isolation from working peers led Roberts (1983) to suggest that the young unemployed are not being socialised into the culture of work. None of the adolescents investigated by Hendry and Raymond (1985) had broken into this 'adult' package of work-related leisure. Financial constraints meant that only very few visits could be made to pubs or discos. Cheap, informal, often passive leisure activities were more usual for both boys and girls.

Although Y.T.S. trainees felt their leisure would improve if they had a 'real' job, their fairly high level of satisfaction with their evening leisure is explained by the fact that they had a purpose to their free time, that is as relaxation from their daily work. Brenner and Bartell (1983) isolated the positive use of free time as being the single most reliable predictor of psychological well-being during unemployment; and Hepworth (1980) and Warr and Payne (1983) also stressed the psychological dangers if time is unstructured and directionless.

As Ingham (1987) has suggested, leisure may be significant in creating opportunities for identity development, social meaning, levels of competence, and intrinsic satisfactions in adolescence. This is possible because alternative forms of self-presentation and style can be tried out without dire consequences should they fail to impress. At the same time these individualistic aspects of behaviour are carried out within institutionally defined roles, with relatively expected and predictable behaviours and rules. Adolescents need to learn these skills in planning, self-orientation, and organisation in the social and leisure domains as well as in cognitive and work-related spheres in order to develop a clear-cut personal and social identity. However, leisure activities do not generate income. Moreover, while they can fill time, leisure pursuits, being voluntary, cannot impose a structure on days, weeks, and months. Insofar as they are practised for intrinsic personal rewards rather than for their value to others, leisure interests cannot become bases for socially esteemed identities. The Association of Recreation Managers (1981) has found scant evidence of successful programmes for the unemployed. This is not only because the unemployed are a fluid population from whom no long-term commitment can be expected, and because reduced charges may still be too high while even free access will not attract the bored and isolated (Town 1983). Free admissions to sports halls are simply no solution to the problems of families struggling on low incomes. Opportunities to play are no answer when people want jobs.

In Hendry and Raymond's (1983) study some adolescents had made no attempt to structure the large amounts of free time available to them. Others had developed a structure revolving around the fact of being unemployed, using visits to 'sign on' or seek work as the organising pivots of their week. Girls, they noted, tended to drift into a structure closely related to a traditional domestic role, becoming unpaid housekeepers to their family. While taking on this role imposes a rigid structure on the individual's time (which may be welcome), it also raises important questions. The decline of work should not mean that women find themselves constrained by domestic roles while the possible development of alternative lifestyles is available to men.

Youth unemployment has become equally prevalent among girls and boys. Competition from experienced married women and labour cutbacks in the light manufacturing industries that once recruited large numbers of female school-leavers have reduced girls' opportunities. During periods out of work, many girls still retreat into their homes, but few revel in the enforced domesticity (Donovan and Oddy 1982). It is considered less acceptable for girls than boys to hang about in pubs, clubs, arcades, and on the streets. Girls who are 'kept in' helping their mothers usually resent their confinement and their isolation from youth scenes; their inability to dress in the latest fashions, attend discos, and socialise with workmates (Roberts *et al.* 1981). Hendry and Raymond's investigation showed that sports and hobbies – the sort of leisure activities encouraged by the schools – were not considered to be important in structuring leisure in the unemployed situation, a fact backed up by the low carry-over effect of school leisure activities among the school leavers.

Jahoda (1979; 1981) has argued that leisure activities cannot replace employment because the latter uniquely provides the necessary conditions for good psychological health. These relate both to the manifest functions of employment (primarily money) and to the latent functions of employment (imposed time structure, regular shared experience and contact outside the family, links to transcending goals and purposes, definition of status and identity, and enforced activity). She proposed that the supportive nature of institutions, and their power, is so taken for granted that their effects only become apparent when they break down, as in unemployment (Jahoda 1984). This 'deprivation hypothesis' has been challenged by Fryer and Payne (1984) on the grounds that some unemployed people respond proactively to their condition and do not appear to suffer the typical negative consequences of joblessness. Further, Fryer and Payne proposed a distinction between unemployment, on the one hand, and leisure, on the other. They criticised the dominant negativity of the former compared with the dominant optimistic mode of the latter. They call for greater attention to be paid to viewing individuals as active agents. The emerging framework:

> should recognise both agency and dependency as fundamental aspects of the human condition, investigate and explain positive and negative features of unemployment and leisure, and operate in a context broader than the left-overs from a time and value structure imposed in employment or what remains when one is deprived of employment.
>
> (Fryer and Payne 1984: 294)

The quality of children's play can have important effects on their subsequent adolescent adjustment by enabling higher levels of intrinsic motivation to be experienced. To the extent that encouraging intrinsic motivation may encourage proactive behaviour, then it could be argued that similar efforts could be made with those adolescents without employment in an attempt to enable more positive (subjectively defined) use of their time.

Related to this area is the increasing interest in the notion of commitment and the nature of meaningful pursuits. Haworth (1984) has pointed to the sparse knowledge in the area concerned with the factors producing individual differences in commitment, and to the different terms by which the relevant variables are labelled (e.g. 'resourcefulness', 'hardiness', 'self-efficacy appraisal', and so on). Some isolated pieces of work have been conducted in this area, for example Stebbins' (1982) analysis of 'serious leisure', which it is felt can provide many of the categories of experience normally provided by employment.

By interpreting the effects of a variety of factors, which may combine to create an overall positive or negative effect, an understanding of particular individual reactions that shape the experience of youth unemployment may be possible. There is an immediate paradox: a number of these factors have the potential either to cause distress or to provide support. This point is illustrated in Figure 8.4, which shows how different orientations of the same factor can (theoretically) have a positive or a disruptive influence on the individual unemployed adolescent.

The unemployed adolescent will usually undergo a mixture of positive and negative experiences. It is only when a number of negative factors impinge on the individual concurrently, and cumulatively, that unemployment becomes an ordeal like other adolescent crises proposed by Coleman (1979). Often the influence of several positive factors can allow the unemployed youth to cope relatively easily with the experience. Rather like

Work, unemployment, and leisure

− Negative orientation   + Positive orientation

− Negative orientation		+ Positive orientation
Low, guilt, self-blame	◄—— SELF-IMAGE	——► Defensively high
Devalued, low	◄—— ASPIRATIONS	——► High
Isolation	◄—— SOCIALISATION with peers	——► Contact with peers
No freedom, low structure	◄—— TIME USE/STRUCTURE	——► Structure, purpose self-responsibility
Pressure, stress	◄—— FAMILY	——► Support, sympathy
Not 'adult', frustrating	◄—— LEISURE	——► 'Appropriate', acceptable
Not useful	◄—— EDUCATION	——► Helpful, useful
Rejected, hostility	◄—— YOUTH Training Schemes	——► Involvement
− Negative orientation		+ Positive orientation

Source: L. B. Hendry (1987) *Unemployment – Personal and Social Consequences,* London: Tavistock.

Figure 8.4 Factors influencing the experience of unemployment.

Coleman's theory of adolescent focal issues, the reality of the process of unemployment can be viewed as a series of different psychological and social issues hitting the individual sequentially. Problems occur when several issues overlap. These factors, in combination, produce the elements around which coping strategies develop or a growing state of distress emerges in the face of unemployment.

Young people in society – rites of passage

Coffield *et al.* (1986) pointed out that leaving school, starting a job, associating with older people, and most important, being treated as an equal by parents and other adults, were judged by young people as crucial elements in growing up. Simply imitating adults was not sufficient: 'Some people think that to become a man all you need to do is drink, smoke and have sex.' (Young man quoted in Coffield *et al.* 1986.) Yet today's young people who do

196

not regard their current employment as lifelong, and who are equipping themselves to cope with economic, technological, and occupational change, are probably better attuned to their future lifestyle than others. Nowadays, young people who are learning to live with impermanence, in temporary relationships, may have stronger claims to maturity than those seeking occupations in which to remain for life, and settling into lifelong liaisons with opposite-sexed partners.

There are many reasons why persistent unemployment in the 1980s has not become a social, political, or economic crisis. Many teenagers have devised effective coping strategies, and these are individualistic and involve seeking personal escapes. These coping strategies are usually successful, which may be why the majority of young people out of work at any time do not progress towards collective political action. Francis (1985) warned of potential political extremism of unemployed individuals denied a purpose in life and treated as worthless. Such a statement is elevated above mere conjecture when one considers that Stokes and Cochrane (1984) in a longitudinal study of redundant workers found increased levels of hostility and criticism of others and society at large after job loss. The more insidious possibilities of denying individuals a substantial place in society is highlighted in the following quote by Carrington and Leaman (1983):

Rioting may come to signify an attempt to gain symbolic control over areas and lives in which people feel they have lost mastery. It can become a reply to the experience of oneself as an object moved around by external forces. Violence has been a frequent resort of those who are denied a substantial identity in the world.

In reality it seems that unemployed individuals are more likely to become isolated, apathetic, and helpless than to collude on some collective rebellion. Where violence does erupt it would appear to be introjected (Stokes and Cochrane 1984) or directed sidewards rather than upwards, in a domestic rather than social setting.

According to Eggleston (1979: 6):

Unless a balanced, satisfying vocational identity can be achieved, then life for the individual is likely to be at best incomplete or compartmentalised; at worst, frustrating, enervating and incompatible.... At no stage in life are these issues of identity more important than in the formative years of adolescence when

predominantly childhood roles and identities have to be replaced or augmented by those of adult life.

(Eggleston 1979)

Several clear responses to the problems and opportunities now
surrounding young people can be distinguished, beyond the retreat into alcohol and drugs which constitutes a coping strategy
even if it is not socially approved.

Roberts (1985) has proposed several:

1. Increasing numbers of young people are devising their own
   forms of 'alternation', using low-paid, often temporary and
   part-time jobs for economic survival and some independence
   while earning the qualifications that may eventually unlock
   more attractive opportunities;
2. Other young people are opting for sub-employment. They drop
   out from education but refuse to commit themselves psychologically to low-status jobs. They work intermittently in order
   to earn 'breaks' (Roberts *et al.* 1982);
3. Some young people are building medium-term careers from
   recently introduced projects, courses and training schemes.
   The stated aim is usually to assist the unemployed towards
   conventional jobs. However, individuals sometimes move from
   scheme to scheme and achieve upward mobility in the process,
   eventually obtaining instructor, supervisor or management
   positions;
4. Soon after completing compulsory education, other young
   people are deciding that the most secure and rewarding careers
   on offer are as welfare claimants. Welfare, especially when
   supplemented by unofficial earnings, often appears a better
   deal than permanent dependence on secondary labour markets.
   In the longer term, however, the claimant role invariably leads
   into a poverty trap;
5. In some countries, the trend towards staying on in full-time
   education instead of facing a choice between unemployment
   and low-status jobs has been particularly strong among females. More are delaying their entry into the labour market,
   earning higher qualifications, then obtaining 'good jobs';
6. There are trends towards pre-marital cohabitational relationships, and towards the formation of temporary households by
   groups of young people who may not be sexually related: these
   developments are explicable in terms of current economic
   insecurity;
7. For women without the prospect of rewarding occupational
   careers, marriage and parenthood have been traditional escapes.

High unemployment makes this route more attractive than ever. Unemployment does not undermine, but to begin with, reinforces traditional feminine aspirations (Wallace 1980; Hendry *et al.* 1984). Unfortunately, for young women whose feminine hopes are reinforced, high youth unemployment makes male breadwinners difficult to locate. The traditional male role is undermined by unemployment. For girls, 'respectable' escapes to economic security and adult status may still be available with older men. However, some young women in high unemployment areas are deciding that the claimant role is more accessible. They know that the quickest route to independent accommodation is to 'get pregnant'. Single parenthood and welfare will not tempt well qualified career women, but may be no greater economic disaster than dependence on a low-paid or unemployed male.

(Roberts 1985)

Loss of producer roles, and the inability of education and training to guarantee lifetime vocations, make young people more dependent on ascribed statuses, sometimes derived from gender and ethnicity, in establishing adult identities and independence. Current trends may also make young people more dependent on leisure activities and environments to sustain these identities, and to establish and maintain relationships that allow other aspects of the transition to adulthood to proceed despite the impossibility of stepping directly from full-time education to stable employment. Hence, we believe that leisure is likely to grow in importance as a source of stability in adults' and young people's lives when most other aspects of society change rapidly, and are beyond individuals' control. Leisure is likely to become one sphere where people are assured of 'returns on their investments'. Access to conventional leisure of various kinds – sporting, musical, political – can assist young people who wish to preserve conventional lifestyles and trajectories. Equally, adolescents who are pioneering less familiar ways of living – as claimants, in marriage, cohabitional relationships, or other households – benefit from leisure environments in which to interact and display their preferred personal and social identities.

Youth is *not* a time of continuous crisis – a sort of developmental disaster area . . . the majority of young people are not in a state of crisis.

(Thompson Report 1982)

199

Chapter nine

Conclusion: a new theoretical approach

It was stated at the outset that the intention in this book was to consider three major theoretical approaches, and then subsequently the empirical evidence which has accumulated on a range of topics within the field of adolescent psychology. This having been done, it is now possible to turn our attention to the question of the extent to which the theories have been corroborated or weakened by this empirical evidence.

As was noted in the introductory chapter, while the two traditional theories differ in many respects, they are united in the view that adolescence is a stressful period in human development. According to the psychoanalytic position, the reason for this is to be found in the upsurge of instinctual forces which occurs as a result of puberty. These forces are said to cause a disturbance in the psychic balance which is believed to lead in turn to regression, ambivalence, and non-conformity. In addition, some form of identity crisis is to be expected among older adolescents. As far as the sociologists are concerned there are a number of factors related to the young person's position in society which may be assumed to result in stress of one sort or another. In the first place, adolescence is a period of both role transition and role conflict. Also, increasing age segregation means less opportunity for young people to be in contact with adult models, making the transition to maturity and the assumption of adult roles more problematic. Furthermore it is argued that teenagers are exposed to a variety of conflicting agents of socialisation, with educational institutions, the peer group, the mass media, and political institutions all pulling in different directions. Finally, teenagers are often seen as reflecting divisions within society itself. Their position is that of the 'marginal man' – being a member of various groups, but belonging to none. Thus they may be said to have an affinity with both conservative and radical forces, owing allegiance to both, but in reality, occupying the battle zone between the two.

In this book the results of a large amount of research have been considered. How does it bear on these theoretical notions? Broadly speaking, as we have noted in the individual chapters, research provides little support for current theories, and fails to subtantiate much of what both psychoanalysts and sociologists appear to believe. To take some examples, while there is certainly some change in the self-concept, there is no evidence to show that any but a small minority experience a serious identity crisis. In most cases relationships with parents are positive and constructive, and young people, by and large, do not reject adult values in favour of those espoused by the peer group. In fact, in most situations peer group values appear to be consistent with those of important adults, rather than in conflict with them. Fears of promiscuity among the young are not borne out by the research findings, nor do studies support the belief that the peer group encourages anti-social behaviour, unless other factors are also present. Lastly, there is no evidence to suggest that during the adolescent years there is a higher level of psychopathology than at other times. While a lot still needs to be learnt about the mental health of young people, almost all the results which have become available so far indicate that, although a small minority may show disturbance, the great majority of teenagers seem to cope well and to show no undue signs of turmoil or stress.

Support for this contention may be found in every major study of adolescence which has appeared in recent years. In summarising the findings which emerged from an extended study of the psychological development of young people in the U.S.A., David Offer (a psychiatrist) had this to say about the concept of 'storm and stress':

The transitional period of adolescence does present the adolescent with a special burden, a challenge, and an opportunity. He has to individualize, build up confidence in himself and his abilities, make important decisions concerning his future, and free himself of his earlier attachments to his parents. Our observations have led us to conclude that the majority of the teenagers in our sample coped with these tasks successfully. They lack the turmoil of the disturbed adolescent precisely because their ego is strong enough to withstand the pressures. ... It seems to us that someone might eventually raise an objection concerning our subjects that, because of their low level of turmoil, they are cases of arrested development. Certain investigators who have also observed the low level of turmoil in a large number of adolescents have interpreted their findings somewhat differently than we have. . . . Implicitly these investigators have adopted the position that lack of turmoil is a bad prognostic sign and must necessarily prevent the adolescent from developing into a mature adult. All of our data, including the psychological testing, point in the opposite direction. The adolescents not only adjusted well; they were also in touch with their feelings and developed meaningful relationships with significant others.

(Offer 1969: 184)

Since 1969 similar conclusions have been drawn by a wide variety of researchers (e.g. Kandel and Lesser 1972; Bandura 1972; Rutter *et al.* 1976; Youniss and Smollar 1985). Most would now agree with the views of Siddique and D'Arcy (1984) who, in summarising their own results on stress and well-being in adolescence, write as follows:

In this study some 33.5 per cent of the adolescents surveyed reported *no* symptoms of psychological distress and another 39 per cent reported five or fewer symptoms (a mild level of distress). On the other hand a significant 27.5 per cent reported higher levels of psychological distress. For the majority the adolescent transition may be relatively smooth; however, for a minority it does indeed appear to be a period of stress and turmoil. . . . The large majority of adolescents appear to get on well with adults and are able to cope effectively with demands of school and peer groups. They use their resources to make adjustments with environmental stressors with hardly visible signs of psychological distress.

(Siddique and D'Arcy 1984: 471)

There would appear to be a sharp divergence of opinion, therefore, between what have been called the 'classical' and 'empirical' points of view (Coleman 1978; 1979). Beliefs about adolescence which stem from traditional theory (the 'classical' view) do not in general accord with the results of research (the 'empirical' view). We need now to consider some of the reasons for this state of affairs. First, as many writers have pointed out, psychoanalysts and psychiatrists see a selected population. Their experience of adolescence is based primarily upon the individuals they meet in clinics or hospitals. Such experience is bound to encourage a somewhat one-sided perspective in which turmoil or disturbance is over-represented. For sociologists, on the other hand, the problem is often to disentangle concepts of 'youth' or 'the youth movement' from notions about young people themselves. As a number of commentators have observed, youth is frequently seen by sociologists as being in the forefront of social change. Youth is, as it were, the advance party where innovation or alteration in the values of society are concerned. From this position it is but a short step to use youth as a metaphor for social change, and thus to confuse radical forces in society with the beliefs of ordinary young people (Brake 1985).

A third possible reason for the divergence of viewpoint is that certain adolescent behaviours, such as vandalism, drug taking, hooliganism and so on, are extremely threatening to adults. The few who are involved in such activities, therefore, attain undue prominence in the public eye. The mass media unfortunately play an important part in this process by publicising sensational behaviour, thus making it appear very much more common than it is in reality. One only has to consider critically the image of the teenager portrayed week after week on the television to understand how, for many adults, the minority come to be representative of all young people. All three tendencies mentioned so far lead to an exaggerated view of the amount of turmoil which may be expected during adolescence, and thus serve to widen the gap between research and theory.

One other factor needs to be considered in this context. In general, psychologists responsible for large-scale surveys have tended to neglect the possibility that individual adolescents may be either unwilling or unable to reveal their innermost feelings. Much depends on the way the study is carried out, but it is important to remember how very difficult it is for anyone, let alone a shy, resentful, or anxious teenager, to share fears, worries, or conflicts with a strange interviewer. Inhibition of this sort may well result in a bias on the part of those writing from the empirical point of view, and cause an underestimation of the degree of stress experienced by young people. Problems of method, therefore, may also be playing their part in widening the gap between theory and research, not by exaggerating the amount of inner turmoil, but by doing just the opposite, namely, causing research workers to miss the more subtle indications of emotional tension. The divergence of opinion referred to earlier can thus be seen to be the result of a number of factors. Both methods and theories have their weaknesses, and the fault cannot be said to lie exclusively with one side or the other.

It has to be admitted that this divergence of opinion has received relatively little attention in the literature over the last decade or so. By and large those involved in the study of adolescence have not, in recent years, given especial prominence to theoretical issues. This may be partly because it has come to seem a sterile debate – most now accept a formulation broadly in line with that of Siddique and D'Arcy (1984), namely that while a minority experience difficulty during the adolescent transition, the majority cope well and do not exhibit signs to indicate that they are grappling with 'storm and stress'. Research attention has undoubtedly come to focus primarily on specific topics – according to Van Hasselt and Hersen (1987) subjects of the greatest concern during the 1980s include the peer group and social competence, communication within the family, step-parents and single parents, puberty and problem adolescents.

Where theory is utilised as a framework for empirical investigation it is quite clear that the lifespan developmental approach is considered to be the most useful. Anne Petersen, in her 1988 article for the *Annual Review of Psychology*, illustrates this trend: 'Recent adolescent-family research is very much in the tradition of contextually based lifespan psychology, examining the reciprocal effects of the family on the developing individual, and of the developing individual on family processes' (pp. 25–26). Another example of the same phenomenon may be found in Simmons and Blyth's *Moving into Adolescence* (1987). Here the authors study the impact of pubertal change and school context on a range of outcome variables including self-esteem, academic performance, and involvement in extra-curricular activities. This important study is conceptualised within the lifespan approach, demonstrating the centrality of many of the principles mentioned in the introductory chapter. As we noted then, this particular theoretical approach has a number of advantages – it stresses the context of human development, it emphasises the fact that growth and change come about only as a result of a reciprocal interplay of forces and pressures, and, last but not least, it underlines the necessity for a multi-disciplinary approach to development.

Of course the lifespan approach also has its limitations. While it may represent a series of important principles, these principles are applicable to human development in general, rather than to adolescence in particular. Such a theoretical stance has no explanation for the adolescent process, nor does it contribute in any way to the debate concerning 'storm and stress'. Assuming that a majority of young people manage well, while a minority struggle through the teenage years, the lifespan developmental model may indicate the criteria by which we should judge acceptable research on the subject, but it has no explanatory power to help us understand why some cope while others do not, and what is likely to distinguish between the two groups. Finally, and perhaps most significant, it cannot help us answer the question: 'In what way, if any, is adolescence fundamentally different from other stages in the life cycle?'

Let us return for a moment to the two traditional theories originating from psychoanalysis and sociology. Obviously these two theories have some value, and it would be wrong to leave the impression that neither are any longer relevant. Perhaps the most important contribution made by these theories is that they have provided the foundation for an understanding of young people with serious problems and a greater knowledge of those who belong to minority or deviant groups. In this respect the two major theories have much to offer. However, it must be recognised that today they are inadequate as a basis for an understanding of the development of the great majority of young people. The most fundamental conclusion of the review carried out in this book is that adolescence needs a theory, not of abnormality, but of normality. Any viable theoretical viewpoint put forward today must not only incorporate the results of empirical studies, but must also acknowledge the fact that, although for some young people adolescence may be a difficult time, for the majority it is a period of relative stability. None the less, there is general agreement that during the teenage years major adaptation has to occur. The transition between childhood and adulthood cannot be achieved without substantial adjustments of both a psychological and social nature; and yet most young people appear to cope without undue stress. How do they do so?

It is this contradiction between the amount of overall change experienced, and the relative health and resilience of the individuals involved in such change, which now requires some consideration. In earlier papers (Coleman 1974; 1978; 1979; 1980) a 'focal' model of adolescence has been outlined, in the hope that this will go some way towards resolving such a contradiction. Before this is explained, however, it will be necessary to sketch briefly the background to this model. The model grew out of the results of a study of normal adolescent development, a study which has been mentioned on a number of occasions throughout this book. To recapitulate, large groups of boys and girls at the ages of 11, 13, 15, and 17 were given a set of identical tests which elicited from them attitudes and opinions about a wide range of relationships. Thus material was included on self-image, being alone, heterosexual relationships, parental relationships, friendships, and large group situations. The material was analysed in terms of the constructive and negative elements present in these relationship situations, and in terms of the common themes expressed by the young people involved in the study. Findings showed that attitudes to all relationships changed as a function of age, but more importantly the results also indicated that concerns about different issues reached a peak at different stages in the adolescent process. This finding is illustrated for boys in Figure 9.1 where it can be seen that simply by considering three of the most important themes there are peak ages for the expression of each of these various concerns. Similar results were obtained for girls.

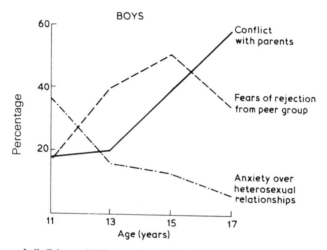

Source: J. C. Coleman (1974) *Relationships in Adolescence*, Routledge & Kegan Paul.

Figure 9.1 Peak ages for the expression of different themes.

It was this finding that led to the formulation of a 'focal' theory. The model suggests that at different ages particular sorts of relationship patterns come into focus, in the sense of being most prominent, but that no pattern is specific to one age only. Thus the patterns overlap, different issues come into focus at different times, but simply because an issue is not the most prominent feature of an age does not mean that it may not be critical for some individuals. These ideas in association with empirical findings such as those illustrated in Figure 9.1, combine to suggest a symbolic model of adolescent development where each curve represents a different issue or relationship. This is portrayed in Figure 9.2.

In many ways such a notion is not dissimilar from any traditional stage theory. However, it carries with it a very much more flexible view of development, and therefore differs from stage theory in

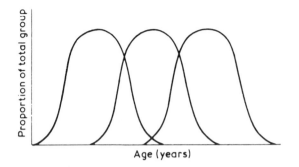

Source: J. C. Coleman (1974) *Relationships in Adolescence*, Routledge & Kegan Paul.

Figure 9.2 Focal theory. Each curve represents a different issue or relationship.

three important respects. In the first place, the resolution of one issue is not seen as the *sine qua non* for tackling the next. In fact it is clearly envisaged that a minority of individuals will find themselves facing more than one issue at the same time. Second, the model does not assume the existence of fixed boundaries between stages and, therefore, issues are not necessarily linked to a particular age or developmental level. Finally, there is nothing immutable about the sequence involved. In our culture it appears that individuals are more likely to face certain issues in the early stages of adolescence, and different issues at other stages, but the 'focal' theory is not dependent on a fixed sequence, and it would be of very great interest to examine other cultures in the light of this theory of development.

It is our belief that the 'focal' model of adolescent development may provide a clue to the resolution of the apparent contradiction between the amount of adjustment required during adolescence on the one hand, and the relatively successful adaptation among the general population on the other. If adolescents have to adjust to so much potentially stressful change, and at the same time pass through this stage of their life with relative stability, as the 'empirical' view indicates, how do they do it? The answer which is suggested by the 'focal' model is that they cope by dealing with one issue at a time. They spread the process of adaptation over a span of years, attempting to resolve first one issue, and then the next. Different problems, different relationship issues come into focus and are tackled at different stages, so that the stresses resulting from the need to adapt to new modes of behaviour are rarely concentrated all at one time. It follows from this that it is precisely in those who, for whatever reason, do have more than one issue to cope with at a time that problems are most likely to occur. Thus, as an example, where puberty and the growth spurt occur at the normal time individuals are able to adjust to these changes before other pressures, such as those from parents and teachers, are brought to bear. For the late maturers, however, pressures are more likely to occur simultaneously, inevitably requiring adjustments over a much wider area.

The 'focal' model is only one of a number of possible ways of conceptualising adolescent development, but it has two particular advantages. First, it is based directly on empirical evidence, and second, it goes at least some way towards reconciling the apparent contradiction between the amount of adaptation required during the transitional process, and the ability of most young people to cope successfully with the pressures inherent in this process. Such a model evidently needs further testing, but since it was first proposed it has come to appear, to some writers at least, as an important contribution to the theoretical understanding of adolescence (see for example Siddique and D'Arcy 1984; Meadows 1986). In addition, two studies have appeared in the literature providing substantial support. In the first Kroger (1985) replicated Coleman's (1974) research on large samples of U.S. and New Zealand teenagers. The results are quite striking. They show almost identical patterns of development in the three countries, and indicate that, in spite of the obvious cultural differences, the same proportions of adolescents appear to face the same inter-personal issues in much the same way in each of the three national settings.

The results of Simmons and Blyth (1987) are equally interesting in this respect. Simmons and Blyth tested the proposition, contained within the focal model, that those who adjust less well during adolescence are likely to be those who have to face more than one interpersonal issue at a time. The authors documented the life changes occurring for the young people in their study, and related the number of life changes to outcome measures such as self-esteem and academic performance. Results are illustrated in Figures 9.3 and 9.4. This is how Simmons and Blyth describe the results:

> While the timing and level of discontinuity of each individual change is important for the adjustment of adolescents, also relevant is the cumulation of life changes at one point in time. Coleman (1974) has advanced the focal theory of change relative to this issue; he has posited that at entry to adolescence, it is easier to deal with life changes one at a time rather than with

all transitions simultaneously. It is easier if one can focus on one major transition before tackling the next. For example, it is easier to cope sequentially rather than simultaneously with environmental changes, physiological differences, the new definition of self as an adolescent, and the alteration in others' expectations.

Findings from this study support the focal theory. Among both boys and girls, those who experience a greater number of major life changes in early adolescence are at greater risk in terms of our key outcome variables. ...

In sum, in early adolescence, social-psychological outcomes are affected in interesting ways by the nature of the changes themselves. There is evidence of detrimental effects if change occurs at too young an age, if it causes the individual to be extremely off-time in development, if the transition places the person in the lowest ranking cohort in the environment, if change is marked by sharp discontinuity, and if many significant changes cumulate and occur close together in time.

(Simmons and Blyth 1987: 350–1)

One other source of support for the focal model comes from an ongoing study of leisure and lifestyles in a sample of 12,000 Scottish adolescents (Hendry *et al*. 1985). Here it is argued that the model is applicable to social aspects of young people's lives, and can be useful in understanding patterns both of leisure and of unemployment. Findings will be reported in due course.

It has to be admitted that the focal model has had its critics too. Coffield *et al*. (1986), for example, take exception to the fact that the model makes no attempt to deal with disadvantage and deprivation.

John C. Coleman's *The Nature of Adolescence* ends by presenting a new focal theory which shows how far academic psychology is at times removed from the real world of young adults. The theory suggests that adolescents cope with one issue or relationship at a time as they grow up; it also contains the reasonable deduction that problems are most likely to occur when young people have more than one issue to deal with at the same time. But why is this thought to be particularly true of adolescents? Could not the same be said of younger children, middle-aged parents or old-aged pensioners? Not even the subsequent modifications and improvements of Leo Hendry (1983) can save the theory from the charge of triviality.

(Coffield *et al*. 1986: 211)

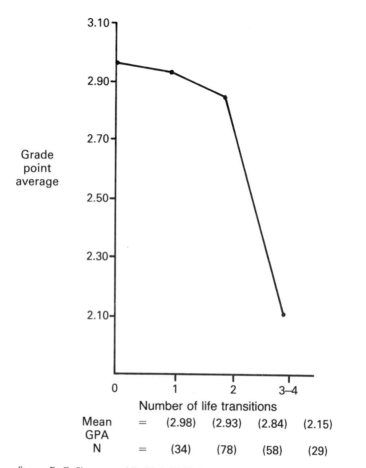

Mean GPA = (2.98) (2.93) (2.84) (2.15)

N = (34) (78) (58) (29)

Source: R. G. Simmons and D. Blyth (1987) *Moving into Adolescence*, Aldine de Gruyter.

Figure 9.3 Grade 7 grade point average and number of life transitions for girls.

Coffield *et al.* present a different model, derived from their experience of carrying out research in the North-East of England with young people, many of whom were unemployed, all of whom were living at the very periphery of British society. In their model class and patriarchy are seen as all-pervading influences which determine to a large extent the options and choices available to young people in this under-privileged section of society (see Figure 9.5). As they write:

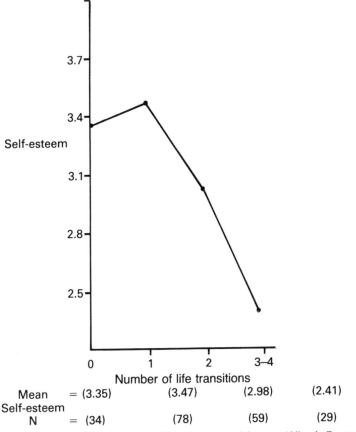

Mean Self-esteem = (3.35) (3.47) (2.98) (2.41)

N = (34) (78) (59) (29)

Source: R. G. Simmons and D. Blyth (1987) *Moving into Adolescence,* Aldine de Gruyter.

Figure 9.4 Grade 7 self-esteem by number of life transitions for girls.

Class and patriarchy are means whereby some gain advantages over others; they are best thought of as relationships between people which accord power, wealth and status to some and deny it to others. Our argument is that *all* of the main factors in our model tend to interact vigorously, creating different patterns of problems and opportunities for individuals. ... In contrast to Coleman, who argues that young adults cope with one issue at a time, we would claim that most of them are struggling to cope with all these different aspects of life, which impinge upon them simultaneously.

(Coffield *et al.* 1986: 213–14)

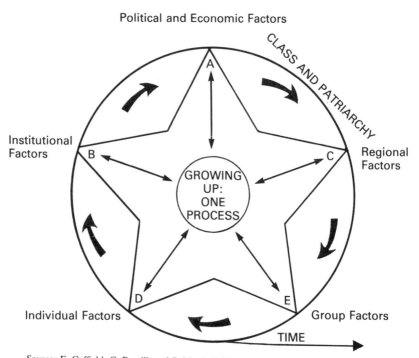

Political and Economic Factors

CLASS AND PATRIARCHY

Institutional Factors

Regional Factors

GROWING UP: ONE PROCESS

Individual Factors

Group Factors

TIME

Source: F. Coffield, C. Borrill, and S. Marshall (1986) *Growing up at the Margins*, OUP.

Figure 9.5 An attempt at an integrating model

Coffield and his colleagues have misunderstood, to some extent, what the focal model is all about. The focal model is to do with the psychological transitions of adolescence, rather than with the economic circumstances of the individual. For example, all young people, irrespective of social background, must negotiate increasing independence from their parents. The focal model suggests that it will be easier to handle the parent issue if the young person is not, at the same time, striving for greater autonomy within the peer group. None the less Coffield is right to draw attention to the social circumstances of the individual, for these will obviously contribute in a substantial way to the adolescent's psychological adjustment. There can be little doubt that in situations of economic hardship it will be more difficult to manage the adolescent transitions in a satisfactory manner. This point has already been made by Hendry (1983) in his argument that ecological factors are as important as psychological ones in understanding the young person's development. Circumstances, many of them unpleasant, will be imposed on the individual, making it less likely that he or she will feel in control of events. This will in turn complicate relationships with friends and family, presenting the young person with a range of additional stress factors on top of all the normal burdens inherent in adolescent development. At present we know far too little about the way in which the psychological development of the adolescent interacts with environmental circumstances, and perhaps we should be considering both Coffield's model and the focal model side by side, rather than seeing them as alternative representations of the adolescent process.

A further criticism of the focal model is that it is nothing more or less than the theory of life events (Dohrenwend and Dohrenwend 1974) applied to adolescence. At one level this is correct. The focal model does imply that the more 'issues' the young person has to cope with, the more indications of stress there are likely to be. The research of Simmons and Blyth (1987) provides excellent validation of this view. However, the focal model goes further – for it is in one highly significant respect quite different from life events theory. While life events theory implies simply that the more events that occur in the individual's life, the more stress there will be, the focal model suggests that the young person is an *agent* in his or her own development, managing the adolescent transition – where possible – by dealing with one issue at a time.

It will be recalled that in Chapter one we mentioned Lerner's seminal paper published in 1985. In this paper the author outlines some of the ways in which the adolescent is active in shaping his or her own maturation. We see this concept as being central to the focal model – not only does the model imply that the young person copes best when facing one issue at a time, the model implies that in most circumstances the young person may actually be determining his or her own rate of development.

Such an idea seems at first to be rather far-fetched. Yet a moment's thought will indicate that the concept is not so extraordinary after all. Consider for a moment the range of choices available to an individual in their current relationships. In any one day a teenager may choose to confront a parent over the breakfast table, to argue with a sibling, to accept the suggestion of a best friend, to stand up to an authoritarian teacher, to conform to peer group pressure, to resist the persuasion of a boyfriend or girlfriend, and so on. Every one of these situations offers the young person a choice, and all may well have a bearing on the interpersonal issues with which the focal model is concerned. We believe that most young people pace themselves through the adolescent transition. Most of them hold back on one issue, while they are grappling with another. Most sense what they can and cannot cope with, and will, in the real sense of the term, be an active agent in their own development.

We see this concept as providing one of the most exciting challenges for adolescent psychology. It is this notion which forms the bridge between lifespan developmental psychology and the concerns of those who, like ourselves, wish to carry forward the understanding of adolescence. The idea also links, significantly, with the interest currently being shown by social psychologists and personality theorists into self-efficacy and locus of control, topics we discussed in Chapter four. Increased knowledge of this process of active agency could provide essential information to help answer the two key questions: 'What distinguishes the majority who cope from the minority who experience manifest stress during the teenage years?' and, 'What is it about adolescence which makes it different from other stages in the life cycle?'

In our view the answers to such questions are almost certainly to do with the nature of the transition and the way it is managed. Yet the focal model and the concept of agency provide – at this stage at least – only signposts in the right direction. We need to address ourselves to a variety of issues. Which young people are able to act in this way, and which are not? What are the circumstances which encourage active agent behaviour? How does economic hardship, or other environmental trauma, affect the young person's capability in this area? Yet if we can make progress in understanding the way in which young people shape their own development, we will surely be taking one of the most significant steps possible towards clarifying the nature of adolescence.

References

Adams, G. R. (1983) 'Social competence during adolescence: social sensitivity, locus of control, empathy, and peer popularity', *Journal of Youth and Adolescence* 12 (3): 203–9.

Adams, G. R., Schvaneveldt, J. D., and Jensen, G. O., (1979) 'Sex, age and perceived competency as correlates of empathic ability in adolescence', *Adolescence* 14: 811–18.

Adams, G. R. and Shea, J. A. (1979) 'The relationships between identity status, locus of control and ego development', *Journal of Youth and Adolescence* 8: 81–9.

Adams, G. R., Shea, J., and Fitch, S. A. (1979) 'Toward the development of an objective assessment of ego-identity status', *Journal of Youth and Adolescence* 8: 223–8.

Adams, G. R., Shea, J., and Kacerguis, M. A. (1978) 'Development of psychosocial maturity: A review of selected effects of schooling', *Urban Education* 13: 255–82.

Adelson, J. (1971) 'The political imagination of the young adolescent', *Daedalus*, Fall, 1013–50.

Adelson, J. (ed.) (1980) *Handbook of Adolescent Psychology*, New York and Chichester: John Wiley & Sons.

Adelson, J. and O'Neill, R. (1966) 'The development of political thought in adolescence', *Journal of Personality and Social Psychology* 4: 295–308.

Aitken, P. P. (1978) *Ten- to Fourteen-year-olds and Alcohol*, Vol. 3, London: HMSO.

Akers, R. L. (1970) 'Teenage drinking and drug abuse', in E. D. Evans (ed.) *Adolescence: Readings in behaviour and development*, New York: Dryden Press.

Allen, I. (1987) *Education in Sex and Personal Relationships*, London: Policy Studies Institute.

Allport, G. W. (1961) *Pattern and Growth in Personality*, New York: Holt, Rinehart & Winston.

Althusser, L. (1985) 'Ideology and the ideological state apparatuses', in V. Beechey and J. Donald (eds) *Subjectivity and Social Relations*, Milton Keynes: Open University Press.

References

Anderson, S. and Messick, S. (1974) 'Social competency in young children', *Developmental Psychology* 10: 282–93.

Archer, J. (1984) 'Gender roles as developmental pathways', *British Journal of Social Psychology* 23 (3): 245–56.

Argyle, M. (1969) *Social Interaction*, London: Methuen.

Arkowitz, H., Hinton, R., Perl, J., and Himadi, W. (1978) 'Treatment strategies for dating anxiety in college men based on real-life practice', *Counselling Psychologist* 7: 41–6.

Ashton, D. N. and Field, D. (1976) *Young Workers*, London: Hutchinson.

Ashton, D. N. and Maguire, M. (1983) *The Vanishing Youth Labour Market*, Youthaid Occasional Paper 3, London: Youthaid

Association of Recreation Managers (1981) 'Recreation programmes for the unemployed – do they work?' in *The Changing Scene: Seminar Report*, ARM: St Annes-on-Sea.

Astley, J. (1985) 'Take a walk on the wild side: Leisure and pop music in a commercial world', *Proceedings of the Leisure Studies Association Conference, Ilkley, Yorkshire*: 4.2.3–4.2.5.

Attenborough, R. E. and Zdep, S. M. (1973) Article in *Proceedings of the 81st Annual Convention of the American Psychological Association*, pp. 237–8, Washington: Office of Technical Services.

Bachman, J. G. and O'Malley, P. M. (1977) 'Self-esteem in young men: a longitudinal analysis of the impact of educational and occupational attainment', *Journal of Personality and Social Psychology* 35: 365–80.

Baittle, B. and Offer, D. (1971) 'On the nature of adolescent rebellion', in F. C. Feinstein, P. Giovacchini and A. Miller (eds) *Annals of Adolescent Psychiatry*, New York: Basic Books.

Ball, S. J. (1981) *Beachside Comprehensive: A case study of secondary schooling*, Cambridge: Cambridge University Press.

Bandura, A. (1972) 'The stormy decade: fact or fiction?', in D. Rogers (ed.) *Issues in Adolescent Psychology* (2nd edn), New York: Appleton-Century-Crofts.

Banks, M. and Ullah, P. (1987) 'Political attitudes and voting among unemployed and employed youth', *Journal of Adolescence* 10: 201–16.

Banks, M., Ullah, P., and Warr, P. (1984) 'Unemployed and less qualified urban young people', *Employment Gazette* August: 343–6.

Barker, D. (1972) 'Young people and their homes: spoiling and "keeping close" in a South Wales town', *Sociological Review* 20: 4.

Baruch, G. K. (1972) 'Maternal influences upon college women's attitudes towards women and work', *Developmental Psychology* 6: 32–7.

Basini, A. (1975) 'Education for leisure: a sociological critique', in J. T. Haworth and M. A. Smith (eds) *Work and Leisure*, London: Lepus.

Bates, I., Clarke, J., Cohen, P., Finn, D., Moore, R., and Willis, P. (1984) *Schooling for the Dole*, London: Macmillan.

Baumrind, D. (1968) 'Authoritarian versus authoritative parents control', *Adolescence* 3: 255–72.

Baumrind, D. (1975) 'Early socialization and adolescent competence', in S. E. Dragastin and G. Elder (eds) *Adolescence in the Life Cycle*, New York: John Wiley.

Baxter, J. L. (1975) 'The chronic job-changer: a study of youth un-employment', *Social and Economic Administration* 9: 184–206.

Becker, H. S. (1963) *Boys in White*, University of Chicago Press.

Becker, H. S and Carper, J. W. (1956a) 'The development of identification with an occupation', *American Journal of Sociology* 61: 289–98.

Becker, H. S. and Carper, J. W. (1956b) 'The elements of identification with an occupation', *American Sociological Review* 21: 341–8.

Bedeman, T. and Courtenay, G. (1983) *One in Three*, Sheffield: MSC Research and Development Series 13.

Bee, H. (1975) *The Developing Child*, New York: Harper & Row.

Bell, A. P. (1969) 'Role modelling of fathers in adolescence and young adulthood', *Journal of Counselling Psychology* 16: 30–5.

Bell, N., Avery, A., Jenkins, D., Field, J., and Shoenrock, C. (1985) 'Family relationships and social competence during adolescence', *Journal of Youth and Adolescence* 14: 109–20.

Belsky, J., Lerner, R., and Spannier, G. (1984) *The Child in the Family*, London: Addison-Wesley.

Belson, W. A. (1978) *Television Violence and the Adolescent Boy*, London: Saxon House.

Benedict, R. (1938) 'Continuities and discontinuities in cultural conditioning', *Psychiatry* 1: 161–7.

Berger, B. M., Hackett, B. M., and Miller, R. M. (1972) 'Child rearing practices in the communal family', in H. P. Dreitzel (ed.) *Family, Marriage and the Struggle of the Sexes*, London: Collier-Macmillan.

Berndt, T. J. (1979) 'Developmental changes in conformity to peers and parents', *Developmental Psychology* 15: 606–16.

Berndt, T. J. (1982) 'The features and effects of friendship in early adolescence', *Child Development* 53: 1447–60.

Berscheid, E. and Walster, E. (1972) 'Beauty and the beast', *Psychology Today* 5: 42–6.

Bigelow, B. J. (1972) 'Children's friendship expectations: a cognitive-developmental study', *Child Development* 48: 246–53.

Bigelow, B. J. and LaGaipa, J. J. (1975) 'Children's written descriptions of friendships: a multidimensional analysis', *Developmental Psychology* 11: 857–8.

Birkstead, I. K. (1976) 'School performance viewed from the boys' perspective', *Sociological Review* 24: 63–77.

Bixenstine, V. E., DeCorte, M. S., and Bixenstine, B. A. (1976) 'Conformity to peer-sponsored misconduct at four grade levels', *Developmental Psychology* 12: 226–36.

Blackburn, R. M. and Mann, M. (1979) *The Working Class in the Labour Market*, London: Macmillan.

Blos, P. (1962) *On Adolescence*, London: Collier-Macmillan.

Blos, P. (1967) 'The second individuation process of adolescence', *Psychoanalytic Study of the Child* 22: 162–86.

Bloxham, S. (1984) 'Social behaviour and the young unemployed', in R. Fiddy (ed.) *Young People's Work: Policy and provision for the young unemployed*, London: Falmer.

217

References

Blyth, D. A., Simmons, R. G., and Carlton-Ford, S. (1983) 'The adjustment of early adolescents to school transitions', *Journal of Early Adolescence* 3 (1–2): 105–20.

Blyth, D. A., Simmons, R. G., and Zakin, D. (1985) 'Satisfaction with body image for early adolescent females: the impact of pubertal timing within different school environments', *Journal of Youth and Adolescence* 14: 207–26.

Bohan, J. S. (1973) 'Age and sex differences in self-concept', *Adolescence* 8: 379–84.

Bone, M. (1972) *The Youth Service and Similar Provision for Young People*, London: HMSO.

Borkovec, T. D., Stone, N. M., O'Brien, G. T., and Kaloupek, D. G. (1974) 'Evaluation of a clinically relevant target behaviour for analogue outcome research', *Behaviour Therapy* 5: 503–11.

Bowlby, J. (1973) *Separation, Anxiety and Anger*, London: Hogarth.

Bradlyn, A. S., Himadi, W. G., Crimmins, D. R., Christoff, K. A., Graves, K. G., and Kelly, J. A. (1983) 'Conversational skills training for retarded adolescents', *Behaviour Therapy* 14: 314–25.

Brake, M. (1973) 'Cultural revolution or alternative delinquency: an examination of deviant youth as a social problem', in R. Bailey and J. Young (eds) *Contemporary Social Problems in Britain*, London: D. C. Heath.

Brake, M. (1980) *The Sociology of Youth Culture and Youth Sub-cultures*, London: Routledge & Kegan Paul.

Brake, M. (1985) *Comparative Youth Sub-cultures*, London: Routledge & Kegan Paul.

Braun, F. (1977) 'Youth unemployment in West Germany: the psycho-social aspect', in B. O. Pettman and J. Fyfe (eds) *Youth Unemployment in Great Britain and the Federal Republic of Germany*, Bradford: M. C. B.

Breakwell, G. M. (1983) 'Young people in and out of work', paper presented at *SSRC Labour Markets Workshop*: Manchester.

Breakwell, G. M. (1985) *The Quiet Rebel*, London: Century Press.

Breakwell, G. M. (1986) 'Political and attributional responses of the young short-term unemployed', *Political Psychology* 7: 575–86.

Breakwell, G. M., Harrison, B., and Propper, C. (1984) 'Explaining the psychological effects of unemployment for young people: the importance of specific situational factors', *British Journal of Guidance and Counselling* 12: 132–40.

Brennan, T. (1982) 'Loneliness at adolescence', in L. Peplau and D. Perlman (eds) *Loneliness: A source of current theory, research and therapy*, pp. 269–90, New York: Wiley.

Brenner, S. O. and Bartell, R. (1983) 'The psychological impact of unemployment: a structural analysis of cross-sectional data', *Journal of Occupational Psychology* 56 (2): 129–36.

Brim, O. G. (1965) 'Adolescent personality as self-other systems', *Journal of Marriage and the Family* 27: 156–62.

218

Brittain, C. V. (1963) 'Adolescent choices and parent-peer cross-pressures', *American Sociological Review* 28: 385–91.

Bronfenbrenner, U. (1974) 'The origins of alienation', *Scientific American* 231: 53–61.

Brooke-Taylor, G. (1970) 'Quality in recreation', in T. L. Burton (ed.) *Recreation, Research and Planning*, London: Allen & Unwin.

Brooks-Gunn, J. (1987) 'Pubertal processes: their relevance for developmental research', in V. B. Van Hasselt and M. Hersen (eds) *Handbook of Adolescent Psychology*, Oxford: Pergamon Press.

Brooks-Gunn, J. and Petersen, A. (eds) (1983) *Girls at Puberty: biological and psycho-social perspectives*, New York: Plenum Press.

Brooks-Gunn, J., Petersen, A., and Eichorn, D. (eds) (1985) 'The time of maturation and psycho-social functioning in adolescence', Parts 1 and 2. *Journal of Youth and Adolescence* 14 (3); 14 (4).

Brooks-Gunn, J. and Warren, M. (1985) 'The effects of delayed menarche in different contexts: dance and nondance students', *Journal of Youth and Adolescence* 14: 285–300.

Brown, B. B. (1982) 'The extent and effects of peer pressure among high school students: a retrospective analysis', *Journal of Youth and Adolescence* 11: 121–33.

Brown, B. B., Eicher, S. A., and Petrie, S. (1986) 'The importance of peer group ("crowd") affiliation in adolescence', *Journal of Adolescence* 9: 73–95.

Brown, B. B. and Lohr, M. J. (1987) 'Peer group affiliation and adolescent self-esteem: an integration of ego identity and symbolic interaction theories', *Journal of Personality and Social Psychology*, 52: 47–55.

Brown, R. (1978) 'Work', in R. Abrams (ed.) *Work, Urbanism and Inequality in U.K. Society Today*, London: Weidenfeld & Nicholson.

Bruggen, P. and O'Brian, C. (1986) *Surviving Adolescence: a handbook for adolescents and their parents*, London: Faber & Faber.

Bryant, B. M. and Trower, P. E. (1974) 'Social difficulty in a student sample', *British Journal of Educational Psychology* 44: 13–21.

Bryne, D., London, O., and Reeves, K. (1968) 'The effects of physical attractiveness, sex, and attitude similarity on interpersonal attraction', *Journal of Personality* 36: 259–71.

Burgoyne, J., Ormrod, R., and Richards, M. (1987) *Divorce Matters*, Harmondsworth: Penguin.

Burke, R. J. and Weir, T. (1978) 'Benefits to adolescents of informal helping relationships with parents and peers', *Psychological Reports* 42: 1175–84.

Bury, J. (1984) *Teenage Pregnancy in Britain*, London: The Birth Control Trust.

Bush, D. E., Simmons, R. G., Hutchinson, B., and Blyth, D. A. (1977) 'Adolescent perception of sex roles in 1968 and 1975', *Public Opinion Quarterly* 41 (4): 459–74.

Carrington, P. and Leaman, S. (1983) *Youth and Policy*, 11 (3): 14.

Carter, M. P. (1966) *Into Work*, Harmondsworth: Penguin.

References

Carter, M. P. (1971) *Home, School and Work*, London: Pergamon.

Carter, M. P. (1972) 'The world of work and the ROSLA pupil', *Education in the North* 9: 61–4.

Cavior, N. and Dokecki, P. R. (1973) 'Physical attractiveness, perceived attitude similarity, and academic achievement as contributors to interpersonal attraction among adolescents', *Developmental Psychology* 9: 44–54.

Cherry, N. (1976) 'Persistent job changing: is it a problem?', *Journal of Occupational Psychology* 49 (4): 203–21.

Ching, J. E. (1970) 'Educational and vocational guidance for the able pupil', *Careers Quarterly* 22: 18–24.

Clasen, D. R. and Brown, B. B. (1985) 'The multidimensionality of peer pressure in adolescence', *Journal of Youth and Adolescence* 14 (6): 451–65.

Clausen, J. A. (1975) 'The social meaning of differential physical and sexual maturation', in S. Dragastin and G. Elder (eds) *Adolescence in the Life Cycle*, New York: John Wiley.

Clifford, E. (1971) 'Body satisfaction in adolescence', *Perceptual. Motor Skills* 33: 119–25.

Closs, J., Downs, S., and Willoughby, J. (1977) 'Me Tarzan, you Jane', *Careers Quarterly* 28 (4): 24–31.

Cloutier, R. and Goldschmid, M. (1976) 'Individual differences in the development of formal reasoning', *Child Development* 47: 1097–1102.

Coffield, F., Borrill, C., and Marshall, S. (1983) 'How young people try to survive being unemployed', *New Society* 2 June: 332–9.

Coffield, F., Borrill, C., and Marshall, S. (1986) *Growing up at the Margins*, Milton Keynes: Open University Press.

Cohen, A. K. (1950) *Delinquent Boys*, London: Routledge & Kegan Paul.

Cole, L. and Hall, I. N. (1970) *Psychology of Adolescence*, New York: Holt, Rinehart & Winston.

Coleman, J. and Husen, T. (1985) *Becoming Adult in a Changing Society*, Paris: OECD.

Coleman, J. C. (1974) *Relationships in Adolescence*, London: Routledge & Kegan Paul.

Coleman, J. C. (1978) 'Current contradictions in adolescent theory', *Journal of Youth and Adolescence* 7: 1–11.

Coleman, J. C. (ed.) (1979) *The School Years*, London: Methuen.

Coleman, J. C. (1980) 'Friendship and the peer group in adolescence', in J. Adelson (ed.) *Handbook of Adolescent Psychology*, New York: John Wiley.

Coleman, J. C. (1987) (ed.) *Working with Troubled Adolescents: a handbook*, London: Academic Press.

Coleman, J. C. and Coleman, E. Z. (1984) 'Adolescent attitudes to authority', *Journal of Adolescence*, 7: 131–41.

Coleman, J. C., George, R., and Holt, G. (1977) 'Adolescents and their parents: a study of attitudes', *Journal of Genetic Psychology* 130: 239–45.

Coleman, J. C., Herzberg, J., and Morriss, M. (1977) 'Identity in adolescence: present and future self concepts', *Journal of Youth and Adolescence* 6: 181–5.

Coleman, J. S. (1961) *The Adolescent Society*, New York: The Free Press.

Collins, J. K. (1974) 'Adolescent dating intimacy: norms and peer expectations', *Journal of Youth and Adolescence* 3: 317–28.

Combs, M. L. and Slaby, D. A. (1978) 'Social skills training with children', in B. B. Lahey and A. E. Kazdin (eds) *Advances in Child Clinical Psychology* 1: 161–206, New York: Plenum.

Conger, J. J. (1977) *Adolescence and Youth*, New York: Harper & Row.

Conger, J. J. (1979) *Adolescence: generation under pressure*, London: Harper & Row.

Conger, J. J., Peng, S. S., and Dunteman, G. H. (1977) *National Longitudinal Study of the High School Class of 1972: group profiles on self-esteem, locus of control, and life goals*, Research Triangle Institute: Research Triangle Park, N.C.

Conger, J. J. and Petersen, A. C. (1984) *Adolescence and Youth*, New York: Harper & Row.

Connell, W. F., Stroobant, R. E., and Sinclair, K. E. (1975) *Twelve to Twenty: studies of city youth*, Sydney: Hicks & Sons.

Coopersmith, S. (1967) *The Antecedents of Self-Esteem*, San Francisco: Freeman.

Corrigan, P. (1976) *The Smash Street Kids*, London: Paladin.

Corrigan, P. (1979) *Schooling the Smash Street Kids*, London: Macmillan.

Costanzo, P. R. and Shaw, M. E. (1966) 'Conformity as a function of age level', *Child Development* 37: 967–75.

Cottle, T. J. (1978) *Black Testimony – Voices of Britain's West Indians*, London: Wildwood House.

Cousins, J. (1987) *Make it Happy: what sex is all about*, Harmondsworth: Penguin Books.

Covington, J. (1982) 'Adolescent deviation and age', *Journal of Youth and Adolescence* 11: 329–44.

Covington, L. V. and Beery, R. G. (1977) *Self-worth and School Learning*, New York: Reinhart & Winston.

Craig-Bray, L. and Adams, G. (1986) 'Different methodologies in the assessment of identity: congruence between self report and interview technique', *Journal of Youth and Adolescence* 15 (3): 191–204.

Crain, W. C. and Crain, E. F. (1974) 'The growth of political ideas and their expression among young activists', *Journal of Youth and Adolescence* 3: 105–33.

Crandall, V. C., Katkovsky, W., and Crandall, W. J. (1965) 'Children's beliefs in their own control of reinforcements in intellectual-academic achievement situations', *Child Development* 36: 91–109.

Crockett, L., Losoff, M., and Petersen, A. C. (1984) 'Perceptions of peer group and friendship in early adolescence', *Journal of Early Adolescence* 4: 155–81.

221

Crowther Report (1959) 15–18, Central Advisory Council for Education. London: HMSO.

Csikszentmihalyi, M. and Larson, R. (1984) *Being Adolescent: conflict and growth in the teenage years*, New York: Basic Books.

Csikszentmihalyi, M., Larson, R., and Prescott, S. (1977) 'The ecology of adolescent activity and experience', *Journal of Youth and Adolescence* 6: 281–94.

Damon, W. (1978) *The Social World of the Child*, San Francisco: Jossey-Bass.

Damon, W. (1983) *Social and Personality Development: infancy through adolescence*, New York: Norton.

Damon, W. and Hart, D. (1982) 'The development of self-understanding from infancy through adolescence', *Child Development*, 53: 841–64.

Davies, E. and Furnham, A. (1986) 'Body satisfaction in adolescent girls', *British Journal of Medical Psychology* 59: 279–87.

Davies, J. and Stacey, B. (1972) *Teenagers and Alcohol*, Vol. 2, London: HMSO.

Davies, J. B. (1978) 'Alcohol: the development of concepts, attitudes and use', *Proceedings of the British Psychological Society Conference, University of Stirling*, Chichester: Wiley.

Davies, R. D. S. (1970) 'Youth service as a part of further education', in J. Bulman, M. Craft, and F. Milson (eds) *Youth Service and Interprofessional Studies*, London: Pergamon.

Davis, F. and Muroz, L. (1970) 'Heads and freaks: patterns and meanings of drug use among hippies', in J. D. Douglas (ed.) *Observations and Deviance*, London: Random House.

Deem, R. (1980) *Schooling for Women's Work*, London: Routledge & Kegan Paul.

De Grazia, S. (1962) *Of Time, Work and Leisure*, New York: 20th Century Fund.

Delamont, S. (1984) 'Sex roles and schooling', *Journal of Adolescence* 7 (4): 329–36.

Dennehy, C. and Sullivan, J. (1977) 'Poverty and unemployment in Liverpool', in F. Field (ed.) *The Conscript Army: a study of Britain's unemployed*, London: Routledge & Kegan Paul.

Department of Education and Science (1983) *Young People in the 80s: a survey*, London: HMSO.

Department of Employment (1970) *At Odds*, London: HMSO.

Dibiase, W. J. and Hjelle, L. A. (1968) 'Body image stereotypes and body type preferences among male college students', *Perceptual Motor Skills* 27: 1143–46.

Diener, C. J. and Dweck, C. S. (1978) 'An analysis of learned helplessness: continuous changes in performance strategy and achievement cognitions following failure', *Journal of Personality and Social Psychology* 36: 451–62.

Dight, S. (1976) *Scottish Drinking Habits*, p. 279, London: HMSO.

Dodd, D. (1978) 'Police and thieves on the streets of Brixton', *New Society* 16 March.

Dodge, K. A., Coie, J. D., and Brakke, N. P. (1982) 'Behaviour patterns of socially rejected and neglected pre-adolescents. The role of social approach and aggression', *Journal of Abnormal Child Psychology* 10: 389–409.

Dohrenwend, B. S. and Dohrenwend, B. P. (eds) (1974) *Stressful Life Events: their nature and effects*, New York: Wiley.

Donald, J. and Hall, S. (1986) *Politics and Ideology*, Milton Keynes: Open University Press.

Donovan, A. and Oddy, M. (1982) 'Psychological aspects of unemployment: an investigation into the emotional and social adjustments of school-leavers', *Journal of Adolescence* 5: 15–30.

Douglas, M. (1966) *Purity and Danger: an analysis of concepts of pollution and taboo*, London: Routledge & Kegan Paul.

Douvan, E. (1970) 'New sources of conflict in adolescence', in J. Bardwick, E. Douvan, M. Horner, and D. Gutman (eds) *Feminine Personality and Conflict*, Belmont California: Brooks Cole.

Douvan, E. (1979) 'Sex role learning', in J. C. Coleman (ed.) *The School Years*, London: Methuen.

Douvan, E. and Adelson, J. (1966) *The Adolescent Experience*, New York: John Wiley.

Dowling, P. and O'Brien, G. E. (1981) 'The effects of employment, unemployment and F. E. upon the work values of school-leavers', *Australian Journal of Psychology* 33 (2): 185–95.

Duck, S. W. (1973) 'Similarity and perceived similarity of personal constructs as influences on friendship choice', *British Journal of Social and Clinical Psychology* 12: 1–6.

Dulit, E. (1972) 'Adolescent thinking à la Piaget: the formal stage', *Journal of Youth and Adolescence* 1: 281–301.

Dunphy, D. C. (1972) 'Peer group socialisation', in F. J. Hunt (ed.) *Socialisation in Australia*, Sydney: Angus & Robertson.

Dweck, C. S. and Elliott, E. S. (1984) 'Achievement motivation', in M. Hetherington (ed.) *Social Development: Carmichael's Manual of Child Psychology*, pp. 643–91, New York: Wiley.

Eccleshall, R., Geoghegan, V., Jay, R., and Wilford, R. (1984) *Political Ideologies*, London: Hutchinson.

Eggleston, J. (1976) *Adolescence and Community*, London: Arnold.

Eggleston, J. (1979) *Work Experience in Secondary Schools*, London: Routledge & Kegan Paul.

Elder, G. H. (1968) 'Adolescent socialisation and development', *Handbook of Personality Theory and Research*, Chicago: Chicago University Press.

Elder, G. H. (1975) 'Adolescence in the life cycle: an introduction', in S. E. Dragastin and G. H. Elder (eds) *Adolescence in the Life Cycle*, New York: John Wiley.

Elkind, D. (1966) 'Conceptual orientation shifts in children and adolescents', *Child Development* 37: 493–8.

Elkind, D. (1967) 'Egocentrism in adolescence', *Child Development* 38: 1025–34.

Elkind, D. (1983) 'Strategic interactions in early adolescence', in W. Damon (ed.) *Social and Personality Development: essays on the growth of the child* pp. 434–44, New York: Norton.

References

Elkind, D. and Bowen, R. (1979) 'Imaginary audience behaviour in children and adolescents', *Developmental Psychology* 15: 38–44.

Elliott, D. S., Ageton, S. S., and Canter, R. J. (1979) 'An integrated theoretical perspective on delinquent behaviour', *Journal of Research in Crime and Delinquency*, 16: 3–27.

Emler, N. (1984) 'Differential involvement in delinquency: towards an interpretation in terms of reputation management', *Progress in Experimental Personality Research* 13: 173–239.

Emmett, I. (1971) *Youth and Leisure in an Urban Sprawl*, Manchester: Manchester University Press.

Emmett, I. (1977) Unpublished draft report to the Sports Council on decline in sports participation after leaving school. London: Sports Council.

Engel, M. (1959) 'The stability of the self-concept in adolescence', *Journal of Abnormal and Social Psychology* 58: 211–15.

Enright, R. D., Shukla, D. G., and Lapsley, D. K. (1980) 'Adolescent egocentrism – sociocentrism and self consciousness', *Journal of Youth and Adolescence*, 9: 101–16.

Entwistle, H. (1970) *Education, Work and Leisure*, London: Routledge & Kegan Paul.

Eppel, E. M. and Eppel, M. (1966) *Adolescence and Morality*, London: Routledge & Kegan Paul.

Epstein, S. (1973) 'The self-concept revisited or a theory of a theory', *American Psychologist* 28: 404–16.

Erikson, E. (1968) *Identity: youth and crisis*, New York: Norton.

Eveleth, P. and Tanner, J. M. (1977) *Worldwide Variation in Human Growth*, Cambridge: Cambridge University Press.

Fagin, L. (1981) *Unemployment and Health in Families*, London: Department of Health and Social Security.

Fagin, L. and Little, M. (1984) *The Forsaken Families*, Harmondsworth: Penguin.

Farley, F. H. and Sewell, T. (1975) 'Attribution and achievement motivation differences between delinquent and non delinquent black adolescents', *Adolescence* 10: 391–7.

Farrell, C. (1978) *My Mother Said*, London: Routledge & Kegan Paul.

Farrington, D. P., Gundry, G., and West, D. J. (1975) 'The familial transmission of criminality', *Medicine, Science and the Law* 15: 177–86.

Faust, M. S. (1960) 'Developmental maturity as a detriment in prestige of adolescent girls', *Child Development* 31: 173–84.

Feather, N. T. (1982) 'Unemployment and its psychological correlates: a study of depressive symptoms, self-esteem and attributional style', *Australian Journal of Psychology* 34 (3): 309–23.

Feather, N. T. and Barber, J. G. (1983) 'Depressive reactions and unemployment', *Journal of Abnormal Psychology* 92 (2): 185–95.

Feather, N. T. and Bond, M. J. (1983) 'Time structure and purposeful activity among employed and unemployed university graduates', *Journal of Occupational Psychology* 56 (3): 241–54.

Ferguson, T. and Cunnison, J. (1951) *The Young Wage Earner*, Oxford University Press.

Fiddy, R. (1983) *In Place of Work*, Lewes: Falmer.

Fincham, F. D. (1982) 'Moral judgement and the development of causal schemes', *European Journal of Social Psychology* 12: 47–62.

Fincham, F. D. (1983) 'Developmental dimensions of attribution theory', in J. Jaspars, F. D. Fincham, and M. Hewstone (eds) *Attribution Theory and Research: conceptual, developmental and social dimensions*, London: Academic Press.

Fine, L. (1977) *After All We've Done For Them*, Englewood Cliffs, NJ: Prentice Hall.

Flavell, J. H. (1977) *Cognitive Development*, New Jersey: Prentice-Hall.

Flexer, B. and Roberge, J. (1983) 'A longitudinal investigation of field dependence-independence and the development of formal operational thought', *British Journal of Educational Psychology* 53: 195–204.

Flude, R. A. (1977) 'The development of an occupational self-concept and commitment to an occupation in a group of skilled manual workers', *Sociological Review* 25: 41–9.

Fogelman, K. (1976) *Britain's 16-year-olds*, London: National Children's Bureau.

Ford, M. E. (1982) 'Social cognition and social competence in adolescence', *Developmental Psychology* 18: 323–40.

F.P.I.S. (1986) 'The legal position regarding contraceptive advice and provision to young people', *Fact Sheet F.3*, July, London: Family Planning Information Service.

Francis, L. J. (1985) *Young and Unemployed*, London: Costello.

Franks, D. D. and Marolla, J. (1976) 'Efficacious action and social approval as interacting dimensions of self-esteem: a tentative formulation through construct validation', *Sociometry* 39: 324–41.

Freedman, B. J., Rosenthal, L., Donahoe, C. P., Schlundt, D. G., and McFall, R. M. (1978) 'A social-behavioural analysis of skill deficits in delinquent and non delinquent adolescent boys', *Journal of Consulting and Clinical Psychology* 46: 1448–62.

Freedman, M. (1969) *The Process of Work Establishment*, New York: Columbia University Press.

French, D. C. and Tyne, T. F. (1982) 'The identification and treatment of children with peer-relationship difficulties', in J. P. Curran and P. M. Monti (eds) *Social Skills Training: a practical handbook for assessment and treatment*, pp. 280–308, New York: Guilford.

Freud, A. (1937) *The Ego and the Mechanisms of Defence*, London: Hogarth Press.

Frith, S. (1978) *The Sociology of Rock*, London: Constable.

Fryer, D. and Payne, R. (1984) 'Proactive behaviour in unemployment: findings and implications', *Leisure Studies* 3: 273–95.

Furnham, A. (1982) 'Explanations for unemployment in Britain', *European Journal of Social Psychology* 12: 335–52.

Furnham, A. (1984) 'Getting a job: school-leavers' perceptions of employment prospects', *British Journal Educational Psychology* 54: 293–305.

Furnham, A. and Gunter, B. (1983) 'Political knowledge and awareness in adolescence', *Journal of Adolescence* 6: 373–86.

Furnham, A. and Gunter, B. (1988) *The Anatomy of Adolescence*, London: Routledge.

References

Furstenberg, F. F. Jr., Brooks-Gunn, J., and Morgan, S. P. (1987) *Adolescent Mothers in Later Life*, New York: Cambridge University Press.

Gaffney, L. R. and McFall, R. M. (1981) 'A comparison of social skills in delinquent and non delinquent adolescent girls using behavioural role-play inventory', *Journal of Consulting and Clinical Psychology* 49: 959–67.

Gallatin, J. E. (1975) *Adolescence and Individuality*, New York: Harper & Row.

Gatherer, W. A. (1982) 'The education of the 16–18 group', *Scottish Educational Review* 14 (2): 93–100.

Gecas, V. and Schwalbe, M. L. (1983) 'Beyond the looking-glass self: social structure and efficacy-based self-esteem', *Social Psychology Quarterly* 46 (2): 77–8.

Geer, B. (1972) *Learning to Work*, New York: Russell Sage.

Gergen, K. J. and Davis, K. E. (1985) *The Social Construction of the Person*, New York: Springer-Verlag.

Gershuny, J. I. (1978) *After Industrial Society?* London: Macmillan.

Gilligan, C. (1982) *In a Different Voice*, Cambridge, Massachusetts: Harvard University Press.

Glueck, S. (1959) 'Theory and fact in criminology', *The Problem of Delinquency*, pp. 241–52, Boston: Houghton Mifflin.

Goldthorpe, J. H. and Payne, C. (1986) 'Trends in intergenerational class mobility in England and Wales 1972–1983', *Sociology* 20 (1).

Gothard, W. P. (1982) *Brightest and Best*, Driffield: Nafferton Books.

Gottman, J. M., Gonso, J., and Rasmussen, B. (1975) 'Social interaction, social competencies and friendship in children', *Child Development* 46: 709–18.

Gow, L. and McPherson, A. (1981) *Tell Them From Me*, Aberdeen: Aberdeen University Press.

Greenberg, M. T., Siegel, J. M., and Leitch, C. J. (1983) 'The nature and importance of attachment relationships to parents and peers during adolescence', *Journal of Youth and Adolescence* 12 (5): 373–83.

Greenberger, E. and Sorenson, A. B. (1974) 'Toward a concept of psychosocial maturity', *Journal of Youth and Adolescence* 3: 329–58.

Griffin, C. (1981) *Cultures of Femininity: romance revisited*, University of Birmingham: Centre for Contemporary Cultural Studies.

Griffin, C. (1982) 'Women and leisure', in J. Hargreaves (ed.) *Sport, Culture and Ideology*, London: Routledge & Kegan Paul.

Griffin, C. (1985) *Typical Girls?*, London: Routledge & Kegan Paul.

Grinder, R. E. (1978) *Adolescence* (2nd edn), New York: Wiley.

Grotevant, H. D. and Adams, G. R. (1984) 'Development of an objective measure to assess ego-identity in adolescence: validation and replication', *Journal of Youth and Adolescence* 13: 419–38.

Grotevant, H. D., Thorbecke, W., and Meyer, M. L. (1982) 'An extension of Marcia's identity status interview into the interpersonal domain', *Journal of Youth and Adolescence* 11: 33–47.

Gunderson, E. K. (1956) 'Body size, self-evaluation and military effectiveness', *Journal of Personality and Social Psychology* 2: 902–6.

Guppy, N. (1970) *Wai-wai*, Harmondsworth: Penguin.

Gurney, R. M. (1982) 'Leaving school, facing unemployment and making attributions about the causes of unemployment', *Journal of Vocational Behaviour* 18: 79–81.

Haan, N. (1977) 'A manual for interactional morality', unpublished manuscript, University of California: Berkeley.

Hale, S. (1971) *The Idle Hill*, London: Bedford Square Press.

Hall, S., Critcher, C., Jefferson, T., Clarke, J., and Roberts, B. (1978) *Policing the Crisis: mugging, the state and law and order*, London: Macmillan.

Hammar, S. L. (1965) 'The obese adolescent', *Journal of School Health* 35: 246–9.

Hargreaves, D. H. (1967) *Social Relations in a Secondary School*, London: Routledge & Kegan Paul.

Hargreaves, D. H. (1972) *Interpersonal Relations and Education*, London: Routledge & Kegan Paul.

Hargreaves, D. H. (1981) 'Unemployment, leisure and education', *Oxford Review of Education* 7 (5): 197–210.

Hargreaves, D. H. (1982) *The Challenge for the Comprehensive School*, London: Routledge & Kegan Paul.

Harré, R. (1984) *Personal Being*, Oxford: Blackwell.

Harter, S. (1983) 'The development of the self-system', in M. Hetherington (ed.) *Handbook of Child Psychology: social and personality development*, New York: Wiley.

Hartley, D. (1985) 'Social education in Scotland: some sociological considerations', *Scottish Educational Review* 17 (2): 92–8.

Hartley, J. F. (1980) 'The impact of self-esteem on the unemployment of managers', *Journal of Occupational Psychology* 53: 147–55.

Hartup, W. W. (1982) 'Peer relations', in C. B. Kopp and J. B. Krakow (eds) *The Child: development in a social context*, pp. 514–75, Reading, MA: Addison-Wesley.

Hartup, W. W. (1983) 'Peer interaction and the behavioural development of the individual child', in W. Damon (ed.) *Social and Personality Development: essays on the growth of the child*, pp. 220–33, New York: Norton.

Haworth, J. T. (1984) 'The perceived nature of meaningful pursuits and the social psychology of commitment', *Society & Leisure* 7: 197–216.

Hayman, S. (1986) *It's More than Sex*, Aldershot: Wildwood House.

Hendricks, L. F. and Fullilove, R. E. (1983) 'Locus of control and the use of contraception among unmarried black adolescent fathers and their controls', *Journal of Youth and Adolescence* 12: 225–33.

Hendry, L. B. (1986) 'Changing schools in a changing society', in J. Evans (ed.) *Physical Education, Sport and Schooling*, London: Falmer Press.

Hendry, L. B. (1978) *School, Sport and Leisure*, London: A. & C. Black.

Hendry, L. B. (1981) *Adolescents and Leisure*, London: Sports Council/ SSRC.

Hendry, L. B. (1983) *Growing Up and Going Out*, Aberdeen: Aberdeen University Press.

References

Hendry, L. B. (1987) 'Young people: from school to unemployment', in S. Fineman (ed.) *Unemployment – Personal and Social Consequences*, London: Tavistock.

Hendry, L. B., Brown, L., and Hutcheon, G. (1981) 'Adolescents in community centres: some urban and rural comparisons', *Scottish Journal of Physical Education* 9: 28–40.

Hendry, L. B. and Gillies, P. (1978) 'Body type, body esteem, school and leisure: a study of overweight, average and underweight adolescents', *Journal of Youth and Adolescence* 7 (2): 181–94.

Hendry, L. B. and Jamie, D. (1978) 'Pupil's self concepts and perceptions of popular qualities', *Scottish Educational Review* 10 (2): 44–52.

Hendry, L. B. and McKenzie, H. F. (1978) 'Advantages and disadvantages of raising the school-leaving age: the pupil's viewpoint', *Scottish Educational Review* 10 (2): 53–61.

Hendry, L. B. and Marr, D. (1985) 'Leisure education and young people's leisure', *Scottish Educational Review* 17 (2): 116–27.

Hendry, L. B. and Percy, A. (1981) 'Pre-adolescents, television styles and leisure', unpublished memorandum, University of Aberdeen.

Hendry, L. B. and Raymond, M. (1983) 'Youth unemployment and lifestyles: some educational considerations', *Scottish Educational Review* 15 (1): 28–40.

Hendry, L. B. and Raymond, M. (1985) 'Coping with unemployment', unpublished Report to the Scottish Education Department, Edinburgh.

Hendry, L. B. and Raymond, M. (1986) 'Psychological/sociological aspects of youth unemployment: an interpretative theoretical model', *Journal of Adolescence* 9: 355–66.

Hendry, L. B., Raymond, M., and Stewart, C. (1984) 'Unemployment, school and leisure: an adolescent study', *Leisure Studies* 3: 175–87.

Hendry, L. B., Shucksmith, J., and McCrae, J. (1985) *Young People's Leisure and Lifestyles in Modern Scotland*. Dept. of Education, University of Aberdeen and Scottish Sports Council: Edinburgh.

Hendry, L. B. and Simpson, D. O. (1977) 'One centre: two subcultures', *Scottish Educational Studies* 9 (2): 112–21.

Henriksson, B. (1983) *Not For Sale*, Aberdeen: Aberdeen University Press.

Hepworth, J. T. (1980) 'Moderating factors of the psychological impact of unemployment', *Journal of Occupational Psychology* 53: 139–45.

Hetherington, E. M. (1972) 'Effects of father absence on personality development in adolescent daughters', *Developmental Psychology* 7: 313–26.

Hetherington, E. M. (1980) 'Children and divorce', in R. Henderson (ed.) *Parent–Child Interaction: theory, research and prospect*, New York: Academic Press.

Hetherington, E. M., Cox, M., and Cox, R. (1978) 'The development of children in mother headed families', in H. Hoffman and D. Reiss (eds) *The American Family: dying or developing*, New York: Plenum.

Higgins, E. T., Rubel, D. N., and Hartup, W. W. (1983) *Social Cognition and Social Development*, Cambridge: Cambridge University Press.

228

Hill, J. (1978) 'The psychological impact of unemployment', *New Society* 19 January.

Hill, M. J., Harrison, R. M., Sargent, A. V., and Talbot, V. (1973) *Men Out of Work: a study of unemployment in three towns*, Cambridge: Cambridge University Press.

Hirschi, S. (1969) *Causes of Delinquency*, University of California Press.

Hoffman, A. D. (1978) 'Legal and social implications of adolescent sexual behaviour', *Journal of Adolescence* 1: 25–34.

Hoffman, L. W. (1974) 'Effects of maternal employment on the child – a review of the research', *Developmental Psychology* 10: 204–28.

Hoffman, L. W. (1979) 'Maternal employment: 1979', *American Psychologist*, 34: 859–65.

Holland, G. (1978) 'M.S.C.: securing a future for young people', *Coombe Lodge Report* 2: 4.

Holt, M. (1983) 'Vocationalism: the new threat to universal education', *Forum* 25 (3): 84–86.

Honess, T. (1984) 'Group membership and personal identity', *BPS Social Section Conference*, University of Sheffield.

Huba, G. J., Wingard, J. A., and Bentler, P. M. (1979) 'Beginning adolescent drug use and peer and adult interaction patterns', *Journal of Consultant and Clinical Psychology* 47: 265–76.

Hunter, F. T. (1985) 'Adolescent's perception of discussions with parents and friends', *Developmental Psychology* 21: 433–40.

Hurlock, E. B. (1973) *Adolescent Development*, New York: McGraw-Hill.

Iacovetta, R. G. (1975) 'Adolescent-adult interaction and peer-group involvement', *Adolescence* 10: 327–36.

Ingham, R. (1987) 'Psychological contributions to the study of leisure, Part Two', *Leisure Studies* 6: 1–14.

Inhelder, B. and Piaget, J. (1958) *The Growth of Logical Thinking*, London: Routledge & Kegan Paul.

Jackson, P. R. and Banks, M. H. (1982) 'Unemployment and risk of minor psychiatric disorder in young people: cross-sectional and longitudinal evidence', *Psychological Medicine* 12: 789–98.

Jahoda, M. (1979) 'The impact of unemployment in the 1930s and the 1970s', *Bulletin of British Psychological Society* 32: 309–14.

Jahoda, M. (1981) 'Work, employment and unemployment: values, theories and approaches in social research', *American Psychologist* 36 (2): 184–91.

Jahoda, M. (1982) *Employment and Unemployment: a social-psychological analysis*, Cambridge: Cambridge University Press.

Jahoda, M. (1984) 'Social institutions and human needs: a comment on Fryer and Payne', *Leisure Studies* 3: 297–99.

Jaspars, J. (1985) 'Social attributions', *ESRC Conference on social beliefs*, Cambridge, March.

Jenkins, C. and Sherman, B. (1979) *The Collapse of Work*, London: Eyre-Methuen.

Jephcott, P. (1967) *A Time of One's Own*, Edinburgh: Oliver & Boyd.

References

Jessor, R. and Jessor, S. L. (1977) *Problem Behaviour and Psychological Development*, p. 281, New York: Academic Press.

Johnson, R. (1981) *Education and Popular Politics*, E353 Block 1, Unit 1, Milton Keynes: The Open University Press.

Johnson, R. E. (1979) *Juvenile Delinquency and its Origins*, London: Cambridge University Press.

Jonathan, R. (1982) 'Lifelong learning: slogan, educational aim or manpower service?', *Scottish Educational Review* 14 (2): 80–92.

Jones, W. H. (1981) 'Loneliness and social contact', *Journal of Psychology* 113: 295–6.

Jones, E. F., Forrest, J. D., Goldman, N., Henshaw, S., Lincoln, R., Rosoff, J., Westoff, C., and Wulf, D. (1985) 'Teenage pregnancy in developed countries: determinants and policy implications', *Family Planning Perspectives*, 17: 53–63.

Jones, M. C. and Bayley, N. (1950) 'Physical maturing among boys as related to behaviour', *Journal of Educational Psychology* 41: 129–48.

Jones, M. C. and Mussen, P. H. (1958) 'Self conceptions, motivations, and interpersonal attitudes of early and late maturing girls', *Child Development* 29: 491–501.

Jorgensen, E. C. and Howell, R. J. (1969) 'Changes in self, ideal-self correlations from ages 8 through 18', *Journal of Social Psychology* 79: 63–7.

Jourard, S. (1967a) 'Automation and leisure', *Humanities* 3: 78–85.

Jourard, S. (1967b) 'Out of touch: body-taboo', *New Society* 9.

Jourard, F. M. and Secord, S. F. (1955) 'Body-cathexis and the ideal female figure', *Journal of Abnormal and Social Psychology* 50: 243–6.

Juhasz, A. M. (1975) 'Sexual decision making: the crux of the adolescent problem', in R. E. Grinder (ed.) *Studies in Adolescence* (3rd edn), London: Collier-Macmillan.

Kandel, D. B. (1978) 'Homophily, selection and socialisation in adolescent friendships', *American Journal of Sociology* 84: 427–36.

Kandel, D. B., Kessler, R. C., and Margulies, R. Z. (1978) 'Antecedents of adolescent initiation into stages of drug use', *Journal of Youth and Adolescence* 7: 13–40.

Kandel, D. B. and Lesser, G. S. (1972) *Youth in Two Worlds: U.S. and Denmark*, San Francisco: Jossey-Bass.

Kaneti-Barry, M., Baldy, R., and van der Eyken, W. (1971) *2100 Sixth Formers*, London: Hutchinson.

Kaplan, H. B. (1980) *Deviant Behaviour in Defense of Self*, New York: Academic Press.

Karlsmith, L. (1964) 'Effects of early father absence on scholastic aptitude', *Harvard Educational Review* 34: 3–21.

Katchadourian, H. (1977) *The Biology of Adolescence*, San Francisco: Freeman.

Katz, P. and Zigler, E. (1967) 'Self-image disparity: A developmental approach', *Journal of Personality and Social Psychology* 5: 186–95.

Keating, D. P. (1980) 'Thinking processes in adolescence', in J. Adelson (ed.) *Handbook of Adolescent Psychology*, New York: Wiley.

Keil, I. (1978) *Becoming a Worker*, Leicester: Leicester Committee for Education and Industry/training Services Agency.

Kelley, H. H. (1967) 'Attribution theory in social psychology', in D. Levine (ed.) *Nebraska Symposium on Motivation*, Lincoln, Nebraska: University of Nebraska Press.

Kelsall, R. K., Poole, A. and Kuhn, A. (1972) *Graduates: the sociology of an elite*, London: Methuen.

Kelvin, P. (1981) 'Work as a source of identity: the implications of unemployment', *British Journal of Guidance and Counselling* 9: 2–11.

Kelvin, P., Dewberry, C., and Morley-Bunker, N. (1984) *Unemployment and Leisure*, University College, London, Mimeo.

Keyes, S. and Coleman, J. (1983) 'Sex-role conflicts and personal adjustment: a study of British adolescents', *Journal of Youth and Adolescence* 12 (6): 443–57.

King, M. D., Day, R. E., Oliver, J. F., Lush, M., and Watson, J. M. (1981) 'Solvent encephalography', *British Medical Journal* 2 (83): 663–5.

Kinsey, A. C., Pomeroy, W. B., and Martin, C. E. (1948) *Sexual Behaviour in the Human Male*, Philadelphia: W. B. Saunders.

Kinsey, A. C., Pomeroy, W. B., Martin, C. E., and Gebhard, P. H. (1953) *Sexual Behaviour in the Human Female*, Philadelphia: W. B. Saunders.

Kitwood, T. (1980) *Disclosures to a Stranger*, London: Routledge & Kegan Paul.

Kohen-Raz, R. (1974) 'Physiological maturation and mental growth at pre-adolescence and puberty', *Journal of Child Psychology and Psychiatry* 15: 199–214.

Kohlberg, L. (1964) 'The development of moral character and moral ideology', in M. L. Hoffman and L. W. Hoffman (eds) *Review of Child Development Research*, Vol. 1, New York: Russell Sage Foundation.

Kohlberg, L. (1969) *Stages in the Development of Moral Thought and Action*, New York: Holt Rinehart & Winston.

Kohlberg, L. and Gilligan, T. F. (1971) 'The adolescent as philosopher: the discovery of the self in a post-conventional world', *Daedalus* 100: 1051–65.

Krause, E. A. (1971) *The Sociology of Occupations*, Boston: Little Brown & Company.

Kroger, J. (1985) 'Relationships during adolescence: a cross national comparison of New Zealand and United States teenagers', *Journal of Youth and Adolescence* 8: 47–56.

Kroger, J. (1986) 'The relative importance of identity status interview components: replication and extension', *Journal of Adolescence* 9 (4): 337–54.

Kuhn, D., Langer, J., Kohlberg, L., and Haan, N. (1977) 'The presence of formal operational thought structures in adolescence and adulthood', *Genetic Psychology Monographs* 95: 97–188.

Kurdek, L. (ed.) (1983) *Children and Divorce*, San Francisco: Jossey-Bass.

Laishley, J. (1979) 'The human relations course', in G. E. Verma and C. Bagley (eds) *Race Relations and Education*, London: Macmillan.

Langford, P. E. and George, S. (1971) 'Intellectual and moral development in adolescence', *British Journal of Educational Psychology* 45: 330–2.

231

References

Larson, L. E. (1972a) 'The influence of parents and peers during adolescence: the situation hypothesis revisited', *Journal of Marriage and the Family* 34: 67–74.

Larson, L. E. (1972b) 'The relative influence of parent-adolescent affect in predicting the salience hierarchy among youth', *Pacific Sociological Review* 15: 83–102.

Lavercombe, S. and Fleming, D. (1981) 'Attitudes and duration of unemployment among sixteen-year-old school leavers', *British Journal of Guidance and Counselling* 9 (1): 36–45.

Lee, L. (1971) 'The concomitant development of cognitive and moral modes of thought: a test of selected deductions from Piaget's theory', *Genetic Psychology Monographs* 83: 93–146.

Leigh, J. (1971) *Young People and Leisure*, London: Routledge & Kegan Paul.

Leming, J. S. (1974) 'Moral reasoning, sense of control and social-political activism among adolescents', *Adolescence* 9: 507–28.

Lerner, H. (1987) 'Psychodynamic models', in V. B. Van Hasselt and M. Hersen (eds) *Handbook of Adolescent Psychology*, Oxford: Pergamon Press.

Lerner, R. M. (1969) 'The development of stereotyped expectancies of body-build behaviour relations', *Child Development* 50: 137–41.

Lerner, R. M. (1985) 'Adolescent maturational changes and psychosocial development: a dynamic interactional perspective', *Journal of Youth and Adolescence* 14: 355–72.

Lerner, R. M. and Karabenick, S. (1974) 'Physical attractiveness, body attitudes and self-concept in late adolescents', *Journal of Youth and Adolescence* 3: 7–16.

Lesser, G. S. and Kandel, D. B. (1969) *Youth in Two Worlds*, London: Jossey-Bass.

Leyva, F. A. and Furth, H. G. (1986) 'Compromise formation in social conflicts: the influence of age, issue and interpersonal context', *Journal of Youth and Adolescence* 15 (5): 441–51.

Lifshitz, M. (1973) 'Internal-external locus-of-control dimension as a function of age and the socialisation milieu', *Child Development* 44: 538–46.

Lindsay, C. (1969) *School and Community*, London: Pergamon Press.

Löchel, E. (1983) 'Sex differences in achievement attribution', in J. Jaspars, F. D. Fincham, and M. Hewstone (eds) *Attribution Theory and Research: conceptual, developmental and social dimensions*, London: Academic Press.

Logan, R. F. M. and Goldberg, E. M. (1954) 'Rising 18 in a London suburb', *British Journal of Sociology* 4: 323–45.

Louden, D. (1980) 'Self-esteem among black teenagers: a comparative study of self-esteem among minority group adolescents in Britain', *Journal of Adolescence* 3 (1): 17–34.

McCarthy, J. D. and Hoge, D. R. (1982) 'Analyses of age effects in longitudinal studies of adolescent self-esteem', *Developmental Psychology* 18: 372–9.

Macoby, E. E. and Jacklin, C. N. (1974) *The Psychology of Sex Differences*, Oxford: Oxford University Press.

Macoby, E. E. and Jacklin, C. N. (1980) 'Psychological sex differences', in M. Rutter (ed.) *Scientific Foundations of Developmental Psychiatry*, pp. 92–100, London: Heinemann Medical.

McCormack, M. (1985) *The Generation Gap: the view from both sides*, London: Constable.

Mackay, D. I. (1971) *Labour Markets Under Different Employment Conditions*, London: Allen & Unwin.

McKeganey, N. P. and Boddy, F. A. (1987) 'Drug abuse in Glasgow: an interim report of an exploratory study', *Report by Social Paediatric and Obstetric Research Unit*, Glasgow: University of Glasgow.

McLoughlin, D. and Whitfield, R. (1984) 'Adolescents and their experience of divorce', *Journal of Youth and Adolescence* 7: 155–70.

McPhail, P. (1977) *And How are We Feeling Today?* Health Education Council Project, Cambridge: Cambridge University Press.

McRobbie, A. (1978) 'Working class girls and the culture of femininity', in *Women Take Issue: aspects of women's subordination*. Edited by the Women's Studies Group Centre for Contemporary Cultural Studies, University of Birmingham, pp. 96–108, London: Hutchinson.

McRobbie, A. and Garber, J. (1976) 'Girls and subcultures', in S. Hall, and T. Jefferson (eds) *Resistance Through Rituals*, London: Hutchinson.

McRobbie, A. and McCabe, T. (1981) *Feminism for Girls*, London: Routledge & Kegan Paul.

Maizels, J. (1970) *Adolescent Needs and the Transition from School to Work*, London: Athlone Press.

Mann, M. (1973) *Workers on the Move*, Cambridge University Press.

Marcia, J. E. (1966) 'Development and validation of ego-identity status', *Journal of Personality and Social Psychology* 3: 551–8.

Marcia, J. E. (1967) 'Ego-identity status: relationships to change self-esteem "general maladjustment" and authoritarianism', *Journal of Personality* 35: 119–33.

Marcia, J. E. (1980) 'Identity in adolescence', in J. Adelson (ed.) *Handbook of Adolescent Psychology*, New York: Wiley.

Marsden, D. (1982) *Workless*, London: Croom Helm.

Marsh, P., Rosser, E., and Harré, R. (1978) *The Rules of Disorder*, London: Routledge & Kegan Paul.

Marsland, D. (1987) *Education and Youth*, London: The Falmer Press.

Martens, R., Christina, R. S., Sharkey, B. S., and Harvey, J. S. (1981) *Coaching Young Athletes*, Champaign, Illinois: Human Kinetics.

Martin, R. (1983) 'Women and unemployment: activities and social contact', paper presented to SSRC Labour Markets Workshop, Manchester.

Matteson, D. R. (1974) 'Alienation vs exploration and commitment: personality and family corollaries of adolescent identity status', *Rapport Fra Projekt for Ungoomsforskning*, Copenhagen, Denmark: Royal Danish School of Educational Studies.

Matteson, D. R. (1977) 'Exploration and commitment: sex differences and methodological problems in the use of identity status categories', *Journal of Youth and Adolescence* 6: 353–74.

Meadows, S. (1986) *Understanding Child Development*, London: Hutchinson.

Meikle, S., Peitchinis, J. A., and Pearce, K. (1985) *Teenage Sexuality*, London: Taylor & Francis.

Melgosa, J. (1987) *Social Influence and Social Change*, London: Academic Press.

Meredith, H. (1963) 'Changes in the stature and body weight of North American boys during the last eighty years', in L. Lipsitt and C. Spiker (eds) *Advances in Child Development and Behaviour*, Volume 1, New York and London: Academic Press.

Merton, R. K., Reader G. G., and Kendall, P. L. (1957) *The Student Physician*, Cambridge, Mass.: Harvard University Press.

Meyerhoff, H. and Meyerhoff, B. (1964) 'Field observation of middle-class groups', *Social Forces* 42 (3): 328–36.

Miller, A. G. (1970) 'Role of physical attractiveness in impression formation', *Psychonomic Science* 19: 241–3.

Miller, K. and Coleman, J. C. (1980) 'Attitudes to the future as a function of age, sex and school leaving age' (unpublished).

Milson, F. (1972) *Youth in a Changing Society*, London: Routledge & Kegan Paul.

Mitchell, A. (1985) *Children in the Middle: living through divorce*, London: Tavistock.

Monello, L. F. and Mayer, J. (1963) 'Obese adolescent girls: an unrecognisable minority', *American Journal of Clinical Nutrition* 13: 35–9.

Montemayor, R. (1982) 'The relationship between parent-adolescent conflict and the amount of time adolescents spend alone and with parents and peers', *Child Development* 53: 1512–19.

Montemayor, R. and Eisen, M. (1977) 'The development of self-conceptions from childhood to adolescence', *Development Psychology* 4: 314–19.

Montemayor, R. and Hansom, E. (1985) 'A naturalistic view of conflict between adolescents and their parents and siblings', *Journal of Early Adolescence* 5 (1): 23–30.

Mortimer, J. T. and Finch, M. D. (1984) 'Autonomy as a source of self-esteem in adolescence', unpublished manuscript.

Mortimer, J. T. and Lorence, J. (1980) 'Self-concept stability and change from late adolescence to early adulthood', in R. G. Simmons (ed.) *Research in Community and Mental Health*, Greenwich, Conn.: JAI Press.

Morton-Williams, R. and Finch, S. (1968) *Enquiry 1: young school-leavers*, London: HMSO.

Moscovici, S. (1976) *Social Influence and Social Change*, London: Academic Press.

Moscovici, S. and Hewstone, M. (1983) 'Social representations and social explanations: from the "naive" to the "amateur" scientist', in M. Hewstone (ed.) *Attribution Theory: social and functional extensions*, Oxford: Blackwell.

Mugny, G. (1982) *The Power of Minorities*, London: Academic Press.

Mundy, J. and Odum, L. (1979) *Leisure*, New York: Wiley.

Mungham, G. and Pearson, G. (1976) *Working Class Youth Culture*, London: Routledge & Kegan Paul.

Murdock, G. and Phelps, G. (1973) *Mass Media and the Secondary School*, London: Macmillan.

Murphey, E. B., Silber, E., Coelho, G. V., Hamburg, D., and Greenberg, I. (1963) 'Development of autonomy and parent-child interaction in late adolescence', *American Journal of Orthopsychiatry* 33: 643–52.

Murphy, G. (1947) *Personality*, New York: Harper.

Murray, C. (1978) *Youth Unemployment: a social-psychological study of disadvantaged 16–18 year olds*, Slough: National Foundation Educational Research.

Musgrove, F. (1963) 'Inter-generation attitudes', *British Journal of Social and Clinical Psychology* 2: 209–23.

Musgrove, F. (1964) *Youth and the Social Order*, London: Routledge & Kegan Paul.

Mussen, P. H. (1962) 'Long term consequences of masculinity of interest in adolescence', *Journal of Consulting Psychology* 26: 435–40.

Mussen, P. H., Conger, J. J., and Kagan, J. (1974) *Child Development and Personality*, New York: Harper & Row.

Mussen, P. H. and Jones, M. (1957) 'Self conceptions, motivations and interpersonal attitudes of late and early maturing boys', *Child Development* 28: 243–56.

Mussen, P. H., Young, H. V., Daddini, R., and Morante, L. (1963) 'The influence of father/son relationships on adolescent personality and attitudes', *Journal of Child Psychology and Psychiatry* 4: 3–16.

Muuss, R. E. (1970) 'Adolescent development and the secular trend', *Adolescence* 5: 267–84.

Muuss, R. E. (1980) 'Peter Blos's modern interpretation of adolescence', *Journal of Adolescence* 3: 229–52.

Muuss, R. E. (1988) *Theories of Adolescence* (5th edn), New York: Random House.

Nava, M. and McRobbie, A. (1984) *Gender and Generation*, London: Macmillan.

Neimark, E. D. (1975) 'Intellectual development during adolescence', in F. D. Horowitz (ed.) *Review of Child Development Research*, Vol. 4, Chicago: University of Chicago Press.

Newman, P. R. and Newman, B. M. (1976) 'Early adolescence and its conflict: group identity vs. alienation', *Adolescence* 11: 261–74.

Nisbet, S. (1957) *Purpose in the Curriculum*, London: University Press.

Noller, P. and Callan, V. (1986) 'Adolescent and parent perceptions of family cohesion and adaptability', *Journal of Adolescence* 9: 97–106.

Offer, D. (1969) *The Psychological World of the Teenager*, New York: Basic Books.

Offer, D. and Offer, J. B. (1975) *From Teenage to Young Manhood*, New York: Basic Books.

Offer, D., Rostov, E., and Howard, K. I. (1981) *The Adolescent: a psychological self-portrait*, New York: Basic Books.

Offer, D., Rostov, E., and Howard, K. I. (1984) *Patterns of Adolescent Self Image*, San Francisco: Jossey-Bass.

Offer, D. and Sabshin, M. (1984) *Normality and the Life Cycle: a critical integration*, New York: Basic Books.

O'Hagan, F. J. (1976) 'Gang characteristics: an empirical survey', *Journal of Child Psychology and Psychiatry* 17 (5): 305–14.

O'Malley, P. M. and Bachman, J. G. (1983) 'Self-esteem: change and stability between ages 13 and 23', *Developmental Psychology* 19 (2): 257–68.

Pahl, R. E. (1978) 'Living without a job: how school-leavers see the future', *New Society* 2 November.

Palmer, V. C. (1964) 'Young workers in their first jobs', *Occupational Psychology* 38: 99–113.

Parker, S. (1983) *Leisure and Work*, London: Allen & Unwin.

Patrick, J. (1973) *A Glasgow Gang Observed*, London: Eyre-Methuen.

Patterson, O. (1966) 'The dance invasion', *New Society* 401–3.

Penk, W. E. (1969) 'Age changes and correlates of internal-external locus of control scale', *Psychological Reports* 25: 856.

Peskin, H. (1973) 'Influence of the developmental schedule of puberty on learning and ego-functioning', *Journal of Youth and Adolescence* 4: 273–90.

Petersen, A. C. (1988) 'Adolescent development', *Annual Review of Psychology* 39: 583–607.

Petersen, A. C. and Crockett, L. (1985) 'Pubertal timing and grade effects on adjustment', *Journal of Youth and Adolescence* 14: 191–206.

Petersen, A. C., Ebatta, A. T., and Graber, J. A. (1987) 'Coping with adolescence: the functions and dysfunctions of poor achievement', paper presented at the Biennial Meeting of the Society of Research in Child Development, Baltimore, Maryland.

Petersen, A. C. and Taylor, B. (1980) 'The biological approach to adolescence: biological change and psychosocial adaptation', in J. Adelson (ed.) *Handbook of Adolescent Psychology*, New York: John Wiley.

Phillips, D. (1973) 'Young and unemployed in a northern city', in D. Weir (ed.) *Men and Work in Modern Britain*, London: Fontana.

Phillips, D. and Zigler, E. (1980) 'Children's self-image disparity: effects of age, socio-economic status, ethnicity and gender', *Journal of Personality and Social Psychology* 39 (4): 689–700.

Piaget, J. (1972) 'Intellectual evolution from adolescence to adulthood', *Human Development* 15: 1–12.

Piaget, J. (1932) *The Moral Judgement of the Child*, London: Routledge & Kegan Paul.

Piers, E. V. and Harris, D. B. (1964) 'Age and other correlates of self-concept in children', *Journal of Educational Psychology* 55: 91–5.

Plant, M. A. (1979) *Drinking Careers: occupations, drinking habits and drinking problems*, London: Tavistock.

Plant, M. A., Peck, D. F., and Stuart, R. (1982) 'Self-reported drinking habits and alcohol-related consequences amongst a cohort of Scottish teenagers', *British Journal of Addiction* 77: 75–90.

Plant, M. A. and Stuart, R. (1984) 'The correlates of serious alchohol-related consequences and illicit drug use amongst a cohort of Scottish teenagers', *British Journal of Addiction* 79: 197–200.

Pollert, A. (1981) *Girls, Wives, Factory Lives*, London: Macmillan.

Pollock, G. J. and Nicholson, V. M. (1981) *Just the Job*, Sevenoaks: Hodder & Stoughton.

Poppleton, P. and Brown, P. (1966) 'The secular trend in puberty: has stability been achieved?', *British Journal of Educational Psychology* 36: 95–100.

Prais, S. J. (1981) 'Vocational qualifications of the labour force in Britain and Germany', *National Institute Economic Review* 98(4): 47–59.

Raffe, D. (1983) 'Youth unemployment in Scotland since 1977', *Scottish Educational Review* 15: 16–27.

Rapoport, R. and Rapoport, R. N. (1975) *Leisure and the Family Life-Cycle*, London: Routledge & Kegan Paul.

Rasmussen, J. E. (1964) 'The relationship of ego-identity to psychosocial effectiveness', *Psychological Reports* 15: 815–25.

Rees, A. M. (1987) 'Housing', in G. A. Causer (ed.) *Inside British Society*, Sussex: Wheatsheaf Books.

Reimer, J. W. (1977) 'Becoming a journeyman electrician', *Sociology of Work and Occupations* 4: 87–98.

Reiss, A. J. and Rhodes, A. L. (1964) 'An empirical test of differential association theory', *Journal Res. Crime and Delinquency* 1: 5–18.

Rest, J. (1973) 'The hierarchical nature of moral judgement: a study of patterns of comprehension and preference of moral stages', *Journal of Personality* 41: 86–109.

Rice, F. P. (1978) *The Adolescent: development, relationships and culture*, Boston: Allyn and Bacon.

Richard, B. A. and Dodge, K. A. (1982) 'Social maladjustment and problem solving in school-aged children', *Journal of Consulting and Clinical Psychology* 50: 226–33.

Richards, M. (1987) 'Parents and kids: the new thinking', *New Society*, 27 March: 12–15.

Riester, A. E. and Zucker, R. A. (1968) 'Adolescent social structure and drinking behaviour', *Personnel Guidance Journal* 47: 304–12.

Riley, T., Adams, G., and Neilsen, E. (1984) 'Adolescent ego-centrism: the association among imaginary audience behaviour, cognitive development and parental support and rejection', *Journal of Youth and Adolescence* 13: 401–8.

Roberts, K. (1970) *Leisure*, London: Longman.

Roberts, K. (1981) 'The sociology of work entry and occupational choice', in A. G. Watts, D. E. Super, and J. M. Kidd (eds) *Career Development in Britain*, Cambridge: Hobsons Press.

Roberts, K. (1983) *Youth and Leisure*, London: Allen & Unwin.

Roberts, K. (1985) 'Unemployment, youth and leisure in the 1980s', *Proceedings of the Leisure Studies Association Conference, Ilkley, Yorkshire*: 1.1.1–1.1.20.

Roberts, K. (1986) *School-leavers and Their Prospects: youth in the labour market in the 1980s*, Milton-Keynes: Open University Press.

Roberts, K., Duggan, J., and Noble, M. (1981) *Unregistered Youth Unemployment and Outreach Careers Work, Part one, Non-registration*, London: Department of Employment Research Paper 31.

Robins, D. and Cohen, P. (1978) *Knuckle Sandwich*, Harmondsworth: Penguin.

Robins, L., West, P. A., and Herjanic, B. L. (1975) 'Arrests and delinquency in two generations: a study of black urban families and their children', *Journal of Child Psychology and Psychiatry* 16: 125–40.

Root, N. (1957) 'A neurosis in adolescence', *Psychoanalytic Study of The Child* 12: 320–34.

Rosen, G. and Ross, A. (1968) 'Relationship of body image to self concept', *Journal of Consulting and Clinical Psychology* 32: 100.

Rosenberg, M. (1965) *Society and the Adolescent Self Image*, Princeton, New Jersey: Princeton University Press.

Rosenberg, M. (1975) 'The dissonant context and the adolescent self-concept', in S. Dragastin and G. Elder (eds) *Adolescence and the Life Cycle*, New York: John Wiley.

Rosenberg, M. (1979) *Conceiving the Self*, New York: Basic Books.

Rosenthal, R. and Jacobson, L. (1968) *Pygmalion in the Classroom*, London: Holt, Rinehart & Winston.

Rothenberg, B. (1970) 'Children's social sensitivity and the relationship to interpersonal competence, intrapersonal comfort and intellectual level', *Developmental Psychology* 2: 335–50.

Rotter, J. B. (1966) 'Generalised expectancies for internal vs external control of reinforcement', *Psychological Monographs* 80: 1: 609.

Royal College of Psychiatry (1979) *Alcohol and Alcoholism*, London: Tavistock.

Ruble, D. N., Boggiano, A. K., Feldman, N. S., and Leobl, J. H. (1980) 'A developmental analysis of the role of social comparison in self evaluation', *Developmental Psychology* 16: 105–15.

Rutter, M. and Giller, H. (1983) *Juvenile Delinquency: trends and perspectives*, Harmondsworth: Penguin.

Rutter, M., Graham, P., Chadwick, O., and Yule, W. (1976) 'Adolescent turmoil: fact or fiction', *Journal of Child Psychology and Psychiatry* 17: 35–56.

Rutter, M., Maughan, B., Mortimer, P., and Ouston, J. (1979) *Fifteen Thousand Hours: secondary schools and their effects on children*, London: Open Books.

Ryrie, A. C. (1981) *Routes and Results*, London: Hodder & Stoughton.

Salmon, P. (1979) 'The role of the peer group', in J. C. Coleman (ed.) *The School Years*, London: Methuen.

Sauer, L. W. (1966) 'Your adolescent's health', *PTA Magazine* 60: 31–2.

Savin-Williams, R. C. and Demo, D. H. (1983) 'Conceiving or misconceiving the self: issues in adolescent self-esteem', *Journal of Early Adolescence* 3 (1–2): 121–40.

Scanlan, T. K. (1982) 'Social evaluation: a key developmental element in the competition process', in R. A. Magill, M. J. Ash, and F. L. Smoll, (eds) *Children in Sport: a contemporary anthology*, pp. 138–52, Champaign, Illinois: Human Kinetics.

Scarlett, C. L. (1975) *Euroscot: the new European generation*, The Scottish Standing Conference on Voluntary Youth Organisations, Edinburgh.

Schofield, M. (1965) *The Sexual Behaviour of Young People*, London: Longman.

Schofield, M. (1973) *The Sexual Behaviour of Young Adults*, London: Allen Lane.

Scholzman, K. L. and Verba, S. (1980) *Insult to Injury*, Cambridge, Mass.: Harvard University Press.

Scottish Council for Community Education (1981) *Community Schools in Scotland*, SCCE, New St Andrew's House, Edinburgh.

Seabrook, J., (1982) *Unemployment*, London: Quartet.

Secord, P. F. and Jourard, F. M. (1953) 'The appraisal of body cathexis', *Journal of Consulting Psychology* 17: 343–7.

Selman, R. L. (1976) 'Social-cognition understanding: a guide to educational and clinical practice', in T. Lickona (ed.) *Moral Development and Behaviour: theory, research and social issues*, New York: Holt, Rinehart & Winston.

Selman, R. L. (1977) 'A structural-developmental model of social cognition: implications for interventional research', *Counselling Psychologist* 6: 3–6.

Selman, R. L. (1980) *The Growth of Interpersonal Understanding: developmental and clinical analyses*, New York: Academic Press.

Serafica, F. C. (ed.) (1982) *Social Cognitive Development in Context*, London: Methuen.

Shamir, B. (1986) 'Self-esteem and the psychological impact of unemployment', *Social Psychology Quarterly* 49 (1): 61–72.

Sharpe, S. (1977) *Just Like a Girl*, Harmondsworth: Penguin.

Shavelson, R. J., Hubner, J. J., and Stanton, G. C. (1976) 'Self-concept validation of construct interpretations', *Review of Educational Research* 46: 407–41.

Shaw, J. (1976) 'Finishing school: some implications of sex segregated education', in D. Barker and S. Allen (eds) *Dependence and Exploitation in Work and Marriage*, London: Longman.

Shaw, J. (1980) 'The causes of increasing drinking problems amongst women', in *Women and Alcohol*, pp. 1–40, Camberwell Council of Alcoholism, London: Tavistock.

Shayer, M., Kuchemann, D. E., and Wylam, H. (1976) 'The distribution of Piagetian stages of thinking in British middle and secondary school children', *British Journal of Educational Psychology* 46: 164–73.

Shayer, M. and Wylam, H. (1978) The distribution of Piagetian stages of thinking in British middle and secondary school children: II', *British Journal of Educational Psychology* 48: 62–70.

References

Sheard, K. and Dunning, E. (1973) 'The rugby football club', *International Review of Sport* 8: 5–24.

Short, F. J. (1968) *Gang Delinquency and Delinquent Sub-cultures*, New York: Harper & Row.

Shotter, J. (1985) *Social Accountability and Selfhood*, Oxford: Blackwell.

Siddique, C. M. and D'Arcy, C. (1984) 'Adolescence, stress and psychological well being', *Journal of Youth and Adolescence* 13: 459–74.

Sigall, H. and Aronson, E. (1969) 'Liking an evaluator as a function of the physical attractiveness and nature of the evaluation', *Journal of Experimental Social Psychology* 5: 93–100.

Sigall, H., Page, R., and Brown, A. C. (1971) 'Effort expenditure as a function of evaluation and evaluator attractiveness', *Reports of Research in Social Psychology* 2: 19–25.

Silbereisen, R. K., Noack, P., and Eyferth, K. (1987) 'Place for development: adolescents, leisure settings and developmental tasks', in R. K. Silbereisen, K. Eyferth, and G. Rudinger (eds) *Development as Action in Context: problem behaviour and normal youth development*, New York: Springer-Verlag.

Simmons, D. D. (1970) 'Development of an objective measure of identity achievement status', *Journal of Projective Techniques and Personality Assessment* 34: 241–4.

Simmons, R. and Blyth, D. A. (1987) *Moving into Adolescence*, New York: Aldine de Gruyter.

Simmons, R., Blyth, D. A., Vancleave, F. F., and Bush, D. M. (1979) 'Entry into adolescence: the impact of school structure, puberty and early dating on self-esteem', *American Sociological Review* 44: 948–67.

Simmons, R., Rosenberg, F., and Rosenberg, M. (1973) 'Disturbance in the self-image of adolescents', *American Sociological Review* 38: 553–68.

Simmons, R. and Rosenberg, S. (1975) 'Sex, sex roles and self image', *Journal of Youth and Adolescence* 4: 229–56.

Simon, M. (1978) 'Young people's attitudes to work', in C. Murray (ed.) *Young in Contemporary Society*, Slough: National Foundation Educational Research.

Simpson, I. H. (1979) *From Student to Nurse*, Cambridge: Cambridge University Press.

Simpson, J. (1973) 'Education for leisure', in M. A. Smith, S. Parker, and S. C. Smith (eds) *Leisure and Society in Britain*, London: Allen Lane.

Sinfield, A. (1981) *What Unemployment Means*, Oxford: Martin Robertson.

Smith, L. S. (1978) 'Sexist assumptions and female delinquency', in C. Smart and B. Smart (eds) *Women, Sexuality and Social Control*, London: Routledge & Kegan Paul.

Smith, R. E. (1986) Concluding article: 'Unemployment and health', in a series entitled: 'Unemployment in my practice', *British Medical Journal*, April.

Smith, T. E. (1976) 'Push versus pull – intra-family versus peer group variables as possible determinants of adolescent orientation toward parents', *Youth and Society* 8: 5–26.

Speier, M. (1970) 'The everyday world of the child', in J. D. Douglas (ed.) *Understanding Everyday Life*, New York: Aldine.

Spender, D. (1982) *Invisible Women: the schooling scandal*, Plymouth: Writers and Readers Co-operative.

Spivack, G., Platt, J., and Shure, M. (1976) *The Problem-solving Approach to Adjustment*, San Francisco: Jossey-Bass.

Stebbins, R. A. (1982) 'Serious leisure: a conceptual statement', *Pacific Sociological Review* 25: 251–72.

Stokes, G. and Cochrane, R. (1984) 'The relationship between national levels of unemployment and the rate of admission to mental hospitals in England and Wales (1950–76)', *Social Psychiatry* 19: 117–25.

Stonier, T. (1983) *The Wealth of Information*, London: Methuen.

Streitmatter, J. L. (1985) 'Cross-sectional investigation of adolescent perceptions of gender roles', *Journal of Adolescence* 8: 183–93.

Stunkard, A. J. and Mendelson, M. (1967) 'Obesity and the body image: characteristics of disturbances in the body image of some obese persons', *American Journal of Psychiatry* 123: 1296–1300.

Sugarman, A. and Haronian, R. (1964) 'Body-type and sophistication of body concept', *Journal of Perspectives* 32: 380–94.

Sugarman, B. (1967) 'Involvement in youth culture: academic achievement and conformity in school', *British Journal of Sociology* 18: 157–64.

Sugarman, L. (1986) *Life-Span Development: concepts, theories and interventions*, London: Methuen.

Sykes, E. G. (1953) 'School and work', *Sociological Review* 1: 29–47.

Tanner, J. M. (1962) *Growth at Adolescence*, Oxford: Blackwell Scientific Publications.

Tanner, J. M. (1978) *Foetus into Man*, London: Open Books.

Thomas, E. J. (1968) 'Role theory, personality and the individual', in E. Borgatta and W. Lambert (eds) *Handbook of Personality Theory and Research*, Chicago: Rand McNally.

Thompson Report (1982) *Experience and Participation: Report of the Review Group on the Youth Service in England*, London: HMSO.

Thornburg, H. D. (1975) 'Adolescent sources of initial sex information', in R. E. Grinder (ed.) *Studies in Adolescence* (3rd edn), London: Collier-Macmillan.

Tiggeman, M. and Winfield, A. (1984) 'The effects of unemployment on the mood, self-esteem, locus of control and depressive affect of school-leavers', *Journal of Occupational Psychology* 57: 33–42.

Tobin, J. M. (1985) 'How promiscuous are our teenagers? A study of teenage girls attending a family planning clinic', *The British Journal of Family Planning* 10: 107–12.

Toder, N. L. and Marcia, J. E. (1973) 'Ego-identity status and response to conformity pressure in college women', *Journal of Personal and Social Psychology* 26: 287–94.

Tome, H. R. and Bariaud, F. (1987) *Les Perspectives Temporelles à L'adolescence*, Paris: Presses Universitaires de France.

Tomlinson-Keasey, C. and Keasey, C. B. (1974) 'The mediating role of cognitive development in moral judgement', *Child Development* 45: 291–8.

References

Town, S. (1983) 'Recreation and the unemployed: experiments in Bradford', *Leisure Studies Association Newsletter*. 4: 5–10.

Toynbee, P. (1978) 'Girls' magazines', *The Guardian*: 30.10.78.

Trew, K. and Kilpatrick, R. (1984) *The Daily Life of the Unemployed: social and psychological dimensions*, Belfast: Queen's University.

Trowbridge, N. (1972) 'Self-concept and socio-economic status in elementary school children', *American Educational Research Journal* 9 (4): 525–37.

Turiel, E. (1974) 'Conflict and transition in adolescent moral development', *Child Development* 45: 14–29.

Turner, R., Bostyn, A. M., and Wight, D. (1983) 'The work ethic in a Scottish town with declining employment', paper presented in *XIth International Congress of Anthropological and Ethnological Sciences*, Vancouver.

Van Hasselt, V. B. and Hersen, M. (1987) *Handbook of Adolescent Psychology*, Oxford: Pergamon Press.

Varlaam, C. (1984) *Rethinking Transition: educational innovation and the transition to adult life*, Lewes: Falmer.

Virgo, P. (1981) 'Learning for change. Training, retraining and life-long education for multi-career lives', London: Bow Publications.

Voss, H. L. (1963) 'The predictive efficiency of the Glueck Social Prediction Scale', *Journal of Criminal Law, Criminology and Police Science* 54: 421–30.

Waddington, P. A. J. (1982) 'Indeterminacy in occupational recruitment: The case of prison assistant governors', *Sociology* 16: 203–19.

Walczak, Y. and Burns, S. (1984) *Divorce: the child's point of view*, London: Harper & Row.

Wallace, C. (1980) 'Adapting to unemployment', *Youth in Society* 40: 6–8.

Wallerstein, J. S. and Kelly, J. B. (1980) *Surviving the Breakup: how children and parents cope with divorce*, New York: Basic Books.

Walster, E., Aronson, V., Abrahams, D., and Rottman, L. (1966) 'The importance of physical attractiveness in dating behaviour', *Journal of Personality Social Psychology* 4: 508–16.

Wan, G. Y., Yamamura, D. S., and Ikeda, K. (1969) 'The relationship of communication with parents and peers to deviant behaviour of youth', *Journal of Marriage and the Family* 31: 43–47.

Warr, P. (1983) 'Work, jobs and unemployment', *Bulletin of British Psychological Society* 36: 305–11.

Warr, P. and Payne, R. (1983) 'Social class and reported changes in behaviour after job loss', *Journal of Applied Social Psychology* 13 (3): 206–22.

Waterman, A. S., Geary, P. S., and Waterman, C. K. (1974) 'Longitudinal study in changes of ego-identity status from the freshmen to the senior year at college', *Developmental Psychology* 10: 387–92.

Waterman, A. S. and Waterman, C. K. (1971) 'A longitudinal study of changes in ego-identity status during the freshman year at college', *Developmental Psychology* 5: 167–73.

Waterman, A. S. and Waterman, C. K. (1972) 'Relationship between freshman ego identity status and subsequent academic behaviour', *Developmental Psychology*, 6: 179.

Watson, J. M. (1980) 'Solvent abuse by children and young adults: a review', *British Journal of Addiction* 75: 27–36.

Watts, A. G. (1983) *Education, Unemployment and the Future of Work*, Milton Keynes: Open University Press.

Weinreich, P. (1979) 'Ethnicity and adolescent identity conflicts', in S. Khan (ed.) *Minority Families in Britain*, London: Macmillan.

Weinreich, P. (1985) 'Identity exploration in adolescence', *International Journal of Adolescence, Medicine and Health* 1: 51–71.

Weinreich-Haste, H. (1979) 'Moral development', in J. C. Coleman (ed.) *The School Years*, London: Methuen.

Weinstein, E. A. (1973) 'The development of interpersonal competence', in D. A. Goslin (ed.) *Handbook of Socialisation Theory and Research*, New York: Rand-McNally.

Weir, D. and Nolan, F. (1977) *Glad To Be Out?*, Edinburgh: SCER.

Weisman, C. S. *et al.* (1976) 'Sex differences in response to a blocked career pattern among unaccepted medical school applicants', *Sociology of Work and Occupations* 3: 187–208

Wells, K. (1980) 'Sexual identity: gender role identity and psychological adjustment in adolescence', *Journal of Youth and Adolescence* 9: 59–74.

Werthman, C. and Piviavin, I. (1967) 'Gang members and the police', in D. Bordua (ed.) *The Police*, New York: Wiley.

West, D. J. and Farrington, D. P. (1977) *The Delinquent Way of Life*, London: Heinemann.

West, M. and Newton, P. (1983) *The Transition From School to Work*, London: Croom Helm.

White, D. (1971) 'Brum's mobs', *New Society* 2 October: 760–3.

White, M. (1987) 'The social world of the unemployed', London: Policy Studies Institute.

Wilkins, L. T. (1955) *The Adolescent in Britain*, London: Central Office of Information.

Willis, P. (1977) *Learning to Labour*, Farnborough: Saxon House.

Willis, P. (1978) *Profane Culture*, London: Routledge & Kegan Paul.

Willis, P. (1984) 'Youth unemployment – 1. A new state', *New Society* March. 'Youth Unemployment – 2. Ways of living', *New Society*, April.

Wilmott, P. (1966) *Adolescent Boys of East London*, London: Routledge & Kegan Paul.

Wilson, D. (1978) 'Sexual codes and conduct: a study of teenage girls', in C. Smart and B. Smart (eds) *Women, Sexuality and Social Control*, London: Routledge & Kegan Paul.

Witkin, H. A. (1965) 'Psychological differentiation and forms of pathology', *Journal of Abnormal Psychology* 70: 5.

Wright, J. D. and Pearl, L. (1986) 'Knowledge and experience of young people of drug abuse 1969–84', *British Medical Journal* 292: 179–182.

Wylie, R. C. (1961) *The Self-Concept: a critical review of pertinent research literature*, Lincoln: University of Nebraska.

Wylie, R. C. (1974) *The Self-Concept: a review of methodological considerations and measuring instruments*, Lincoln: University of Nebraska Press.

Wylie, R. C. (1979) *The Self-Concept: theory and research on selected topics*: 2, Lincoln: University of Nebraska Press.

Yablonsky, L. (1967) *The Violent Gang*, Harmondsworth: Pelican.

Yamamoto, K., Thomas, E. C., and Karns, E. A. (1969) 'School-related attitudes in middle-school age students', *American Educational Research Journal* 6 (2): 191–206.

Young, I. M. (1980) 'Throwing like a girl: a phenomenology of feminine body comportment, mobility and spatiality', *Human Studies* 3: 187–90.

Young, J. (1971) *The Drug Takers*, London: Paladin.

Young, J. and Crutchley, J. B. (1972) 'Student drug use', *Drugs and Society* 2 (1): 11–15.

Youniss, J. (1980) *Parents and Peers in Social Development: a Sullivan-Piaget perspective*, Chicago: Chicago University Press.

Youniss, J. and Smollar, J. (1985) *Adolescent Relations with Mothers, Fathers and Friends*, Chicago: University of Chicago Press.

Youthaid (1979) *Study of the Transition from School to Working Life*, London: Youthaid.

Zelnick, M. and Kantner, J. F. (1980) 'Sexual activity, contraceptive use and pregnancy among metropolitan-area teenagers: 1971–1979', *Family Planning Perspectives* 12: 230–7.

Zieman, G. L. and Benson, G. P. (1983) 'Delinquency: the role of self-esteem and self values', *Journal of Youth and Adolescence* 12 (6): 489–99.

Zimbardo, P. G. (1977) *Shyness*, Reading, MA: Addison-Wesley.

Name index

Subject index